A BRIEF HISTORY OF CRIME

A BRIEF HISTORY OF CRIME

The Decline of Order, Justice and Liberty in England

PETER HITCHENS

Atlantic Books
London

First published in Great Britain in 2003
by Atlantic Books, an imprint of Grove Atlantic Ltd

The author and publisher wish to thank the following
for permission to quote from copyrighted material:
David Higham Associates for *Chronicles of Wasted Time* by
Malcolm Muggeridge (1979); Simon & Schuster for
The Closing of the American Mind by Allan Bloom (1987).

1 2 3 4 5 6 7 8 9

A CIP catalogue record for this book is available
from the British Library.

ISBN 1 84354 148 3

Printed in Great Britain by
CPD, Ebbw Vale, Wales.

Atlantic Books
An imprint of Grove Atlantic Ltd
Ormond House
26–27 Boswell Street
London WC1N 3JZ

To my parents

Society cannot exist unless a controlling power
upon will and appetite be placed somewhere,
and the less there is within, the more
there must be without.
Edmund Burke

There are more instances of the abridgment
of the freedom of the people by gradual and
silent encroachments of those in power
than by violent and sudden usurpation.
James Madison

Contents

Acknowledgements

My thanks to David Miller, Toby Mundy and Clara Farmer, for helping to turn an idea into a book; to Peter Wright, Editor of the *Mail on Sunday*, for encouraging and helping me to pursue this most important subject, and likewise to Eric Bailey; to Fred Broughton and Tony Judge (whose book *The Force of Persuasion* was invaluable to me) for indispensable advice on how to find what I was looking for; to Louise Stemp of the Home Office Library, who helped me far beyond the call of duty both with a superb bibliography and access to unique documents, and to her colleagues Lorna Brook and Marilyn Saklatvala; also to Wendy Sainsbury and Ian Harris of the Prison Service Headquarters library and Paul Levay, Assistant Librarian of the National Police Training Library at Bramshill; to Brian Butler, head of information at the Home Office, to many diligent press officers at the Home Office and the Lord Chancellor's Department who responded so willingly to my requests for arcane information; to the librarians of the London Library, the British Library and the Leicester Square Public Library for always finding what I needed, however ancient and obscure; to the librarians at Associated Newspapers, superb keepers of one of the best archives in Britain; to Norman Dennis, for his dissection of the Macpherson report; to Colin Greenwood, a real expert; to Stephen Moore, for allowing me into prison at Wormwood Scrubs, and letting me out again even though he knew how sceptical I was about the modern prison service; to Neil Clark, for pointing out the Labour Party's changing view of the death penalty; to the many readers of the *Mail on Sunday* who have written to me about their experiences as police

and prison officers, or as victims of the scourge of crime and disorder; above all, and as always, to my wife Eve for companionship,
support and comfort – and to Ribs, Daniel and Jonathan for the
encouragement that only they could give. All these should share in
any credit. I take all the blame.

P.H.,
Oxford,
December 2002

A BRIEF HISTORY OF CRIME

Introduction

Necessity is the plea for every infringement of
human freedom. It is the arguments of tyrants;
it is the creed of slaves.
William Pitt

Let us at least agree that there is something wrong.

Once it was modish to argue that we were suffering from an ailment called 'moral panic' and to make light of worries that crime and disorder were at perilous levels. Then the liberal left began reluctantly to admit that perhaps the problem might exist even though conservatives said it did. From that came the seemingly simple slogan 'Tough on crime – tough on the causes of crime' which the Labour Party used before 1997 to suggest that it had grown out of its anti-police phase.

That slogan hides an awkward truth, which its apparent ferocity is designed to conceal. The left is still convinced that crime is a social and economic disease, produced by poverty, bad housing, poor schools and all the other ills that socialism claims to be able to cure. This is understandable. If this belief were false the left would lose most of the justification for its existence. Why have all that high taxation, those regiments of social workers and that maze of targeted benefits, not to mention the bureaucracies needed to organize them, if they do not actually make people more content and better behaved? Being 'tough on the causes of crime' means continuing to accept that public officials and public money can cajole and bribe the people into being good, when they would otherwise be bad.

Being 'tough on crime', on the other hand, means that Labour can from now on ignore what is left of its liberty-loving wing and cheerfully enact laws that increase the power of the state and the police to search, listen, file, survey, arrest, hold suspects and seize property, while weakening jury trial and the other safeguards that our wiser ancestors devised to protect us if evil times should come again.

Behind this recipe for repression lies another problem – too large for this book to deal with in full but bound to grow in importance in the coming decades – the accelerating growth of a European legal system, police force and prosecution service. These are bound to conflict with existing English institutions because they draw their power from different courts and documents. They know nothing of the common law, Magna Carta, the English Bill of Rights (a document that seems genuinely to be unknown to many human rights campaigners who noisily demand a British Bill of Rights as if this were an entirely new idea), habeas corpus, the English law's great safeguard against unlimited detention without trial, or the right to trial by jury.

Consciously or unconsciously, the English legal authorities appear at the start of the twenty-first century to be adapting the English system to fit the very different pattern of Continental law. This unpleasant change has been hastened by the ugly collection of repressive and irrelevant measures gathered into one bill by David Blunkett, the Home Secretary, ostensibly in response to the terrorist massacres in the United States on 11 September 2001.

These include the right to detain certain suspects without trial, a breach of the principle of habeas corpus that is not only bad in itself but also shows a willingness to plead necessity as an excuse for destroying liberty, an attitude that threatens many other freedoms if it is not checked. Mr Blunkett dismissed opposition to this bill as 'airy-fairy', a view shared by the Prime Minister, who was and is quite unmoved by the traditions of English liberty or by the left's own strain of libertarianism.

Mr Blair has often spoken with contempt of civil liberty and those who defend it, notably after his government had suggested that everyone who is arrested should be forcibly tested for traces of illegal drugs, even before being convicted. Mr Blair told the Labour Party conference on 28 September 1999:

> It is time to move beyond the social indifference of right and left, libertarian nonsense masquerading as freedom. This generation wants a society free from prejudice but not from rules. I can announce that we will provide the extra resources for a database where every known offender will have their DNA recorded, and evidence from any scene of crime will be matched with it. And I saw that what we said on drugs and new powers was attacked by civil liberties groups. I believe in civil liberties too: civil liberty to me means just that: the liberty to live in a civil society founded on rights and responsibilities, and in dealing with the drugs menace, that is the society we can help to build.

Incoherent as this is, like most of Mr Blair's speeches, it betrays a powerful man's scorn for the irritating rules that get in the way of his grand and benevolent plans. His impatience with those who have doubts about such measures is a common failing in messianic political leaders. They believe themselves to be exempt from the normal laws of life because of their special goodness.

The September 2001 massacre was also used as a pretext for the introduction of a European Arrest Warrant which will permit prosecuting authorities in any EU country to order the arrest of citizens of other EU nations for a number of vague offences. Several of the offences listed are not actually crimes under English law. They include 'xenophobia', which is not an offence, as such, anywhere in Britain. There is also no safeguard against a Continental magistrate obtaining a warrant for one of the listed offences and then charging the arrested person with a wholly different crime once he is in custody. This measure effectively demolishes the boundaries between the criminal justice systems of EU member states. Since the overwhelming majority of EU countries lack habeas corpus, the presumption of innocence or jury trial it indirectly, but gravely, undermines all of them.

Corpus juris is a plan to give the EU a common legal space, which entails a common jurisdiction, a European prosecutor and a European police force. Ultimately, it will not be able to function unless a common code is in being throughout the EU. Since only England, Wales and Ireland – and to a lesser extent Scotland – differ significantly from the systems used on the Continent, it is more likely that Britain and Ireland will eventually be brought under this civil code system than that the other states will adopt common law, habeas corpus and jury trial. Much of this new system is already in existence or in preparation, justified by supposed campaigns against fraud, and probably in future by similar campaigns against illegal immigration and drug trafficking or any other form of lawbreaking that crosses frontiers and can be portrayed as a public menace so serious that freedom must be abridged in order to deal with it. It is likely to increase its powers much as the FBI has done in the USA, allowing federal intervention in national affairs. The difference, from an English point of view, is that the EU's federal system will lack English protections, whereas the FBI is still restrained by habeas corpus, the Bill of Rights and a universal right to trial by jury. The recent experience of British plane-spotters arrested for spying in Greece has alerted many people to the possible drawbacks of the Continental system. However, it has done little or nothing to halt the changes. Europol, for instance, already has the legal right to operate in the UK and its officers have immunity from prosecution for any action that they may take here.

Other parallel developments, especially the incorporation of the 1950 European Convention on Human Rights into English law, have weakened the specifically English tradition of unconditional liberty – everything is legal unless officially banned. They have replaced it with the codified and conditional Continental system, under which all rights are granted by the authorities and everything is illegal unless specifically allowed. The rights contained in the ECHR are often devices for altering the moral and cultural balance rather than actually for protecting liberty. The Convention contains grandiose provisions such as the right to life and liberty, and the right to respect for private and family life. But it does not offer the effective provisions found in the US Bill of Rights which prevent the state from acting in such a way that these rights would be infringed, by debarring it from making certain laws. 'Congress shall make no law abridging the freedom of speech' is much more use in a court of law (and in a crisis) than a right to free speech which is balanced by a right to privacy and perhaps cancelled by the right of the state to act in self-defence.

This is only the beginning. There is a likelihood that in the long term a European constitution will be created and enforced by the European Court of Justice, a wholly different body from the Strasbourg-based European Court of Human Rights. The EU has already drafted its own Charter of Rights and Freedoms, a rival to the ECHR which gives significantly more rights to the state and fewer to the individual. Many of the rights enshrined in these documents are political or group rights, given to people supposedly discriminated against under the existing system. They are not rights as the English Whigs of 1689 or the American revolutionaries of 1776 would have understood them – freedom from autocratic power, arbitrary arrest, indiscriminate searches or indefinite detention without charge. On the contrary, modern human rights charters tend to be very weak and vague on such issues. They have generally been written by idealists from free countries with little experience of the methods and mechanisms of oppression.

This book cannot deal in detail with Scotland, although much of what has gone wrong in England has been replicated north of the border. Scotland's legal and criminal justice systems have never been fully merged with England's, and now never will be – except perhaps as part of a final all-European code which will submit the whole of the British Isles to the Code Napoléon and corpus juris. Scottish juries are significantly different from English ones; England has no procurators fiscal (a kind of examining magistrate who can decide on prosecutions); and the office of constable is far newer and less significant in Scotland than in England. Northern Ireland's problems are so different and special that they form a whole separate subject, although it is interesting that one of the greatest battles over the political future of the province has involved the nature of its police force. This is why all the facts and figures in this book refer only to England and Wales. Even so, many of its themes affect all parts of what is still officially a United Kingdom. The recent collapse of the rule of law in Northern Ireland has had many subtle and demoralizing effects on law enforcement and trust in the rule of law in the rest of the country.

My purpose is to show that much of the public debate on crime and punishment in modern England is based on mistaken beliefs, misunderstood figures and cheap slogans – especially on the death penalty, imprisonment, drugs, policing and the right to bear arms. None of the major parties appears to have given any serious thought to the issue for many years. As a result, the actions taken by government in the name of fighting crime are often quite worthless for that purpose. They have, however, gravely damaged the liberty of the law-abiding citizen, which government ministers dismiss as the concern of tiresome eccentrics.

If the new armoury of police and state powers had had the slightest effect on levels of crime and disorder, the government's arguments might have some force. However, these measures have proved useless, as well as menacing to liberty in general. The wicked, the selfish, the loud, the oafish, the inconsiderate and the bully are all freer to behave as they wish than at any time for a hundred and fifty years. Their actions often go unrecorded or are dismissed as petty by the authorities. Yet their effects on people's lives are deep and painful. Even the well-massaged crime figures and the new emphasis on the British Crime Survey (a household survey using random sampling, now generally believed to be more accurate than the centralized crime figures amassed by the police and courts) instead of on classical statistics cannot obscure the truth. England is rapidly becoming a place where the good are afraid of the bad and the bad are not afraid of anything.

The real paradox in the argument is one that the genuinely liberal left needs to grasp swiftly if it is to act in time. The left has now captured the machinery of government and the great bulk of the media and the education system. It alone has the opportunity to put matters right. If it refuses to do so, it is likely that the slide into disorder will soon become unstoppable as the last vestiges of authority and obedience disappear from the streets and the unpoliced countryside. Even at this late stage, there is little sign that the left is prepared to look at the issue as anything other than a propaganda problem. One of the Prime Minister's closest advisers, Peter Mandelson, wrote in *The Times* on 10 June 2002 that the left is failing to cope with 'tough issues that are "cultural" rather than ideological'. Among these he included crime. But he clearly saw this as a question of fighting against the right for a propaganda victory rather than of re-examining principles:

> Fundamentally, we must connect with issues that are
> disturbing voters and not vacate space to be occupied by
> the Right. This does not mean pandering to prejudice or
> headline grabbing; it means advancing workable policies
> that reflect the essentially tolerant values of the majority.
> At the heart of the Centre Left's strategy should be
> building security through strong community action;
> vigorously promoting economic opportunity, ensuring
> that everyone gets a proper share of economic success;
> advancing fairness as a responsibility issue (rewards for

those who work and do the right thing as well as lifting the poor and disadvantaged out of need); and investing heavily in education as the key to social mobility.

What this actually means is open to interpretation. None of the leading thinkers of New Labour writes in clear English – either because they do not really know what they intend to say or because they are nervous about saying it. But the warning against 'pandering to prejudice' is a prohibition against conservative common sense, always dismissed as prejudice by the left. The 'essentially tolerant values of the majority' are the essential social liberalism of the intolerant elite. 'Security through strong community action', on the other hand, is authoritarianism justified by the general will. The adherence to 'economic opportunity' and 'proper share[s] of economic success' is a reassertion of economic and social egalitarianism, the very policy that has done so much to promote crime and disorder in the first place. The fact that this sort of thing passes for advanced thinking in Downing Street is profoundly dispiriting. It is a warning that the official left views public concern about crime as a threat to its popularity rather than as a threat to society, and that it would much rather undermine liberty than re-examine its principles in the light of experience. These are people who would rather infringe the freedom of others than change their minds. We must hope that there are others on the left with more open minds, for the left is so entrenched in power that it alone will carry the responsibility if the law crumbles and the country then turns to authoritarian government to impose a crude sort of order.

The paradox is this: the more harshly we treat wrongdoers and the greater the power of the state to punish and pursue them, the more we preserve liberty for the enormous majority who keep to the laws. A society that clearly and decisively punishes wicked actions will have no need to document, restrict or spy on the many millions who do not do such actions.

Conversely, the more generously and considerately we create

safeguards for transgressors, the fewer freedoms will remain for those who behave themselves. The more we treat crime as the symptom of a social and economic disease, requiring treatment rather than penalties, the more the state will need to become an apparatus of repression. The more the police are required to treat individual offenders with care and consideration, the more the law-abiding population will have to be restrained by the authorities from taking actions in their own defence. The less free ordinary citizens are to use their initiative in dealing with wrongdoers, the more they will yearn to do so. The more bureaucratic and formal the criminal justice system becomes, the less use it will be against the disorderly and disobedient. Such people treat a prison record as a career risk, do not pay fines (huge amounts are uncollected, although the middle class still tend to pay), fail to turn up at court or do not stay long at the same address. It is then simpler and more convenient for the police to pursue the settled and orderly members of society. They are easy to find, can have their regular earnings raided to pay fines and still fear the stigma of a criminal record.

A society where crime is an endemic disease to be contained and placated needs to treat all its citizens as potential suspects all the time. This approach will only reduce crime when the state becomes all-powerful. Even then, it may fail to do so; its failure so far is so blatant that any rational society would long ago have abandoned it. The end of this process, of repression followed by failure followed by yet more repression, will be wretched. If it is not soon halted, it will create a social and legal system so stifling and intrusive as to be uncomfortably close to dictatorship.

When I first sat down to write this book, those words would have seemed overheated. However, since the publication of the Anti-Terrorism Bill in the autumn of 2001 and the contempt of the government for the bill's responsible critics, such alarm is completely justified. Enlightened and thoughtful members of the liberal left ought to remember that they were originally moved to action by a desire for both justice and liberty. In their own interests, they should think again about this tremendous issue. What follows should at least give them some material to consider. I hope it may even create a few doubts in their minds.

Returning to Labour's dishonest and misleading slogan about being 'Tough on crime – tough on the causes of crime', I hope to show why these words are both false and dangerous. I also intend to show why and how the current government and its Conservative forerunners have failed to stop the growth of disorder – and how they have unintentionally encouraged it. I would like to demonstrate that we can do better than this. However, our political leaders, of all parties, cannot make progress until they understand the real nature of a problem that they seem barely to have thought about at all.

The sheer concrete-headed stupidity of most political statements about crime defies belief. Anyone who calls for 'more bobbies on the beat' simply reveals that he – or, in many cases, she – knows nothing about what has happened to the police, especially that there is no longer any 'beat' for 'bobbies' to go on and that the word 'bobby' simply cannot be applied to the paramilitary social workers, jangling with clubs, handcuffs, radios and gas sprays, who have replaced the traditional English constable.

As for those who demand 'tougher' sentences, 'fast-track' prosecutions, juvenile curfews and similar measures, they are announcing that they have not recently visited their own country, let alone taken any interest in it. One of the most astonishing recruits to the 'tough sentences' campaign is the Lord Chief Justice, Lord Woolf, who in February 2002 suddenly urged long prison terms for thieves who steal mobile telephones. Lord Woolf had until then been seen as a member of the liberal wing of the judiciary. His 1991 report on the Strangeways prison riot had been sharply critical of the usefulness of prisons as a whole. His intervention is a worrying sign that the liberal elite, far from recognizing that their whole approach is mistaken, is suffering from the moral panic of which it normally accuses others. Lord Woolf's plan could only work if there were a constant police presence on the streets. Had he been paying attention to real life, he and his fellow campaigners for 'tough' measures would have observed that proper police patrols to catch thieves or enforce curfews are a rarity in most parts of the country, and that most patrolling that does take place takes the form of random appearances by officers in cars. They might also have noticed that even 'long' prison sentences are, in effect, automatically halved as they are passed. They would know that prisons themselves are only terrifying to the innocent or the harmless because they are run by the bad and the strong. They would realize that prosecutions could never keep pace with the quantity of offences now committed unless the rules of justice and evidence were entirely abandoned.

As for the crime figures, in whatever form they are served up, they are not to be trusted fully or taken literally. Like all politically important statistics they have suffered what ought to be called the 'bikini effect' – the things concealed are more interesting than those revealed. This is not to say that they are meaningless: they cannot conceal the grave increase in dishonesty and disorder. However, it is well to bear in mind that police forces campaigning for extra funds or increased manpower may be diligent in recording crime, while forces under pressure to produce results for their political masters may be far less diligent and might even be tempted to 'combine' several offences into one or to reclassify a theft as lost property. In an era when central government assumes responsibility for so many aspects of life, such figures are always susceptible to gentle (and sometimes quite rough) massage. British inflation figures, absurdly, exclude the price of houses. Unemployment figures exclude the 'long-term sick', who may not be sick at all. Anyone with the slightest knowledge of schools knows that league table pressure sometimes prevents weak candidates from taking exams when their performance might drag down the average. It would be sensible to assume that similar rules apply to the collection of crime figures. Certainly, the repeated claims of the current government that crime is falling are risible.

In judging them, we should always ask ourselves what story they are trying to tell and make allowances for it. So, before showing that something enormous and damaging has happened to English society since the Second World War, it is worth quoting an astonishing footnote from Jose Harris's social history of Britain before the First World War, *Private Lives, Public Spirit: Britain 1870–1914*. Dealing with pre-1914 crime figures, she states:

> A very high proportion of Edwardian convicts were in
> prison for offences that would have been much more
> lightly treated or wholly disregarded by law enforcers in
> the late twentieth century. In 1912–13, for example, one
> quarter of males aged 16 to 21 who were imprisoned in the
> metropolitan area of London were serving seven-day
> sentences for offences which included drunkenness,
> 'playing games in the street', riding a bicycle without
> lights, gaming, obscene language and sleeping rough.
> If late twentieth-century standards of policing and
> sentencing had been applied in Edwardian Britain,
> the prisons would have been virtually empty; conversely,
> if Edwardian standards were applied in the 1990s then
> most of the youth of Britain would be in gaol.

As it happens, 1913 was a fairly bad year by the standards of the time, with 98,000 serious offences recorded. This level would not be surpassed again until 1920 when the total rose to 101,000 after a wartime truce during which annual crime tallies sank to as low as 78,000 in 1915. Even convicts were reported to be showing patriotic zeal as they broke their rocks. Measure this against the figure of 2,521,000 recorded in 1980 and, even when you grant that the population had risen from 36 million to 49 million, the figures could be from different planets as well as from different eras.

Set beside A. J. P. Taylor's famous statement that the Edwardian Englishman hardly came into contact with the state at all, except to see a policeman walking past or a postman coming up his front path, these figures raise an interesting point. The numbers of recorded crimes in England and Wales had remained fairly stable for sixty years before the outbreak of war. Occasionally falling to as low as 79,000 (1886) or rising as high as 105,000 (1908 and 1909), the annual figure generally remained between 85,000 and 95,000. Murder, the worst of all crimes, seldom rose above 170 and often fell below 130 in a year (these numbers include deaths from backstreet abortions and infanticides). Courts at that time were far less likely to accept pleas of manslaughter, and primitive medical treatment meant that almost any serious wounding could result in death whereas nowadays thousands of such injuries are successfully treated by the National Health Service.

These totals are striking for a society far poorer than most of us can imagine, in which millions lived in disgusting and miserable slums or survived on wages that would be barely enough to feed a twenty-first-century pet cat. There were no laws restricting the ownership of guns or knives. Transportation and the hulks had been abolished, as had public execution. Even hanging itself had become more humane, a swift breaking of the neck instead of a slow strangulation. There were no social services and very few benefits, targeted or otherwise, offered by the state or local authorities, apart from the workhouse. Nobody had a National Insurance number and hardly anyone had a tax code. Trade union membership was small, council housing non-existent and state pensions for the elderly unknown until the very end of the period. Even if recent suggestions that the crime figures of this era were manipulated are true – and, given that most English police forces were locally controlled and that crime was not a major political issue, one has to wonder why anyone should have manipulated them – the difference between then and now still cannot be explained by worsening social conditions.

What makes the figures for the late Victorian and Edwardian age still more telling is that they cover a period when the population of

Year	Population (England and Wales)	Recorded crime (England and Wales)
1921	37,886,689	103,000
1931	39,948,000	159,000
1941	41,748,000	359,000
1951	43,745,000	525,000
1961	46,166,000	807,000
1971	48,604,000	1,666,000
1981	49,011,000	2,963,000*
1991	49,890,000	5,276,200
2001	53,137,000	5,200,000**

*Changes in the law mean that post-1980 figures are not strictly comparable with pre-1980 totals, but no other statistics are available and there appears to be some continuity.

**These figures have been disputed, with suggestions that there is some undercounting – for example, because of failures by the uninsured to report thefts and because police have recorded multiple thefts in one block or street as if they were a single offence. Few who lived through the period believe that crime did not rise between 1991 and 2001. The alternative British Crime Survey gives a different picture but is itself criticized for under-reporting crimes affecting the young. By this time, crime figures had become politically significant and therefore subject to massage and adjustment.

England and Wales increased more rapidly than ever, and when multitudes exchanged the ordered and ancient ways of the countryside for the fetid chaos of the new cities. In 1861, when the annual crime figure was 88,000, the population stood at 20,066,224. In 1911, when the crime figure was 97,000, the population had risen to 36,075,269. This was, in fact, a significant drop in the crime rate and one that was to continue, less sharply but just as convincingly, until the 1930s.

The table above shows the growth of population and of crime in the twentieth century. The idea that poverty or social conditions are causes of crime melts away in the hot blast of these truths. The increase in wrong-doing of all kinds is so huge that supposedly reassuring factors, such as temporary surges in the numbers of young men or a greater temptation to steal caused by the presence of so much portable property, are simply too limited to explain the colossal rise. The evidence, which shows that the highest levels of crime in memory have occurred at a time of unheard-of prosperity, health, social welfare provision, good housing and material content-ment, also destroys the idea that increased welfare leads to a reduction in crime. On the contrary, it raises the possibility that well-meaning state intervention to improve the lot of the poor can actually lead to increased crime.

Gertrude Himmelfarb argued in *The Demoralisation of Society* that the Victorian achievement of peaceful order owed far more to Sunday Schools and moral values than to any other factor. Exactly the same argument, but in reverse, should be applied to Britain's descent from lawful peace to lawless chaos since the early 1930s. It is the decay and destruction of moral values and self-restraint, acceler-ated by two terrible wars, that have led to the misery of the modern poor – poor in spirit rather than in goods.

In the companion to this book, *The Abolition of Britain*, I sought to show that there had been a cultural revolution in this country as thor-oughgoing as the Chinese upheaval under Mao. The subject of crime, order and justice was too big to be considered properly in that book. It deserves separate treatment – yet, like the rest of the cul-tural revolution, it has involved changes that were often minute, seldom understood or even noticed at the time they were made, and which, in this case, would be surprisingly easy to reverse. The still better news is that, by correcting these mistakes, an enlightened government could help to revive ideas of responsibility, good and bad, guilt and innocence. This would greatly strengthen the position of the large number of citizens who still believe in self-discipline based on a common morality. It would help in the remoralization of our country. It would be pointless to try to deal with the rise in dis-order solely through changes in the law and in police methods. A moral counter-revolution is also needed. Practical reforms, however, would help such a counter-revolution to begin and hasten it once it had started, provided they were not attempted in isolation.

The balance of power in England, between the criminal and lawless on one hand and the civilized and law-abiding on the other, has been disturbed by a number of measures and changes which could quite easily be repealed or amended. The revolution in the police force could be reversed by a determined Home Secretary with the support of Parliament and people. The Police and Criminal Evidence Act 1984 (PACE), with its many pages of absurd codes for detention and identification, its guaranteed lawyers and tape recordings, seems to have been devised by left-wing lawyers *for* left-wing lawyers. It is astonishing that it was passed without serious protest by a Conservative government at the height of its strength. Based on a complete mistrust of the police, it assumed that a small number of real miscarriages of justice were typical of police behaviour. It destroyed what remained of police independence of action. It ensured that constables could no longer do what the people wanted them to do.

Let us not decieve ourselves about this. The police in former times repressed crime and criminals without much gentleness or finesse. We knew, if we were honest, that we were guarded by men who kept the rough world away from us with rough methods. Now the police are all but powerless because of regulations imposed by unrealistic utopians who do not have to live with the consequences of their reforms. Millions of others do, and long for help. Can anyone now say that what has followed is better than what went before, for anybody except the wicked? Now it is the criminals who rule many parts of Britain with boot and fist. Intimidation of witnesses and juries makes a mockery of hundreds of trials each year while ensuring that many crimes are never prosecuted at all. Few innocent people went to prison under the old rules. Too few guilty people go there now. From the moment it came into effect, PACE – with the Police Complaints Authority standing behind it to punish those officers who broke its codes – spelt the end of order for honest poor people. However, it made wealthy liberals feel good about themselves, and made many liberal lawyers wealthy enough to live in places where they could avoid its consequences. Its repeal would be a symbolic break with the folly of the past which would give hope to all now suffering at the hands of criminals.

Even the prisons, those hopeless warehouses of failure and lassitude largely controlled by their inmates, could at last be given a purpose once again. Their inmates could be forced to work to pay for their keep and provide restitution to those they had wronged. They could be deprived of all but the most austere necessities of life. They might then discover that wrongdoing has severe and unpleasant consequences, and so learn to avoid it.

But before we can begin, all those concerned about this great problem must understand what has gone wrong. Then they must grasp the central and worrying truth, which ought to unite principled men and women of the left as well as the right, that without a serious attempt to restrain crime our liberty will soon be in danger. What are generally dismissed as harsh and illiberal attitudes are actually essential for the preservation of individual freedom and the protection of the kind and gentle. Put simply, if the wicked are not disciplined and afraid, then the good and the bad alike will have to live in a prison state, subject to unending surveillance, surrendering freedom to a powerful armed police force, accepting lower standards of proof in the courts and permitting government interference in the legal system. Quite likely we shall also have to accept censorship of printed and electronic media. Revulsion at the licence of the pornography business is likely to grow. So is the demand for controls on broadcasters who know that violence increases ratings and refuse to accept that there are any limits on their behaviour apart from commercial ones.

The book that follows describes in detail the way in which the best police force in the world has been reduced to bureaucratic uselessness. It shows how egalitarian socialism and limp, unrealistic conservatism withdrew the law's protection from the poor and left the English people defenceless in their own homes.

It shows how actual moral panic led to the destruction of the Englishman's ancient right to bear arms, which most Englishmen do not even know they possess. It sets out the implications of this momentous change in the constitution.

It explains how and why the prison system has lost all sense of purpose and is a place where the wicked flourish, while the innocent and the harmless are punished.

It argues against the fashionable surrender to the drug culture by amoral liberals and supposedly libertarian conservatives. It states unequivocally that the spread of stupefying narcotics creates demoralization and crime. It suggests that decriminalization or legalization will lead to an increase in human misery.

It urges an open-minded reconsideration of the case for the death penalty as being preferable by far to the rapidly emerging alternative – arming of the police and the resultant increase in unofficial execution without due process. It contrasts the careful use of the death penalty in a free society with an unfettered press and independent juries, with its careless abuse in tyrannies without such freedoms. It notes that the left seems readier to accept the latter than the former.

It examines and dismisses the claims that the police are 'institutionally racist'. It argues that the Brixton riots and the murder of Stephen Lawrence were employed by social liberals to destroy the old conservative ethos of the police and to subject them to a politically-correct inquisition which left them unable to function as a crime-fighting body. It also maintains that this was a serious betrayal of the great majority of black and other minority peoples in England, who badly need the law to be enforced on their behalf.

It shows that juries are not in principle weak and foolish, but that rash egalitarian reforms and liberal tampering have made them so.

Finally, it warns that if these things are not dealt with swiftly, then all but the very rich face a future of increasing danger and insecurity.

This will become so severe that ignorant and unscrupulous calls for the abandonment of valuable liberties will grow in strength. Political forces may be unleashed that will lead to the extinction of liberty itself. We may, even now, be living in the British equivalent of the Weimar Republic. Fortunately, we have time for amendment and reconsideration before night falls.

I

The causes of crime

He shall keep the simple folk by their right:
defend the children of the poor, and punish
the wrong-doer.
Psalm 72

The single most serious mistake made by modern democracies is to imagine that criminality can be contained or discouraged by being more considerate or kinder to criminals. By doing so, they make it plain that they think that crime is caused, and thus excused, by bad conditions. They imply that they do not believe crime to be absolutely wrong in itself. The next step in this logic, which its supporters tend to hide from themselves, is that everybody is a potential criminal whose good behaviour depends only on his good fortune. In that case, those who are prosperous are good only because they *are* prosperous, rather than prosperous because they are good.

This belief demolishes the whole idea of a middle class, open to all who are diligent and self-disciplined, who will then be rewarded by a more abundant life. It helps to explain the modern left-winger's contempt for middle-class values, such as respectability and conventional moral and social behaviour. It also explains our cultural elite's withering scorn for the lower middle class, the most aspirant group of all, the most respectable and conventional of all because they are so close to the frontier. It may even solve the mystery of that elite's destructive hatred for the grammar schools where the poor learned the virtues of the middle class and were enabled to join it. The comprehensive system, with its equally passionate loathing for selection by ability, is actively designed to ensure that the process of individual self-improvement is halted. Its main effect is to trap its pupils in whatever social, economic, racial and cultural place they happen to be at the age of eleven. What else could explain the governing party's refusal to adopt for the national education system a principle – selection by ability – that governs every other field of life from science to football?

The socialist state-worshipper thinks that virtue consists of him confiscating other people's money and power for the higher good. He wants all that virtue for himself. Those who believe in this religion of government must design society, as we have, on the assumption that goodness is imposed from above by the wise generosity of the elite state. They will be guided by the belief that, without such wisdom and generosity, people will naturally behave badly. Implicit in this creed – a sort of socialist version of original sin – is the belief that everyone who *can* do bad deeds *will* do bad deeds unless he has the correct housing, income and health care. Usually, however, these correct levels are slightly out of reach, thus forever justifying further intervention by the state – somehow the task is never finished. To help people overcome their sinful state, they need subsidies, handouts, counselling, intervention from social workers, help and treatment. They have no vice or virtue of their own and cannot be expected to behave well unless they are looked after. The elite state has taken all virtue upon itself. Deterrence and punishment are therefore not merely cruel but wrong.

The old, pre-1960s law, based on unchanging moral codes, assumes that conscience is individual rather than social, that man can improve himself by work and free will. It assumes that he can refrain from committing crime through self-control and, if that fails, can be deterred from repeating it by exemplary punishment. If these things are true, then man does not need to rely on his rulers for a better life. This is why a belief in self-reliance, self-control and conscience is now the great heresy.

By sucking all personal responsibility out of the population, government actually does the opposite of what socialism claims and hopes to do. It creates a society of endemic crime which must be unceasingly placated by welfare. If an ungrateful people persist in their violence and dishonesty despite the elite's goodness towards them, it has nothing left with which to control them (and assert its goodness) except external force and fear. This requires the weapons of the strong state, an armed and obedient gendarmerie separate from the people and owing its allegiance directly to the state, with great powers of arrest, search, interrogation, investigation and detention. Communist countries, despite being allegedly based on the popular will, all eventually created harsh legal systems based on naked force, restrained by nothing.

Although social democracy has failed to abolish or even reduce crime and wrongdoing, despite decades of trying to do so, it cannot accept that its ideas are wrong and have failed. The suggestion that socialist reforms might actually have increased crime by undermining morality is impossible for the left to accept. Instead, it insists that it has failed because it has not yet gone far enough, and so demands yet more taxation, yet more spending, yet more social workers, yet more treatment. Forced to admit that crime, disorder and bad behaviour have *still* not responded to this treatment, it reaches increasingly for the crude bludgeons of authoritarian rule, curfews, surveillance, confiscations, limitations on the liberties of all to control the licence of a criminal few. Taken much further than it has already been, this idea will lead to the destruction of personal freedom for all but a very few powerful or rich people.

Lord Woolf's conversion to 'tough' sentencing is the first sign of a general collapse into crude authoritarianism. In the early months of 2002, it was followed by two other interesting straws in the wind. On 8 March, the radical left-wing Labour MP, Tony Banks, made a speech in the Commons bemoaning the decay of order and calling for the arming of the police and the stationing of armed paramilitaries at London railway termini. Mr Banks had recently been the victim of a street robbery. In May 2002 the prominent left-wing intellectual Jonathan Miller complained of graffiti in his wealthy north London street – and not just graffiti. He told the *Evening Standard:*

'More and more you notice these gangs of local youths lurking ever closer. They leave their telltale signs in the street – empty KFC boxes and cans of Fosters....

Drug dealing is rife in the high street and around the Tube station and you really have to watch out for yourself.'

Dr Miller said: 'Because of London street crime people here will now avoid going out at night unless they really have to.

It's not worth popping along to the off-licence for a couple of bottles.'

Dr Miller – who has twice had his bank card snatched while attempting to draw cash in Camden High Street – added: 'Call it middle class timidity, but if I travel by bus or Tube at night I always find these gangs – and they are black and white mixed – wearing their hoods and you really do need to avoid making eye contact with them.'

This retreat from liberal complacency – usually via a sudden epiphany when the new barbarism bursts into a previously sheltered life – has been summed up in the phrase 'A conservative is a liberal who has just been mugged'. Yet it is not an open or even a deliberate and conscious process, and the new enthusiasts for armed police forces or 'tough' prison sentences usually fail to see that what they used to advocate may have helped to bring about the disorder which they now protest against. If they would only recognize this connection, they might seek to preserve and defend the old system of liberty under the law before it is too late. Those who support liberal authoritarianism do not really mean to produce the results they obtain. It happens subtly, like many of the most damaging changes of the recent past. These changes soak slowly into the law and the state, thanks to the general acceptance of a series of dangerous but attractive ideas.

Those who believe that crime is committed in response to social conditions must begin to believe a number of other risky things. First, they must think that the job of the law is no longer to punish the wrongdoer but instead to mediate between the 'offender' (that carefully neutral word) and the 'victim'. One astonishing example of this, taken to its outer limits, occurred in Somerset in February 1999 when a woman complained to the police that her car had been vandalized. The constabulary wrote her a letter saying that the culprits 'could be considered to be victims themselves'. For those who find this incredible, here is the full account from the *Daily Mail*:

> When Rebecca Trebble found that her car had been vandalised, she expected the police to treat her as a victim of crime. Even when they told her they would not be sending an officer to investigate what they regarded as a minor matter, she thought they would at least care about her plight.
>
> But when she wrote to them complaining about her treatment, the local police chief in Taunton, Somerset, replied that whoever had damaged her car was a victim deserving of sympathy, too.
>
> Superintendent John Snell wrote back: 'Whilst I have every sympathy with you being the victim of crime, the position regarding victims is not limited to those who suffer as you have done.
>
> 'Many of those who are responsible for the commission of such minor crimes could be considered to be victims themselves.

'To my knowledge some of our prolific offenders are heroin addicts who live in the very worst of housing conditions in our area in relative poverty. It is also true many of them are from broken homes and really have miserable family backgrounds.

'I know this is no excuse and it is difficult to sympathise with such individuals when they commit crime; however, I do think sometimes we should give a thought to those less fortunate than ourselves.' Miss Trebble, a 21-year-old financial assistant, said yesterday: 'I was shocked. I felt I was being patronised and that he was lecturing me. To suggest the criminal was as much the victim was amazing. That's just not what you expect from the police.'

There is another unpleasant side to this excuse-making approach. While helping the 'victim' to cope with his victimhood, you must work on the assumption that his misfortune may well be partly his own fault. Although he must not risk the use of force in guarding his life and property, he may be to blame if he fails to protect his possessions strongly enough with the passive methods that are still permitted, such as alarms, lights, fences and locks. He may own more than he ought to, or be too obvious about his wealth. He may be weak, old or ill and therefore vulnerable, and well-advised to stay indoors as much as possible.

In short, wealth greater than the average is itself immoral, probably obtained at the expense of others. Those who draw attention to their wealth, or fail to protect it, or are too feeble to do so, can reasonably expect to be relieved of it by others. They have no absolute right to it. A frightening sign of how deeply this view has penetrated our society is the way in which criminals, like the muggers who recently attacked the Prime Minister's eldest son in north London, will often describe the ownership of expensive clothes and cars as 'greed' and their robberies of those better off than themselves as 'taxing'. They speak more truly than they know. They did, after all, learn something in their long years at comprehensive school: the dim falsehood that the rich and the middle classes are wealthy at the expense of the poor. This is an argument both for expropriation and for its little brother, theft.

Rather than seeking to frighten, punish and deter those who would prey on the 'victim', the socialist state seeks to educate the 'victim' in how he must fortify his house or alarm his car, how he must not walk in certain areas or leave valuables where a criminal might observe them. Millions are spent on advertising campaigns telling us not to leave our property where a thief might see it. The inability to resist the temptation to steal is seen as an unavoidable fact of life. Theft is treated as an uncontrollable force of nature, like the wind and the rain, against which we must shelter ourselves. Policemen who once patrolled the streets to deter thieves now visit homeowners, calling themselves Crime Prevention Officers and advising on fences, lighting and alarm systems. These are designed to deal with a world in which it is assumed that housebreakers will take any opportunity they can, and will almost always escape detection or capture.

If householders fail in their duty of protecting the dishonest from themselves, then they may lose their insurance against theft. When householders are injured or killed during robberies, police spokesmen are often quoted as saying such things as 'this was a burglary that went wrong'. This implies that, in their minds, there is such a thing as 'a burglary that went right' – presumably one in which nobody is hurt. Neighbourhoods are plastered with posters warning that 'pickpockets operate in this area' or 'thieves operate in this locality, do not leave valuables in your car'.

Even if it does catch him, the system will seek to understand the 'offender' so thoroughly that he will probably not be dealt with in any way that will upset or inconvenience him. At the same time, the 'victim' must be placated, because he cannot be offered the reassurance that his attacker will be punished. He is offered counselling, told the outcome of the case and sometimes asked if he wishes to meet the person who has attacked or robbed him, in a process known as 'restorative justice'. Despite its name, this does not restore the things he most wants – his lost property and his lost peace of mind. Instead he may get an apology.

This managerial, morally empty approach was sharply exposed in an article in the *Daily Telegraph* in May 2000 by its home affairs expert Philip Johnston, dealing with the new type of chief constable now emerging. Johnston, an acute observer of the modernised system, wrote:

> The present generation of senior officers is far removed in social and educational background from most of their predecessors. Almost to a man, they grew up in the Sixties, an era of permissiveness which some say led to the development of the current liberal orthodoxy. Thirty of the 43 chief constables in England and Wales are 55 or under. All but seven have degrees. Thirteen have degrees in social sciences, psychology or business studies; a further 13 graduated in law or criminology. The remaining 10 read a variety of subjects.
>
> A decade ago, only a quarter of chief constables had a degree and none was a graduate when he entered the service. The characteristics of chief officers have also changed. Before the last major police reorganisation in the mid-Sixties, many would have been retired Army officers or civil servants. It was not necessary to have been a policeman. Nowadays, every chief constable has come through the police service and few have ever worked outside it. They have all been on specialist courses at the Bramshill police college in Hampshire. They are far more adept than their predecessors in the law, in criminal theory and in detective techniques. The new generation of police chiefs has been much

influenced by the adoption of management techniques in the public services. It would be wrong to see the 43 chief officers as a homogeneous group but they increasingly speak as one through the Association of Chief Police Officers.

Johnston quoted Robert Reiner, professor of law at the LSE, as saying that many of the new chiefs saw themselves as business executives:

> 'That is what they are groomed for. Basically, they are running very large organisations, with the Home Office as their main client,' he said. The type of degrees some chief constables possess may make them more inclined to a 'society causes crime – don't blame us' approach. During the recent debate about policing, that view was prevalent.
>
> Richard Childs, chief constable of Lincolnshire, said: 'The quick and populist way today is to blame the police for getting it wrong. While sometimes we do, we are, I believe, the messengers of a broader problem of change and unrealistic and insatiable expectations.' The Police Federation, with which chief officers have an uncomfortable relationship, once called them 'clones and butterflies', career officers who possessed a similar outlook and flitted from force to force looking for promotion.

As Johnston pointed out, critics of the existing system believe it rewards caution and conformity and reinforces the culture that has already taken root. Most senior officers are reluctant to offend the Home Office or stray from current orthodoxies because this could threaten their promotion. Some of them also feel entitled to join in the political debate. On 26 April 2000 William Hague, then the

Conservative leader, championed what were subsequently denounced as 'populist' views on law and order. In a speech in Alcester, Warwickshire, he said :

> 'The Tony Martin case lit a touch paper that has led to an explosion of anger and resentment among millions of law-abiding British people who no longer feel the state is on their side.' He said that the foremost responsibility of the state was to protect its law-abiding citizens. One of those who did not seem to agree was Mr Crispian Strachan, Chief Constable of Northumbria, who accused the Conservative leader of promoting American-style gun law that could 'seriously increase' levels of violent crime and murder.
>
> Kenneth Williams, 56, the Chief Constable of Norfolk, scene of the Tony Martin episode, said it was not the job of his officers, 'to make value judgments about the crimes we investigate'. He said he had been shocked at the ferocity of public reaction to Martin's life sentence, expressed in a flood of abusive phone calls to the police.

Johnston's account explains why chief constables seem so immune to public pressure and why they seem so keen on technological solutions – the favourite resort of the modern managerial reformer. It also gives a clue as to why they are so resistant to returning to the tried methods of the past.

The results of this on the street are far from happy. Instead of the reassuring presence of police constables walking the beat, there is the disturbing electric shrieking of sirens as the police rush to the scenes of crimes that have already been committed, all too frequently killing or injuring innocent pedestrians (and sometimes killing themselves as well) as they hurtle at excessive speeds down shopping streets and suburban roads. In 1999–2000, twenty-five people were killed in high-speed police chases, three times the figure of three years before. Six more died when police cars answering 999 calls crashed. Roughly two thousand people are injured each year in accidents involving police cars chasing suspects or answering 999 calls, according to the Police Complaints Authority and the Home Office.

This miserable wailing racket, together with the fear and danger it betokens, only spreads the idea that crime is abroad and chaos is near. This is exactly the opposite of what a police force should be doing. Its cost in lives and injuries is greater than that of some recent wars. It is worth asking whether the outcomes of most of these calls justify such a level of risk. It is hard to see what the point of it is, except to emulate what police chiefs have seen on American TV shows, where the strobe-lights and howling may conceivably be justified by the conditions of the south Bronx or north Philadelphia but certainly are not in the suburbs of Wolverhampton.

This is not the only demoralizing and dispiriting result of modern absentee policing. Many city areas, especially in London, are punctuated with bright yellow 'murder boards' detailing horrific crimes that have taken place nearby, about which the police are seeking information. First used in the mid-1980s to seek witnesses to murders, when one or two might be displayed each month, they are now part of the London landscape, with about two hundred now being deployed each month, describing crimes such as street robbery, serious assault, serious sexual assault, murder and racial crime. They may be effective in finding witnesses, but they are even more effective at spreading the idea that evil is abroad and unrestrained. It is much easier to find such boards than to find a police officer on patrol, as one London borough wittily pointed out when it displayed similar boards asking if anyone had seen a police officer in the area recently.

This sort of reactive, fire-brigade policing is doubly useless. Many of the incidents to which the cars are hurrying with their sirens of doom and their spaceship strobe-lights are not worth the fuss. Some, such as pub fights, would sort themselves out quietly if left alone and simply do not merit the level of attention they receive. Others, such as burglaries, are over and done with before the officers can get there. It is a harsh and unwelcome fact that, unless trained in first aid, a police officer is almost entirely useless *after* most crimes have been committed. All he can do is take notes, offer sympathy and launch a legal process that will probably end in failure. Even Sherlock Holmes reincarnated would be unlikely to be able to track down most culprits. Even then, the Crown Prosecution Service may well decide that it is not worthwhile to proceed. If the CPS does go ahead, the case may collapse at the last minute for bureaucratic reasons. If it is taken to its conclusion, the criminal will probably be punished so lightly (if at all) that he will in future be even less afraid of the law.

Yet this is not the worst of it. There are grim and totalitarian implications in the social-work approach to crime which will not be widely obvious until they are far advanced. We should think about them now. The new system refuses to believe that there are people who are so morally unrestrained that they are prepared to do wicked acts. It cannot accept that they must be punished for those acts and deterred from repeating them by hard and memorable retribution. Instead, it bases all its actions on the view that crime results from inequality, mental disturbance or unpleasant experiences such as child abuse. Authority must then assume that everyone is a potential wrongdoer. The law, the police and the authorities must treat everyone as a suspect.

We are supposed to accept that it is necessary for the police to retain DNA details of as many citizens as possible. Pressure to compel us all to be photographed and fingerprinted is great and growing. Terrorism is only the latest pretext for the Home Office to bring out – once more – its long-prepared plans for identity cards. If these cards are successfully introduced, they will contain great quantities of encoded information as well as fingerprints and photographs. They will be of little use to the police unless citizens are compelled to carry them at all times – a measure that would completely change the relationship between the citizen and the state.

Many of our movements in public and semi-private places, from shopping centres to churches and offices, are monitored without our knowledge or permission by closed-circuit TV cameras. Sadly, as in the case of the abducted child James Bulger, this surveillance is of no use in preventing crime unless someone happens to be watching at the very moment it is committed. If only the cameras that tracked the abduction of James Bulger had been able to cry out a warning or call out a question. They merely recorded the disaster, so that experts could stare at the miserable footage too late to save James Bulger from death or his killers from their crime.

Our most personal details are shared with increasing willingness among government departments. Our recorded telephone calls and e-mails are to be stored. The Regulation of Investigatory Powers Act, now likely to be combined with European legislation and Europol powers, is the basis for this enormous intrusion into places that would once have been considered absolutely private.

While still formally presumed to be innocent until proven guilty, we may have our assets seized without any such proof. The Drug Trafficking Offences Act 1986 gave a court powers to order the seizure of property connected with narcotics offences. Later, through the Criminal Justice Act 1988, this power was extended to the profits from all crimes. These Acts were conviction-based, so that there could be no confiscation of assets without the defendant first having been convicted. However, the Proceeds of Crime Act 2002 gives the police powers to confiscate assets *without a conviction* from persons whom they suspect of drug dealing or other crimes. Drug-dealers, for reasons explained elsewhere in this book, are convenient hate-figures against whom such measures might be popular at present. But this does not alter the fact that an important legal principle, of no punishment before conviction, has quietly but definitely been breached.

We may be detained for long periods if we are accused of 'terrorism'. This is a crime the government pretends to treat with special horror but with which it is in truth happy to negotiate when it suits it. So, if the horror is false, we have the right to suspect that 'terrorism' is no more than an excuse for the taking of powers that the state wants anyway. If we engage in certain kinds of demonstration or political movement, the police have extraordinary new powers, almost always granted with the public's willing support, to detain and obstruct us as if we were threats to the state. The Criminal Justice and Public Order Act 1994, originally passed to deal with unpopular 'rave' parties, is the main basis of these new powers. Our passports can be taken from us if we are believed to be football hooligans. How long before this totalitarian power is extended to cover other people?

Police officers, when we do encounter them, are ostentatiously equipped with devices to restrain, gas and club us, when once they managed with no more than a tactfully concealed truncheon. The new equipment makes it plain that the public are not to be trusted and may at any time need to be pursued, gassed or manacled. The modern police officer is not a public servant except in name. Like his Continental counterparts, he is a powerful representative of the state with whom it is unwise to argue. The old police deference to the middle class was not just the consequence of simple snobbery. It was an expression of the old truth that the law was our servant, not our master. The new type of officer, who defers to nobody but his chiefs, does not care who you are, if you support the law or loathe it. It is all the same to him, although stardom and celebrity, the classless society's aristocracy, may gain his deference. He is the state and you are not. That is why he now has far greater licence to enter our homes and search them than ever before, to listen to our telephone conversations and read our mail. Our right to have our guilt assessed by a jury of people like ourselves has also been seriously undermined and may, in effect, soon disappear for ever for most accused people.

This is a physical expression of a new type of thought. The liberal state has redefined crime in such a way that many actions that used to be seen as common sense are now dangerous breaches of the law. Teachers who smack or even restrain children, householders who catch vandals smashing their fences and frogmarch them to their parents for punishment, citizens who put up barbed wire to defend their homes against thieves, shopkeepers who try to fight off violent thieves with force, all find that the police are likely to view them as offenders. The new law believes that the family is itself a seething nest of abuse from which battered wives and molested children may at any time need to be rescued. By means of the Children Act 1989 it openly undermines adult authority, zealously pursuing allegations against teachers accused of 'abuse'.

This enthusiasm for pursuing allegations against authority figures widens the gulf between the police and citizens who once saw themselves as being on the side of the law. Actions that would at one time have been seen as helpful to the police are now prosecuted and punished. Faced with such actions – defence of homes, citizens' arrests of street robbers and so forth – police chiefs complain about citizens 'taking the law into their own hands'. This is an interesting use of language. The law, as it has existed for centuries, is in the hands of the English people and is shared by them with a police force who are supposed to be citizens in uniform.

However, there is now such deep disagreement between the public view of right and wrong and that held by the state that this is no longer so. In the one area where the two do apparently agree – dislike of disorder and disapproval of certain spectacular and unpopular crimes – there are interesting clashes between appearance and reality. The disapproval that used to be aimed at sexual deviation of all kinds has now been focused on paedophilia, the one sexual perversion of which liberals disapprove as much as the rest of the population. Red light districts and blatant prostitution now flourish on the verge of legalization. The laws against under-age intercourse are rarely enforced. In a recent case, police refused to prosecute a man in his twenties for alleged sexual relations with thirteen-year-old girl because the girl herself had not complained and would not complain, despite the powerful evidence that an offence had been committed and the grief and distress of the girl's parents. What would once have been called 'public indecency', heterosexual or homosexual, is quite unchecked. Sexual and violent abuse of children is made vastly more likely by the breakdown of the stable family. All our fears and worries about sexual exploitation, licence and the victimization of the young must now be assuaged by one of the few remaining laws that acknowledges (quite rightly) that some sexual behaviour is wrong and that children need protection from adult evil.

Perhaps this is why this offence, quite bad enough to start with, has become the focus for angry street demonstrations and for special police and court procedures not applied to any other crime. People accused of this offence – and it is important to remember that they *are* accused until convicted – are subject to trials that are often breathtakingly unfair. Police are allowed to trawl for witnesses, childish denunciations are given the same weight as adult statements, under-age witnesses are protected from the normal rigours of cross-examination and guilt is effectively presumed from the start. Dawn swoops, computer searches and similar tactics, often well publicized by press leaks, seem designed to show the police are doing at least one thing that is popular. Celebrities, although usually rather faded ones, are accused surprisingly often of this offence, again as if to show that the law's old impartiality between great and small still exists, since celebrities are the only privileged aristocracy permitted to exist in our egalitarian times.

One effect of this development is that perfectly reasonable doubts about such prosecutions are liable to be viewed as sympathy for child-molesters, by even well-educated and intelligent people who are unaware of the manipulation being practised upon them. Some readers may even find themselves thinking that this passage is some sort of attempt to excuse or minimize paedophilia. No such sentiment is expressed or intended by the author, who views sexual assaults on children as serious offences deserving harsh punishment and who loathes pornography of all descriptions. It is a sign that something is wrong with our laws and our society when such a disclaimer is necessary. This atmosphere makes it harder for reasonable doubts to be expressed, for fear of the mob cry of 'you must be one too'. Concern for justice and due process is dismissed as tenderness for perverts or killers. The modern show-trial of an alleged paedophile is therefore unfair even before it begins. Even where the charges are obviously true, such trials leave a nasty taste. The same end could have been achieved without breaking the basic rules of English justice.

Rape is also now viewed as a crime against feminism rather than merely an offence against decency, kindness and trust. Thanks to its new ideological importance this offence is treated with politicized horror and subject to special rules, notably the anonymity of the victim and restrictions on the right of the accused to defend himself. The presumption of innocence is damaged beyond repair by the treatment of defendants and accusers in such cases. Most such cases involve 'date-rape' where both parties know each other and the alleged assailant claims that consent was given. The name of the accused is made public, in a case where it is generally one person's word against another's and there are no independent witnesses. Even if acquitted, he is subject to the exposure of his private life and behaviour which can never be expunged or forgotten. The accuser, however, retains her anonymity even if the charge is dismissed. This appallingly one-sided procedure cannot fail to impress jurors with the idea that the Crown's mind is already half made up before the trial has begun. It also often fails in its objective. A large number of rape cases end in acquittals, very probably because the law makes little distinction between 'date-rape' and violent assaults by strangers, and juries are reluctant to convict on the basis of an uncorroborated accusation. In November 2002 the government proposed to make it harder for a man accused of rape to claim he believed the woman had consented. This will have the effect of compelling male defendants to prove their innocence of such charges. It is political-law-making.

Another strange development raises suspicions that the justice system has become more politicized than it would care to admit. Conservative politicians such as Jonathan Aitken or Jeffrey Archer seem especially liable to accusations of perjury, a crime that is breathtakingly common (the witnesses in many contested trials could in theory face such charges if their side lost) and remarkably rarely prosecuted among the non-political classes, especially in civil cases. Again, the point is not that anyone should feel sympathy for either of these two. The author has no such sympathy and views both men as an embarrassment to the causes they espouse. They are proven liars who deserved to be punished. Nobody should object to such prosecutions if they were intended to discourage lying on oath, a terrible crime which poisons the wells of justice. However, was that their true purpose? Would their prosecutions have taken place at all, or would their sentences have been so long, if they were not prominent members of the dethroned Conservative elite? Were they imprisoned for being perjurers, or for being *Conservative* perjurers? The apparently selective nature of these cases raises questions about their real justification. Susan Edwards of Buckingham Law School found that Archer's four-year sentence was unprecedented in such a case. Between 1981 and 2000 only nine perjurers were imprisoned for three years or more. They had told lies in serious criminal trials involving murder or large-scale corruption. Archer's perjury was in a civil trial.

The ludicrous affair of the sexual allegations against the former Tory MP Neil Hamilton and his wife Christine, attended with phalanxes of police cars and seizure of computer equipment, all taking place in conditions of total publicity, gave yet more force to fears that the police have become far too sensitive to political fashion and media stardom. The Hamiltons have made public fools of themselves and deserve little sympathy, but the willingness of the police to take seriously these laughable allegations against them is disturbing. For whose benefit was this charade intended?

Murder, a shockingly common crime treated with increasing leniency by the courts, is a different matter when the victim is a child or a celebrity. Police forces cannot catch as many killers as they once did and prosecutors often reduce murder charges to manslaughter in order to achieve a swift conviction. However, they will concentrate enormous resources on prominent murder cases. Something akin to a show-trial often results. It is reasonable to wonder whether these spectacular tribunals are designed to prove, at almost any cost, that the law is actually effective after all. In some recent cases, notably those of the Russell murders in Kent and the killing of the TV presenter Jill Dando, there are serious doubts about the quality of the evidence used to convict the suspects.

The law of the new elite, based on utopian social engineering, is displacing the older law, based on common sense and Christian morals, because that elite controls the courts and the modernized police. One of the most important duties of the modern police force is to ensure its total monopoly of violence and enforcement. The common law has been taken from the common people, and their attempts to enforce it themselves are punished more harshly than crime itself. This is why citizens who unintentionally kill suspects during attempted crimes, such as the farmer Tony Martin, are prosecuted and imprisoned while police officers who do the same thing are generally exonerated. It is not the action itself that is wrong – or police officers who have mistakenly shot suspects would be languishing alongside Mr Martin. It is the fact that a private individual rather than a representative of the elite state has done the shooting.

The police are now a special body of armed men with special powers far beyond those of the ordinary citizen. Such harsh and determined prosecutions are designed to educate the public into realizing that the law no longer belongs to them, that the police are not citizens in uniform any more. They are servants of the elite state, which owns the law and uses it for its own supposedly wise purposes. The same reasoning lies behind the rapid and determined disarming of the English people, who were once obliged by law to bear arms in support of the civil power and who, a century ago, were as free to bear arms as any American is today.

This division, between what people think the law should be and what it actually is, leads to a permanent suspicion and near-hostility between police and citizens. The police are operating a law that they know to be unpopular. This shatters the old sympathy between police and respectable law-abiding people. The police themselves must in many cases be neutral referees between offender and victim. Their new rules tell them that the offender may have good social and economic reasons for his behaviour. They also tell them that the victim may have brought his trouble upon himself by behaving foolishly, for instance by failing to conceal his unfair wealth or status, failing to bar and bolt and alarm his house and car, or just assuming that the streets of an English city are safe at night.

The new police will often be harsher with the victim than with the offender, especially if he has used violence to defend himself or his property. The point must be made that the old idea, that the police are there to defend life and property against those who attack it, has been repealed. It has been replaced by a new 'civilized' or 'social' law. This calls on the police to seek to understand criminals and help them to return to normal life. It has turned them into the uniformed front line of the equality-loving state. This unspoken rule lies behind the zealous prosecution of those who 'take the law into their own hands'. Once, such people would have been more or less the allies of the police. Now they are trying to enforce an obsolete and abolished law and challenging the state's monopoly over law enforcement. It is not merely insensitivity to public opinion when these things happen, or the result of bureaucrats sticking too closely to the rules. It is a cold and deliberate policy aimed at destroying old assumptions about a citizen's right to protect himself and his property. Once we had the Queen's peace, which was ours. Now we have the people's police, who belong to the elite state.

II

'Bobbies on the beat'

The purpose of a trial is to find out the truth.
But we no longer have trials about who did it –
the trial is always about whether somebody
broke the rules in trying to find out who did it.
Sir David Phillips, Chief Constable of Kent

For years British politicians of all parties have been calling for 'more bobbies on the beat' and audiences have been applauding them for doing it. Most citizens, in town and countryside, keenly support the idea that there should be more police officers walking the streets or bicycling down country lanes to reassure the good and frighten the wicked.

One of the most noticeable facts about modern England is that there are hardly any police officers to be seen. Large regiments of them appear during football matches or at demonstrations, kitted out in glowing yellow jerkins whose main purpose seems to be to emphasize that they are there at all. Sometimes, irregularly and unreliably, they are to be found on the busier streets of major cities or sitting, waiting for something to happen, in vans parked round corners. From time to time there are announcements that plainclothes officers 'may be required to go back on the beat'.

There are even schemes for the police to do their main task, which is tacitly admitted to be paperwork, in public places such as shops and cafés, so that they can at least be seen to exist. They may be observed soaring overhead in helicopters or hunkered down on rooftops, in baseball caps and bullet-proof jackets, during state visits or outside the trials of alleged terrorists. They were active in suppressing perfectly peaceful and legitimate demonstrations against the visit of the Chinese tyrant Jiang Zemin to Britain in October 1999. They can often be seen hurrying by in cars, usually in pairs absorbed in each other's conversation. Even London's Royal Parks Police, a force whose territory is almost entirely made up of lawns, woodlands and narrow footpaths, tends to patrol (when it does so at all) in cars.

If we call on them in distress or emergency they will eventually arrive, complaining of an impossible backlog of unsolved cases, to give us a crime number, offer us counselling for our grief or loss and advise us to buy new locks, bolts, lights and alarms, while going through the motions of an investigation that will rarely yield any result. Even this form of activity is now in decline, since the number of robberies, burglaries and car thefts is so great that it is often unwise for them to raise hopes of justice or recompense that are bound to be dashed. They can be found milling around the criminal courts, all too often on wasted journeys for trials that are mysteriously cancelled or postponed.

Those trials, once a contest between prosecution and defence attempting to establish guilt or innocence, are now an elaborate game to see if the enormous safeguards and protections given to defendants by law have been fully exercised. The Police and Criminal Evidence Act 1984 was a response to a series of police scandals and wrongful convictions. Rather than seeing these as errors that might be corrected by punishing those responsible, the elite state chose to blame the entire police force. They enacted a great Domesday Book of mistrust and regulation which assumes that every police officer is a latent evidence planter, quote inventor, liar and brute. Every action must be tape-recorded or logged. Every suspect must be provided with a lawyer at the earliest possible moment. The streets must be trawled for people to take part in identity parades, a regulation that has created a minor cottage industry in many cities, where a useful tax-free income is available to those with time on their hands and a vaguely criminal appearance who can take part in the endless parades. Other measures and judicial decisions have also forced prosecutors to disclose almost everything they are doing to the defence. And any long delay – perhaps caused by the need to assemble mountains of files, stacks of tapes and battalions of busy witnesses – is likely to lead to the cancellation of the trial.

One slip and the case collapses. Sir David Phillips, Chief Constable of Kent, complained in April 2001 that the court system was quite simply too soft on criminals, following the revelation that one offender was so undeterred by the majesty of the law that he had been arrested 186 times before he was seventeen. Sir David pithily described the new justice system in words that ought to be written up outside the country's courthouses: 'The purpose of a trial is to find out the truth. But we no longer have trials about who did it – the trial is always about whether somebody broke the rules in trying to find out who did it.' He reflected a general feeling that there are now too many laws and regulations that give privileges to defendants. Worse, even when they are tried and found guilty the courts are reluctant to do anything to them. For instance, during 1999, thirty-seven thousand people admitted or were convicted of burglary, a serious attack on the peace of mind of many thousands of people. However, seven thousand of those were let off with a caution, the authorities' way of saying they could not be bothered to do anything about it.

Home Office focus groups found in the same year that respect for the law had seriously declined. Most people now believe that criminals run little risk of being caught. Those that are caught will be given short sentences by an elite of out-of-touch judges. This is slightly unfair to judges, who come under unending pressure to keep the prisons from overflowing and so are reluctant to hand out prison sentences unless they absolutely have to.

In an amoral society with feeble courts today's police officer has a difficult task. Even so, the missing police cannot escape blame for being absent from their proper place of duty. Many of them can be seen in the columns of the newspapers, suing their forces for sexual or racial discrimination. Others, who have yet to understand that the job has changed beyond recognition, are hauled before disciplinary tribunals, and sometimes the courts, for chastising wayward youths, having wrongly imagined that this was what they were paid to do. Large numbers have joined the force – now more usually known as a 'service' – since its transformation into a motorized bureaucracy. They simply do not know what traditional policing involves and are surprised that anyone should expect it of them.

Some officers even speak about the health problems that arise in what is now semi-officially a sedentary occupation. In April 2000, the *Daily Mail* interviewed a young policewoman, Gill Moriaty, then aged thirty-three. She explained: 'When you join the police you acquire a really good level of fitness because you train regularly for the first 20 weeks. After that there is no mandatory fitness regime and you are left to your own devices. I spend a lot of the time cruising around in a patrol car.' She said there was 'a certain amount of walking around'. A fitness expert, Doug Robertson, concluded that, while she was quite fit, 'it's true to say that Gill's job is not very active and any exercise outside working hours – even chasing her toddler around – will not go amiss.' A waitress and a gardener both had higher fitness scores.

If we try to seek them out in police stations, we will find that these places have often been closed, both in country districts and in city areas. Where they still exist, they are often sited away from town centres and are open during office hours only. When they are open, their counters are frequently not staffed by police officers. In many cases, especially in small country towns, they are deserted for much of the time and equipped with special telephones. The frightened or angry citizen can use these to reach a control room many miles away. Those who answer the phone, often not police officers, may never have heard of the street where the victim lives. They will frequently explain that lack of manpower means that no swift response can be expected.

The same is true of the 999 service, hugely overloaded because it is the only guaranteed route through which most people can make contact with the police at all. By early 2002, BT was dealing with six hundred and twenty-five thousand 999 calls each week; its competitor, Cable and Wireless, handled a further one hundred and twenty-five thousand (these figures are for the whole of the UK; separate statistics for England and Wales are not available). Genuine emergencies have to fight their way past citizens making daft requests for information, needlessly worried old ladies and cranks – exactly the sort of people who would once have accosted a constable on the beat or queued up for a word with the station sergeant.

The history of the 999 service neatly illustrates the changes that have overtaken British society and policing. It was set up in London following a fatal fire in Wimpole Street in 1936 in which five women died. A neighbour complained that, by the time she reached the operator, the fire engines were already at the scene. The Post Office, which then controlled the telephone system, began the 999 service in London in July 1937 so that emergencies could jump the queue. The system was eventually copied throughout the world, but before the Second World War it was confined to London and Glasgow. In its first month, thirteen thousand Londoners used it. The small number of telephones, public and private, limited its use even when it was expanded to most of the UK in the 1950s. At that time there were fewer than half a million 999 calls each year, 65 per cent of them to the police. By the early 1960s this figure had risen to two and a half million per year, rising to four million in 1970, nine million in 1978, nineteen million in 1988, and over twenty-three million in 1998. By 2001 the explosive increase in the number of mobile phones meant that there were more than thirty-one million calls each year, many of them false or accidental. About 80 per cent of mobile emergency calls are to the police rather than the other emergency services, compared with about 56 per cent of calls from fixed lines. How the police can be expected to respond to this number of calls, or sort them into a reasonable priority, is a mystery. In reality, they cannot be expected to and they do not.

Senior police officers and the Police Federation respond in chorus when complaints are raised about this and the other problems that result from the absence of foot patrols. They cling to the belief of all inefficient nationalized industries, that their problems are caused by a 'lack of resources' rather than by their own actions or failures. They say that more manpower is needed. Opposition politicians sing the same silly song. Governments have several different answers. One is to pass laws – the only thing they can actually do – even if those laws already exist in another form and are not being enforced. Another is to increase police numbers, a hard task at a time when many experienced officers are leaving early and it is all the force can do to maintain its strength. When they cannot afford to provide these resources, they massage the crime statistics and claim that everything is getting better. The Home Secretary, David Blunkett, ludicrously claimed in January 2002 that people were safer from crime than they had been for twenty years. In a speech in Sheffield he said that crime was not as bad as people thought it was. Despite a recent spate of street robberies and a huge increase in mobile phone thefts, he said that the chances of becoming a victim were at their lowest for twenty years. 'Anyone reading recent reports would think that crime and violent crime in particular is now spiralling out of control,' he said. 'The reality is very different. There is a growing problem with street robbery and mobile phones in particular. But overall crime is now falling and has been for some time.'

Politicians also use the public's justified discontent to seek closer and tighter central control of the nation's police – something they have always wanted – on the grounds of increasing efficiency. The Conservative Home Secretary, Kenneth Clarke, did this through the Sheehy Report, much hated within the police force itself. Mr Blunkett, in late 2001, likewise promised an attack on poor working practices and excessive sickness claims, while quietly seeking unprecedented powers to dismiss chief constables, the real point of his measures. Both governments failed to realize that cumbersome organization, unwarranted sickness claims and early retirement, not to mention the endless industrial tribunal and other court cases affecting the police, are the result of their own past reforms. In the end, they both accepted the lazy fiction that the problems of the police can be solved simply by increasing the numbers of officers doing the wrong thing in the wrong place, combined with giving them powers that they are unable to use.

The constant allegation that police operations are hampered by a manpower crisis is the first and most amazing Big Lie of the law and order debate. It is astonishing that it goes unquestioned, although it is so often used and so easily exploded. Examine the figures in the table below for population and police strength in England and Wales throughout the twentieth century.

Year	Population (England and Wales)	Police strength (England and Wales)	men	women
1901	32,527,843	42,484		
1911	36,075, 269	51,203		
1921	37,886,689	56,914		
1931	39,948,000	58,656		
1941	41,748,000 (estimated)	56,193	55,868	325
1951	43,745,000	63,116	61,610	1506
1961	46,166,000	75,161	72,829	2332
1971	48,604,000	95,759	91,937	3822
1981	49,011,000	118,081	107,379	10,702
1991	49,890,000	125,294	110,396	14,898
1995	n/a	124,710	107,022	17,688
1999	n/a	123,051	103,084	19,967
2001	53,137,000 (estimated)			

The changes that have taken place over this period are boundless: in health and strength, wealth and housing, education, morality, religion, diet, means of transport, general social welfare, migration, the role of women. One of those changes is shown by the startling increase in the number of female officers (insignificant before the Second World War) which began nearly thirty years ago. What is more, these women officers, who were once given separate duties, are now treated exactly as if they were men, an interesting change in an organization whose effectiveness once depended heavily on the size and strength of its members. The far greater use of women, who simply cannot be as strong and imposing as male colleagues, is a symptom of the change in the role of the police officer. The modern police is an increasingly bureaucratic service rather than a preventive force whose impact used to depend on the implied ability to intervene and on sheer force of personality.

Now-discarded height regulations and rules against the wearing of glasses did not discriminate specifically against women (or myopic bookworms) but against all, male or female, who would be unlikely to overawe a drunken troublemaker on the midnight streets. Plainly, there are women who can produce such an effect and women who are happy to take part in physically demanding operations. Such atypical individuals do this despite the fact that female upper-body strength is seldom more than 60 per cent of that of men. There is no doubt that many women have the necessary courage or personality. But no amount of such qualities can make up for raw strength and size. Attitudes towards women among the educated middle class have been transformed over the past forty years. However, the educated middle class do not need the police to keep them in order. Attitudes remain largely unchanged among the sort of people the police are supposed to control. Few football hooligans, drunks or wife-beaters are *Guardian* readers and it is no use women officers – or small, bespectacled male officers, come to that – appealing to their progressive instincts when the punches start to fly. Thanks to the censorship of any dissent as 'sexism', few in the police now dare to express such doubts. Those who are still free to debate in public have a duty to ask whether this change is good for the police, the public or the individual women involved.

Many of the recent changes in our world might be thought likely to make for a more law-abiding society rather than a more lawless one. For much of the twentieth century they did have exactly that effect. Perhaps the most peaceful single year was 1951, with a low level of crime, especially violent crime, following a brief increase in bad behaviour following the war. The average daily prison population for that year was 21,370. Forty years later, in 1991, we were recognizably in modern times. The average daily prison population stood at 44,809, and crimes of all kinds were rising sharply and were far more common than forty years earlier. Over the same period the number of police officers increased from roughly 1.4 per thousand in 1951 to roughly 2.5 per thousand in 1991. It is true that the number of officers has fallen slightly since the late 1990s while the population has risen but it is still the case that there are far more police officers per head than in any other era.

This increase has coincided with an increase in crimes of all kinds. It is important to add that the police have been joined in their large new office buildings by tens of thousands of back-room staff whose job is to do the tedious paperwork that is supposed to be tying down so many officers. They have also been relieved of many duties – enforcing car-parking rules, checking shops and factories by night, organizing prosecutions. These are done, respectively, by local authorities, private security firms and the Crown Prosecution Service. So the true increase in manpower is even greater than appears from the figures.

Excuses about overstretched resources and poor manning are also undermined by a great number of other developments which might be thought to make the job of the police easier rather than harder. In roughly the same four decades, the management experts have been set loose on every police force in the land. They have been merged into larger units, supposedly to cut down on bureaucracy and increase efficiency. They have been given huge fleets of cars and vans, computerized central records, personal radios and greatly increased powers of search, surveillance and arrest. They clatter as they move, their belts hung with costly equipment supposedly designed to make them more effective. They even have a small air force of helicopters and the active help of broadcasters, through programmes such as *Crimewatch*, allowing them to hurry details of suspects to millions rather than the few hundred who might have seen a poorly printed 'Wanted' poster in the old days. Enormous networks of closed-circuit TV cameras survey hundreds of town centres, railway stations and shopping malls, supposedly doing the work of dozens of constables.

A deliberate policy of graduate recruitment has raised educational levels to previously unknown heights. Senior officers are more likely to have a university degree than ever before. This may actually be a disadvantage. A university degree in modern Britain is not necessarily a sign of great attainment or intelligence. However, it is almost always a sign that its holder has been indoctrinated in the modern ideology of social welfare, egalitarianism and moral relativism that has dominated the campuses of this country for thirty years. Perhaps, while developing an interest in anarchism like the Oxford-educated Metropolitan Police commander, Brian Paddick, they have forgotten what they are employed to do. This may help to explain why they seem so absent and so ineffiicient, why they no longer patrol the streets and why they respond with indifference or excuses to calls for help from the public.

Like so many of the problems of modern England, this one has its origins in the 1960s and in the mind of Roy Jenkins. To begin with at least, it seems to have been mainly a matter of fashionable innovation, coping with shortages of recruits and cost-cutting, without any co-ordinated political motive at all. Only later did it turn into an opportunity to amend the country's constitution. Economic crisis, like war, is the reformer's ideal opportunity to ram through long-desired change.

From the first patrols of Sir Robert Peel's Metropolitan Police in 1829, the purpose of the force was to prevent crime from happening in the first place, to reassure the lawful and discourage the wrongdoer. Peel deliberately excluded middle-class and officer types from his force because he wanted men who could deal easily with the man in the street. The uniform, originally intended to be scarlet and blue finery, was in the end kept deliberately dull and understated so as not to overawe or stand out too much. The constable's oath was not a declaration of loyalty to the state but to the law, which in England is the property of the whole people. This distinction is deeply significant, which is why there was alarm when during 2002 there were proposals to give it a more politically-correct form. A typical version (each force has its own) runs:

> I do declare that I will well and truly serve Our Sovereign
> Lady the Queen in the office of constable without favour
> or affection, malice or ill-will; and that I will to the best of
> my power cause the peace to be kept and preserved, and
> prevent all offences against the persons and properties of
> Her Majesty's subjects; and that while I continue to hold
> the said office I will to the best of my skill and knowledge
> discharge all the duties thereof faithfully according to
> law. So help me God.

Legally, this gives the individual policeman great powers of initiative and independence so long as he remains within the law. It does not separate him from his fellow citizens or raise him above them.

From the beginning, the English police force was not intended to be a separate gendarmerie. As the 1929 Royal Commission on Police Powers emphasized, the office of constable is very ancient in England, with its powers rooted in the common law. The Commission stated: 'The police of this country have never been recognized, either in law or by tradition, as a force distinct from the general body of citizens.' And the Commission reiterated to the

Home Secretary that there was

> an instinctive feeling that, as a matter of principle, they
> should have as few powers as possible which are not
> possessed by the ordinary citizen, and that their authority
> should rest on the broad basis of the consent and active
> co-operation of all law-abiding people... the utmost
> discretion must be exercised by them to avoid
> overstepping the limited powers which they do possess.
> A proper and mutual understanding between the police
> and the public is essential for the maintenance of law
> and order.

From the start of English policing the chosen method of activity was designed to embody the special relationship between constable and public: that of allies on the same side in support of a law that belongs to all. Plenty of other models were available. This one was chosen because it was the only one that was not likely to threaten liberty.

The standing instructions then given to officers were consciously based on the idea of the constable as a uniformed citizen who kept the peace by persuasion, example and tact, whose influence depended on close contact with the public:

> The primary object of an efficient Police is prevention
> of crime, the next that of detection and punishment of
> offenders if crime is committed. To those ends all the
> efforts of Police must be directed. The protection of life
> and property, the preservation of public tranquillity, and
> the absence of crime, will alone prove whether those
> efforts have been successful.
> In attaining these objects, much depends on the
> approval and co-operation of the public, and these have
> always been determined by the degree of the esteem and

respect in which the Police are held. Therefore every member of the force must remember that it is his duty to protect and help members of the public, no less than to bring offenders to justice. Consequently, while prompt to prevent crime and arrest criminals, he must look on himself as the servant and guardian of the general public and treat all law-abiding citizens, irrespective of their race, colour, creed or social position, with unfailing patience and courtesy.

By the use of tact and good humour the public can normally be induced to comply with directions and thus the necessity for using force, with its possible public disapproval, is avoided. He who in this way secures the object he has in view is a more useful police officer than his comrade who, relying too much on the assertion of his authority, runs the risk of seeing that authority challenged and possibly, for the time being, overborne.

The chosen method was regular, intensive patrolling so that every-one knew that an officer was never far away. Sir Richard Mayne, first Commissioner of the Metropolitan Police, said he intended to achieve his objectives by having constables in uniform walking the streets observing and being observed by members of the public. The constable was to be alert and to see every part of his beat once every ten or fifteen minutes so that a citizen in need of assistance had only to remain in one place until the law arrived.

A century after the founding of the Metropolitan Police, the introduction to the 1929 Royal Commission on Police Powers still stated that the first duty of the police was the 'Prevention of crimes and offences, rightly regarded by the police themselves as their most important duty'. Investigation was said to come second, fol-lowed by 'other duties which have been imposed on the police', by which they meant mainly the control of traffic, already becoming a serious diversion and preoccupation.

There had been no change in this attitude when another Royal Commission reported more than three decades later, in 1962. Nothing had happened to persuade them that the preventive beat was outmoded or useless. On the contrary, they were convinced of the importance of having 'a sufficient quantity of constables on beat duty in close touch with the public'. They believed that this view was shared by both police and public. It is interesting that it had clearly survived not just two world wars but the transformation, already well under way, of the English cityscape into widespread suburbs linked by busy roads in which the car was fast becoming the main method of travel. It is also interesting that forces were beginning to worry about the decline of beat policing, even though they recognized that it was superior to any known alternative and had proved itself thoroughly in practice. The then Metropolitan Police Commissioner, Sir Joseph Simpson, said: 'The policeman in a car, on a motorcycle or absent from his beat becomes a cypher... the greatest safeguard of public relations, as well as the greatest preventive measure against crime, lies in making good deficiencies on the beats.'

These expressions of confidence and continuity seem prehistoric now. This is not because there was any sudden revolution in the science of policing. There was not and never has been. It was because the next few years were to see a series of revolutions in police organization and methods, and also in law and justice, which have changed policing out of all recognition and for the worse. These new methods have also wiped out the memory of the far more effective system that went before. The old system, which existed continuously from the days of Peel and Mayne to the 1960s, is nowadays often ignorantly mocked by the defenders of the disastrous status quo. Any sort of comparison between current levels of crime and disorder and those of the early 1960s must make any unbiased person wonder if the changes were for the better.

So what happened to abolish the long and successful career of the constable on the beat? It may seem unbelievable now, when a far larger police force is equipped with cars and motorcycles, computers and helicopters, and supplied with multitudes of clerical staff, but it seems that by the late 1960s the Home Office felt that it could not afford to continue policing at existing levels. It was also worried by the problem of patrolling the large new council housing estates that had sprung up all over the country, as both major parties pledged to solve the post-war housing crisis. The Chief Constable of Lancashire, one of the few graduates in the police force of those days, was Eric St Johnston, an innovator much liked by civil servants and by 'progressive' politicians. He was a rare survivor of the controversial, pre-1939, Trenchard proposal to recruit an 'officer class' of graduates, which had been swiftly killed off by resistance from the ranks. He seems never to have served as an ordinary constable on the beat. He would later become Chief Inspector of Constabulary (and Sir Eric) and his influence over police methods in the past forty years has been profound.

In the early 1960s, police officers were still almost entirely independent as they made their rounds. They had no personal radios and would contact headquarters through police boxes of the type immortalized by the Tardis in BBC TV's *Doctor Who*. They might also summon help from neighbouring beats with whistles or by hammering their truncheons on the pavement, still a realistic way of attracting attention in those days of light traffic at night. Car patrols were rare and mainly aimed at controlling what traffic there was. This state of affairs did not appeal to Eric St Johnston, who saw himself as the first of a new generation of visionary police chiefs. He was much admired by the Labour Prime Minister and Merseyside MP, Harold Wilson, as well as by Roy Jenkins. Wilson, the great enthusiast for creating a 'New Britain', plainly saw in St Johnston the pattern of the sort of police force he wanted. He wrote an effusive preface to St Johnston's memoirs, *One Policeman's Story*, in which he pictured St Johnston as a sort of modernizing Hercules, cleansing stables of outmoded practices. He described how, when St Johnston took over the Lancashire force, 'appalling problems faced him, the territory of the county authority was honeycombed with independent police authority enclaves, large and small, over which the County Constabulary had no jurisdiction. Equally he had a police authority which knew it all, resisted reform and the modernising ideas of one of the most progressive Chiefs in police history.' Wilson leaves no doubt that his government viewed St Johnston as an ally in its sweeping reforms of the country, against a supposedly bone-headed establishment.

> Not all the civil servants of the Home Office viewed his revolutionary ideas with enthusiasm, or would be happy to see him as either Metropolitan Police Commissioner (which he never became) or Her Majesty's Chief Inspector of Constabulary, a post which the [1962 Royal] Commission [on the Police] recommended should be created. It was Roy Jenkins as Home Secretary, despite some Home Office resistance, who appointed him Britain's first HM Chief Inspector.

St Johnston's breezy autobiography reveals that Wilson and Jenkins had chosen wisely, if their intention was to appoint a radical. He was a keen innovator and modernizer of the sort who would nowadays appeal greatly to Anthony Blair. He loved technology and publicity and was personally involved in an event that for ever changed the image of the police in England. In the early 1960s, when there were only two TV channels and a single programme could have a far greater effect than today, the weekly drama *Dixon of Dock Green* kept alive the image of the honest British copper treading the beat in size twelve shoes, an image that still lingers many years after it flickered off the screen. The BBC of Sir Hugh Greene (Director-General 1960–69) viewed *Dixon*, which it saw as 'middle class' (and therefore bad) and cosy, with some scorn. Jack Warner, the reassuring actor who practically became Dixon, was a national icon much loved by the unfashionable middle-aged and lower middle class, which Sir Hugh's new wave wanted to shock and unsettle. Greene's BBC, whose heyday of innovation and radicalism coincided with the fall of Harold Macmillan and with most of the 1964–70 Labour government, also felt it needed to win back viewers who had deserted to ITV's pioneer soap opera *Coronation Street*. The BBC approached various forces, including Lancashire, saying that *Dixon* was now too paternalistic and asking for ideas that were more modern. They also wanted to move away from portraying a man on the beat to men in cars, probably influenced by American police series such as *Highway Patrol*, then being shown for the first time in Britain. St Johnston recalled being told specifically that they were worried by the success of *Coronation Street* and its northern appeal. 'They wanted to compete by launching a new programme based on working-class life in the north of England.'

St Johnston was aghast at the slovenly, undisciplined image of the police provided by the first episode of *Z Cars*. He expected to be in serious trouble with his colleagues and political masters as a result. He forgot about his objections when the series immediately turned out to be a surging success. Its main characters continued to appear in *Z Cars* and its successors *Softly Softly* and *Task Force* for years to come. Its personalities, 'Fancy' Smith, Sergeant Lynch and Inspector Barlow, and its theme music completely supplanted those of *Dixon* in the public mind. Given the way that realistic TV drama first reflects real life and then influences it, St Johnston's decision to help and advise the BBC may well have had as much effect on English policing as all his other actions put together. To be fair to Sir Eric, this is saying a good deal.

Lancashire Constabulary was one of the biggest forces outside London and covered one of the largest areas in the days when most local forces were quite small. It had always been open to new ideas. It introduced VHF radio in 1936 to maintain contact between head-quarters and patrol cars, then rare in English policing. By 1939 it was operating 140 radio-controlled road patrols, known as 'wireless cars'. It also took part in a now-forgotten pre-war scheme to improve relations between police and motorist which could have changed the whole history of policing, the so-called Courtesy Cops system. This created a separate corps of traffic policemen whose main task was to improve driving standards by offering advice and warnings, rather than prosecuting motorists. An idea of the innovating genius Leslie Hore-Belisha, it had a highly successful start but was abandoned on the outbreak of war in 1939. The failure of the police to find a way of overcoming the growing friction with middle-class car-owners has so seriously damaged their standing with those whose support they most need that it is a great pity that this scheme has been entirely forgotten.

In the 1950s and 1960s, the Lancashire force still wanted to be first with new ideas, although of a rather different kind. It introduced radar speed traps in 1957, consciously copying an American idea, as it was to do several times. Much like modern speed cameras, the traps had a great effect to start with but that faded once drivers realized that there were so few of them. However, the impulse to try new methods did not fade. St Johnston recalled: 'Of all the innovations that we introduced into Lancashire during the time that I was there, undoubtedly the one which has had the most lasting effect on police technology was the introduction of personal radio.' However, even he did not see this as substitute for traditional beat policing. On the contrary, he wrote in his autobiography:

> I am a great believer in the traditional methods of
> policing in this country. If one could only have a
> policeman on his feet in every street in every town,
> the amount of crime and public disorder would be
> minimal. Of course this is not practicable but the fact
> remains that once policemen are taken off their feet
> and put into motor cars, they do lose touch with the
> public. However well-marked the police car may be,
> they are not seen by pedestrians in the same way and
> therefore not available for the passing of information

from the public at large to the policeman.

For this reason I came to the conclusion that we must
attach the wireless to the man rather than to the vehicle,
so that even when away from his car he was still in
contact with his station.

This huge change in the role of the police officer began in the
Lancashire town of Chorley in 1961. Superintendent Frank Gee can
claim to be the man who made personal radios truly portable by
reducing the weight of the equipment from just under three
pounds to less than sixteen ounces. Thanks to his work, the
Lancashire force became the first in the world in which individual
policemen could be constantly in touch with their stations. If modernization had stopped there, it would have been radical enough. A
constable who *can* be in permanent touch with headquarters *will* be
in permanent touch with headquarters. He will come to rely on its
advice, to expect its guidance and to seek it when once he would
have used independent judgement. Without meaning to, Eric
St Johnston had severely weakened the idea that the constable
embodies the common law and the will of the people. The constable was now, more than ever before, the servant of his superior
officers, a man able to call on plenty of support but without initiative
or independence, half his mind always tuned to a radio frequency.
This was a mixed blessing and a mixed curse.

It is possible to argue that the radio brought more benefits than it
took away. We cannot know, because this change was so quickly
followed by another even more radical one. Had constables stayed
on foot patrol, they would still have been influenced by their
regular contact with normal citizens. They would have been able
to observe the streets in a way that is simply impossible from a
passing car.

St Johnston's next step was to introduce what were at first called
Panda Cars. He chose this method because he could not find
enough policemen to give proper cover to the fast-growing town of

Kirkby, on the outskirts of Liverpool. The area, in Harold Wilson's parliamentary constituency, was famous in its early years for being so rough that it was known locally as 'Mob Town'. It was thinly disguised as Newtown in *Z Cars*. The original police sent to live there had very bad relations with the public, although after a short while these improved, along with standards of behaviour. Thanks to the unimaginative building policies of the local authority – matched in scores of similar estates elsewhere – the area was utterly bleak when the first residents moved in, with no shops, pubs, cinemas or even playing fields. St Johnston recalled: 'We were unable to find enough policemen to send to Kirkby and we had at the most only six uniformed men patrolling the town at any one time, and this in a community which had risen to 60,000 by 1963.' This was a serious lack. No old-established town of the same size would have put up with such a miserably small police presence and urgent action was obviously necessary. The pity is that St Johnston and his colleagues chose the solution they did. It was the pivotal moment in the history of policing and crime prevention in modern Britain. While it offered a short-term answer to a special problem, it would come to affect the whole country in an astonishingly short time:

> We decided the foot patrol beat must go, and in May 1965, the eleven foot patrol beats were re-organised into five mobile beats patrolled throughout the 24 hours by a policeman in a car, only the pedestrian shopping precinct being covered on foot. More important, each man carried in his pocket a personal radio which enabled him at all times, whether in the car or out of it, to keep in touch with his station.

Note the use of the words: 'We decided the foot patrol beat must go'. Someone else was shortly to take a similar decision affecting every corner of England and Wales. Parliament never debated it, there was no White Paper, no Royal Commission, no real awareness of what was going on. It was revolution by secret decree, like so many of the changes under governments of both parties that have revolutionized the English justice system in recent years. The introduction of the police in the first place occupied Parliament for nearly forty years and plunged the ruling class into controversy, and it spread across the country entirely because it was so successful and there was a popular demand for it. The new style of policing crept into existence virtually undebated. It spread partly because it appeared to be cheaper and partly because Whitehall bullied forces into adopting it. It was also apparently successful, although this may be because it was pursued so keenly and given all the resources it needed to make it work. Its defenders would certainly say that its later failure was caused by its being starved of men and time. There is little doubt that the Kirkby pilot, like the Accrington one which would follow soon after, was pursued with great enthusiasm and plentiful resources. It has all the signs of an experiment designed in advance to succeed and given ideal conditions in which to do so. St Johnston wrote an article for *The Times* in 1966 in which he said that in the last eight months of 1965 Kirkby experienced a decrease of 31 per cent in reported crimes, while detection rates rose from 29 to 37 per cent. Damage cases fell by 53 per cent, with detection rising from 9 to 21 per cent. Even the number of street accidents was reduced by 16 per cent, a miracle of modern times.

St Johnston also copied American police forces by making the patrol cars stand out from their surroundings, an innovation that now seems commonplace but that symbolized a social revolution. In the grey, brown and dark blue England of those times, the new style was startling. The cars were painted in Cambridge blue with white doors and boldly marked with the words 'Lancashire Constabulary'. Until then, police cars had been deliberately sober and discreet, painted navy blue or funereal black. When the first of the new cars appeared in the garage one mechanic remarked, 'Have you heard the latest mad idea of the Chief? He wants the Kirkby cars to look like bloody pandas.' Hence the name.

The rapidity of the revolution that then followed is typical of the reforms that were unleashed on Britain during this period. Two essential conditions were present: an existing system with no articulate or organized defenders and a determined group of reformers with official backing from the centre. The abolition of the bobby on the beat was never discussed or voted on at an election. To this day, most people believe that, in some way, the old system of policing continues to exist and only lacks enough men and women to restore it to its former splendour. The change was not just a matter of technology and money, but was part of a much wider process of political and social reform. It took hold only after Labour's decisive victory at the polls in March 1966, which transformed Harold Wilson's tentative government into the first full-powered Labour administration since 1950, with a majority of ninety-seven. Those in the Home Office who sought change now had an ally at their side in Roy Jenkins, who had taken over from the more cautious Sir Frank Soskice. While Kirkby was important, it was a special case where special methods were justified. The new type of policing had to be tried on a traditional community if it were to be applied everywhere. So it was.

On Monday, 19 September 1966, the ancient city of Carlisle began its own experiment in what was already being called 'unit beat' policing. The trial was 'at the request of the Home Office'. Frank Williamson, Chief Constable of Cumberland, Westmorland and Carlisle, paid the usual empty compliment to tradition before the scheme got under way: 'There has always been a powerful argument for retaining the foot patrol on the beat to keep contact with the public. In recent years there has been equally forceful argument for increasing mobility at the expense of losing some of this contact. The unit beat policing scheme is an attempt to answer both these arguments.'

The Times reported that the plan aimed 'to increase police efficiency and cultivate a better understanding with members of the public by closer contact with men on the beat and swifter response to calls for assistance.' In a pattern to become very familiar, the city was divided into five areas, each given twenty-four-hour cover by a constable in a car. All the cars would be 'prominently signed' and given a distinctive colour. Each car area would be divided into two beats and on each beat there would be a resident constable. On 7 December *The Times* carried a highly significant report of a supposedly successful experiment in the new methods – yet again in Eric St Johnston's Lancashire. It dealt with what came to be seen as the model for unit beat policing, the town of Accrington. Under the prophetic headline 'Policeman on beat may disappear – Accrington "neighbourhood officer" success', it provided an enthusiastic and uncritical survey of what had happened. The report must have rejoiced the hearts of officials in Whitehall. Civil servants had apparently been yearning to replace the constable on the beat since a system of district policing, mixing radio cars and foot patrolmen, had been introduced in Aberdeen in 1949 and in parts of London in 1953.

Once again, this was no Kirkby New Town in need of special treatment but a traditional place set in its ways and unaware that it desired or needed change. Its only police problem was a shortage of men which (as we have seen) would not last much longer. Previously, Accrington and the surrounding area had been divided into twelve regular beats effectively unchanged since Victorian times. In theory, men worked three shifts per day to keep the beats patrolled for all twenty-four hours. In practice, there were not enough men to go round. In June 1966, obviously influenced by the Kirkby experience, the system was changed. Instead of regularly patrolled beats, eight policemen were given areas to look after. They were supposed to live in these areas and became, in effect, neighbourhood policemen. Times of duty were left to the men, but four other officers in distinctive blue-and-white cars were used to supplement them. A publicity campaign was run in the local newspaper to introduce the policemen to their areas and, said *The Times*, 'according to all reports, the public have responded well. Local information from each area goes back to the main station and the crime figures have so far showed a fall.' A PC Ted Dean was quoted as saying happily: 'This has increased the status of the ordinary policeman... Now the policeman is recognised as a specialist.' Another, John Pilkington, explained that it increased his job satisfaction: 'If I get a complaint here I follow it up myself.' An officer driving a car on duty for the first time said: 'An emergency before depended on your being near a telephone. Now you have a radio and car and you can get there quickly.'

These experiments in Carlisle and Accrington had been under way for a few short months when Whitehall's campaign to abolish the Robert Peel system intensified, with the first trial of the new method in a major city centre. On 10 October 1966, once again 'at the suggestion of the Home Office', the so-called 'neighbourhood' system began trials in the heart of Birmingham. Eight constables would each be responsible for a beat. They would decide their own times of duty. Instead of calling at the station in the morning, they would use personal radios to say they were on duty and telephone reports to a tape-recorder. Typing would be done in the station. Every two beats would also be 'overseen' by a turquoise-and-white patrol car. There was some interest in the fact that the project would cover Balsall Heath, described in the coy language of the time as an 'area with a vice problem'. (Many years later it was to be the scene of a famous confrontation between a prostitution racket and the Muslim community.)

It now became clear that what had begun as a local initiative had become a national campaign. On 18 November 1966 no fewer than three Home Office working parties reported on radical police reform. Their reports were considered and largely accepted by a body called the Police Advisory Board, chaired by none other than the Home Secretary, Roy Jenkins. This meeting of the Police Advisory Board, on 7 December 1966, must count as being one of the most revolutionary gatherings in post-war British politics. Among the ideas discussed was the extension of the responsibilities of traffic wardens, turning them into underpowered traffic policemen, a notion regularly revived and abandoned and most recently dusted off in August 2001. Much more significant was a general 'reshaping of the beat system'. Chief constables were to be told to re-examine their systems of patrolling and to continue with the traditional beat system only in special circumstances. Police should patrol city centres in much the same way as before, but in other parts of the country more use should be made of the Accrington system.

The language of the working party reports, which were published by HMSO in January 1967, shows the force and fierceness of the Home Office's desire for change. It makes it clear that it was driven from the centre, not from below. On the beat system, the working party asserted: 'there is no doubt that the system of policing large areas of the country – which still follows the principles of the beat system started over 100 years ago – should be reviewed as a matter of urgency.' Already, the snobbery of the plain-clothes specialist towards the beat was emerging. The working party felt that there was 'a tendency for beat patrol duties, which account for over half the manpower of the service, to be regarded as inferior to duties in specialist departments'. This, it believed, hindered co-operation within the force and led to the 'lessening of the sense of personal responsibility of the man on the beat'. It also believed that the introduction of lightweight personal radios 'opened up the prospect of new techniques in policing'. At the end came what may have been the most pressing reason for change, the recruitment and retention problems of running a disciplined, semi-military service in an increasingly undisciplined, relaxed and prosperous society. Veterans of the Second World War were ageing. The abolition of National Service in 1958 had left most young people unfamiliar with discipline, uniform or unquestioning obedience to the apparently pointless orders of superiors.

As had become usual with such documents, the working party gave a powerful defence of the Peel system even as it recommended its abolition:

When it is properly worked (that is, when enough men are available to work it), it is possible to arrange for every street in an urban area to be visited by a uniformed policeman at least once in every 24 hours, and in many cases more frequently. By his mere presence the uniformed policeman undoubtedly prevents some crime and affords a degree of protection to life and property. He contributes to the maintenance of order and is available to control traffic, prevent accidents and establish close relations with the people living in his area. By these means mutual confidence and respect can be fostered. And *the concept of a policeman as a citizen in uniform gains reality* [my italics]. Moreover, the 'beat' policeman is able to feed information to his colleagues in the specialist branches of the force, since he knows the movements of people in the locality and is in a position to report irregularities in the routine of day-to-day living. Thus he knows when people are on holiday and houses are shut up, has a keen eye for open windows and gates, and knows in advance the man who is likely to make trouble at closing time on Saturday nights – or rather he would know these things where the same beat is worked regularly.

Its main argument for abandoning the Peel system was that it was no longer practicable with the current manpower shortage: 'There is clearly much of value in this concept of the beat system but we think it also embodies an idealisation from the past which, in the conditions of modern society and, given the chronic shortage of police manpower, is unfortunately no longer attainable.' It spoke of an incompatibility between the original system and the society it was meant to serve. It also noted that many chief constables had already moved away from a rigid beat system. There was also the problem of getting post-war recruits to submit to the sort of discipline needed:

There are probably many young policemen who find it
difficult to derive much interest or satisfaction from
working their beats in the traditional manner in urban
areas... many intelligent young men, fresh from a police
training centre, are unlikely to be convinced that their
mere presence on a street deters potential wrong-doers;
and they are therefore liable, particularly on beats where
little occurs, to suffer from boredom or frustration.

In other words, many policemen did not enjoy the work for which
they were being paid. This was, of course, a problem. However, it
was not by itself an argument for getting rid of a system that was still
working well. Other solutions must have been possible. The order
of the working party's conclusions, in typical nationalized industry
style, placed the welfare of the employees above the needs of their
customers, the tax-paying public.

The working party also shifted delicately from the issue of
recruitment, a matter of fact, to the efficiency of the beat, a matter of
opinion:

Our first ground for criticising the system in its traditional
form is the discouraging effect it undoubtedly has on
many policemen. Our second ground is the doubt we
entertain about its efficiency as a method of policing
many areas in modern conditions.

The question must now be asked whether there is
any longer good reason to retain a system which had its
heyday in totally different conditions from those which
obtain today, when populations tended to be static, crime
was adequately contained, traffic problems barely
existed, and the police lacked the modern resources
of mobility and electronic equipment.

The working party admitted:

> no comprehensive operational research has been
> undertaken in this country into the comparative
> efficiency of different systems of policing until the
> creation, three years ago, of the Home Office Research
> and Planning Branch made systematic research possible.
> Even so, some time must elapse before we shall be able
> to establish conclusively that one form of policing a
> particular area (taking account of its physical nature, the
> character of its population and the hazards) is more
> efficient than another.

In the manner of hundreds of other 1960s' reformers, it was not going to let such doubts stand in its way. Asking whether, in this 'interim period, while we are waiting for the fruits of research, the police forces of England and Wales should continue to rely primarily on the beat system in its traditional form, or whether a definite move should now be made towards the introduction of the more flexible systems of policing made possible by the availability of scientific and technological aids', the working party gave itself the answer it wanted:

> We have no doubt what the answer to this question
> should be. Together, the two broad criticisms of the beat
> system which we have advanced – its lack of appeal to
> the young man of today and the inefficient use of
> manpower which it involves – constitute a formidable
> indictment of the system as a universal means of
> policing; and when to these criticisms is added the fact
> that the system fails to exploit to the full the advantages
> of modern equipment, we think that the case for a very
> early change to more flexible systems of policing in many
> areas of the country becomes unanswerable.

Even in the light of the suspiciously encouraging results of the experiments thus far, this might be described as a rush to judgement. The working party could with justice be said to have made up its mind in advance. There was now pressure on every force to change as rapidly as possible. Those that hung back were to be swept aside by the compulsory mergers that would come two years later. When these took place, traditionalist chiefs and senior officers could more easily be ignored or removed. The new men could step into the leadership of amalgamated super-forces which, for the first time, owed more of their authority to central government than to the locality they served. Any rearguard action to save the beat system would have been crushed by central authority and local ambition.

The working party advised that in future the traditional system should be operated by chief constables only when they believed it had positive advantages over other systems. The traditional method had a 'discouraging effect' on many policemen (that is to say, they found it hard work and rather boring) and there were doubts about 'its efficiency as a method of policing many areas in modern conditions'. More flexible systems should be introduced. It stated that unit beat policing had been introduced not by the local forces that first introduced it but by the Home Office Research and Planning Branch. Kirkby may well have been a genuine individual experiment. What followed, it is now clear, was centrally planned and centrally desired. It comes as no surprise to find that by April 1967 the unit beat system had been 'officially' shown to be a 'success'. The reported results were so extraordinarily good that one can only wonder why its general adoption did not instantly lead to a startling drop in the national crime figures.

The Accrington report showed that total crime in the area had dropped by 19 per cent over ten months. There had been a 30 per cent reduction in breaking and entering. The overall detection rate had risen from 36 to 49 per cent and the rate of detection for breaking and entering offences from 21 to 48 per cent. At Kirkby, there had been a 20 per cent reduction in all crimes with an increased detection rate from 27 to 42 per cent. These figures compared with recent national increases in crime of about 6 per cent. Officers also claimed a great improvement in the amount of information gained about the activities of known criminals.

The working party reports contained many other modernizing ideas which are now commonplace but that were then radical. More graduates were to be hired. There were also proposals for greater use of computers, with a national system as the goal. The abolition of police drill parades, more personal radios and more cars were suggested. Reducing the height requirement, then a minimum of five feet eight inches, and allowing constables to wear glasses were discussed but not agreed on. The issue was fudged with a proposal to recruit 'able and intelligent people who lack stature but could make a useful contribution'. The complete dismantling of the old requirements would come later, during the 1980s and 1990s.

The hiring of more civilian staff, then numbering only sixteen thousand, was agreed in order to tackle paperwork and to include fingerprint experts and school-crossing patrols. The use of the expression 'civilian' has helped to undermine the idea that the police are civilians. It has encouraged them to consider themselves as a special body set above the rest of the citizenry. It has also nurtured the idea that the police are mainly a detective and record-keeping organization, rather than an active preventive force. A proposal to abolish the traditional helmet was rejected, although everything it represented was being jettisoned. It would instead be allowed to disappear slowly and quietly, the British establishment's favoured method of abolishing something that is popular. In another hint of the future direction of English policing, plans were revealed to start the experimental use of helicopters. The tests were not always successful and at least once had ludicrous results. In August 1967 six policemen were said to have been bitten, presumably by their captives, after three men wanted for questioning were run to ground by a police helicopter at a lonely farm at Ash, Surrey.

The men ran from the farmhouse but the helicopter kept track of them as they waded through a canal and crossed a railway, only to be arrested, despite defending themselves with their teeth, by officers on foot. Nobody seems to have wondered whether they might have been arrested without the helicopter and without so much fuss.

In November the police began 'intensive helicopter training' over London. Officers dressed in militaristic berets and battledress-type uniforms with shoulder flashes marked 'Police'. The army provided the pilots. This was the first faint whisper of what would become a powerful trend among the police to abandon their 'citizen in uniform' appearance and kit themselves out in militaristic or storm-troop outfits which emphasized their separation from the rest of us.

In January 1968 police revealed that an experiment with closed-circuit TV had quietly begun in Croydon, following a similar scheme in Liverpool. Unknown to the public, the tests had been going on for several weeks. The cameras had mainly been used to film and arrest men spotted trying the doors of parked cars. A Chief Superintendent Hall said that the main advantage was that it saved manpower: 'I have just not got that number of men to cover the area effectively by policemen alone.' He said there was no moral difference between secret camera surveillance and being looked at by a man in plain clothes. At least, unlike most modern advocates of CCTV, he was aware that there might actually be a moral issue involved. Neither he nor anyone else dealt with the other disadvantages of this technology. First, to be at all effective, it requires somebody to watch it all the time. The more cameras that are installed the more people will be needed for even the most basic vigilance. Secondly, if it does not cover an entire area, then it will have the effect of driving crime into the districts where it does not exist – whereas if it is installed everywhere it will be at least as labour-intensive as the Peel beat system. Thirdly, CCTV cameras have serious technical limitations: they see poorly in the dark and cannot see through masks or round corners, which means that recorded tapes are often useless and even if a central control point 'sees' the crime nobody will be able to reach the scene in time to make an identification. As it happens, the monitors are often so distant from the scenes they are watching that, even if the police do react swiftly, they are bound to be too late to prevent crimes. Wrongdoers know all these things and behave accordingly.

These objections, clearly foreseeable, are at least as powerful as the working party's criticism of the beat system, which was scrapped at the same time that the CCTV network was founded. It is not clear from the reports whether the cameras were concealed or clearly visible. Scotland Yard said it was too early to make an assessment but results thus far had been encouraging, with thirty suspects stopped and questioned and eight arrests, although these were 'not necessarily a direct result of the existence of the television cameras'. The Yard asserted that there had been a considerable decrease in all types of crime. The claim is puzzling given that the experiment was secret.

It is fascinating to find that so many of the changes and concerns of the 1990s and today were prefigured in this hectic period of reform. The Police Advisory Board, in a thin bat's squeak of early political correctness, even noted that there was 'not nearly enough attention paid to the recruitment of women and there should be sustained effort in this field'. No doubt it would have mentioned institutional racism too, if it had been invented. The whirlwind of change continued to howl across the country. Many developments that would subsequently become the subject of widespread complaint and discontent began in this era. In Cornwall the police abandoned their Victorian whistles – which would be revived by some forces more than thirty years later when they turned out to be quite useful despite being unfashionable. In October 1966 the Devon and Exeter police pioneered the retreat from the countryside, introducing a new telephone system that allowed small police stations to be left unmanned. Installed at forty-one stations, it connected callers to an answering machine that gave them the number of divisional headquarters or allowed them to leave a message if the matter was not urgent. Colonel R. B. Greenwood, Chief Constable of Devon and Exeter said: 'The time has gone when policemen should be waiting in police stations for something to happen.' It is hard to think of a more misleading thing for him to have said. Such methods were to lead to policemen spending more and more time in bigger and more remote stations, waiting until after crimes had happened before leaping into high-powered cars festooned with sirens and lights. It would also lead to them arriving long after the criminals were over the horizon. There would be a grave increase in rural crime as professional burglars realized that large parts of the English and Welsh counties now had no police presence at all.

The mighty scythe of reform, which somehow never seems to have cut state spending, has swept away many of the police stations which once offered reassurance to city and countryside alike. Mighty fortresses of policing, such as Rochester Row and Tottenham Court Road in London, both located in active, inhabited and busy centres of business and shopping, were closed and boarded up. While they awaited their fate they were plastered with posters and graffiti, a symbolic triumph of the new culture that governs the unpatrolled streets. The scythe has swung far beyond the capital. The Victorian network of police stations has been lopped as drastically as were the railways by the half-witted Beeching cuts of the sixties. The rash pruning has had similarly unpleasant and unintended results. The effect of this policy on rural life, just at the time when new roads made it possible for urban thieves to make swift raids on rural areas, is only just becoming clear. Even the fastest response times will not act as a deterrent when the nearest police presence may be thirty or forty miles away.

In the years 1990 to 2000, according to Home Office figures, England and Wales lost 630 police stations, mostly small ones in country districts. Even those that remain are often working much shorter hours than the nearby pubs which generate so much of the disorder the police stations once deterred. The *Daily Mail* reported in the summer of 2002 that one thousand stations, one in three, had closed their doors over the previous ten years, and conducted a survey that showed that six out of ten of those that remained in operation were open only during office hours and not at all at weekends. In small towns many police stations are in fact unmanned for much of the time. These closures are not popular and are frequently resisted by local people. A group of pensioners took over and started to man an abandoned station at Old Molesey in outer London in an attempt to reassure the inhabitants of the area. The gesture did not deter the modernizers.

Essex police closed forty-two stations in two years. Of the seventy-two that remain, a mere twelve are open round the clock. A look at the official tally of station closures shows that it is country districts that have suffered most from the cull. Between 1990 and 2000, Avon and Somerset lost forty-three of their eighty-two stations; Derbyshire thirty-two out of eighty-nine; Devon and Cornwall thirty-three out of ninety-eight; Gloucestershire twenty-four out of seventy-one; Hampshire thirty-two out of 126; Hertfordshire an incredible thirty-four out of fifty-five. London alone has almost the same number as before, having opened forty-three and closed forty-four between 1990 and 2000. The new stations, serving a different purpose, tend to be more remote from the high streets than the old ones. Greater Manchester lost twenty-two of its ninety-six stations in the same period; Merseyside nine out of fifty-three. Many more stations may yet close. There seems to be a general policy of abandoning the idea of a station as a physical and obvious presence. The new police service prefers the modern and remote headquarters, designed with custody suites and computer facilities to suit the post-Peel style of policing.

Like all such changes, this revolution has been carried out in the name of efficiency and economy. Those who criticize it meet the standard response of police chiefs to all such complaints: that it is all a matter of manpower and resources, that they just cannot cope, that to man a desk at a police station means taking officers off the beat. The embarrassing truth, that police manpower and non-uniformed back-up have increased by a third in the last thirty years, is seldom admitted.

Much of the thinking behind the closures was summed up in a report from the Audit Commission published in March 1999, although it is obvious that the ideas behind this document date from much further back. In the dreary Newspeak of modern government, it talks of 'improving the management of the police estate'. The buildings, it claims, are often in the wrong place to support police operations, or they are 'outdated and unable to cope with modern technology: 87 per cent are more than 20 years old'. It suggests that 'many stations are not conveniently situated for the public', which may be true but is an odd argument for shutting them down so that they are situated nowhere at all. Perhaps more significant is the appeal to the accountants, summed up in the words 'opportunities to generate income and reduce costs through rationalisation are being missed'. The report goes on to say that most public contact with the police now takes place by telephone. This is true out of necessity rather than public choice. The chance of direct personal contact with a helicopter two thousand feet overhead or a patrol car hurtling by are necessarily limited.

The Audit Commission urges 'strategic thinking', including asking the question 'Is there still a role for the traditional police station?'. While it admits that 'for many people, the traditional police station is a tangible reminder of the police's presence, a source of reassurance second only to the sight of a "bobby on the beat"', it seems to think that this is less important than the fact that many station buildings are not new. However, the real problem is explained in one brief paragraph of the Commission's document, which states: 'Policing styles have also changed, with a greater need for rapid response and an investment in "behind the scenes" intelligence-gathering.' Prevention, based on police stations in the hearts of towns or villages, has been abandoned in favour of 'rapid response' after the crime has already begun.

The idea of policing by remote control was closely connected to the abolition of the beat, which at last reached London, again through 'experiments' that mysteriously never failed, in March 1967. Pilot schemes were announced for unit beat patrols in Harlesden and Bromley, which, 'if they prove successful', were to be extended to all parts of the metropolitan area. Cleverly, the innovation was sold as a return to a homely past and the car-based system was described in the press as a new form of 'old-fashioned village-type bobby'. Almost every future reform of the police would be portrayed in the same way, although the one change that no force would consider was a return to the regular beat. Chief Superintendent Stanley Hebbes set a rather low standard for the success of the tests, pronouncing: 'If after a year we find that this new scheme has cut down the amount of crime in this area by even 1 per cent we shall consider it a success.'

In the same month, *The Times* reported, under the headline 'More police drop beat system', that three British police forces were to scrap the traditional beat system and change to neighbourhood policing. Birmingham, it stated, had announced the decision the previous day. The unnamed reporter, obviously well briefed, added: 'I understand that Lancashire and Bedfordshire will also change this year.' The story asserted that one of the new method's chief advantages was improved contact between police and public, which would turn out to be the opposite of the truth. The changes were portrayed as 'part of a Home Office drive to reduce crime'. They coincided with an announcement by Roy Jenkins that crime had increased by 5.8 per cent during 1966, reaching a total of almost 1.2 million indictable offences.

This was a time of general turmoil and unprecedented change. A vast Criminal Justice Act had just been passed, introducing a series of profound reforms in the court and penal system. Parole, suspended prison sentences and majority verdicts were all brought into the English system in that year. The death penalty had just been abolished. The country had been dismayed and alarmed by the murders in August of three policemen in Shepherd's Bush: PC Geoffrey Fox (aged forty-one), DC Stanley Wombwell (twenty-five) and DS Christopher Head (thirty), shot dead in Braybrook Street outside Wormwood Scrubs prison.

This gruesome event led to angry confrontations between Roy Jenkins and rank-and-file police officers demanding the return of the gallows. Jenkins cut short his holiday because of the killings but said during a visit to the local police station that he would not make any changes in the law because of a wave of emotion caused by one incident. 'I will not change my policy in the shadow of recent events, however horrible,' he declared. Many officers saw his view as condescending and weak. Interestingly, Jenkins did then make changes in policy that suited him, including tighter gun controls. He also took the opportunity to suggest 'modifying' the right to silence, a favourite target of penal 'liberals', although this suggestion would have to wait until the Criminal Justice and Public Order Act of 1994 to find a House of Commons feeble and dim enough to enact it.

Public feeling about the killing of the policemen, who at the time were popular and generally well loved, was also bitter. The event was so shocking to a then-peaceful country that the three dead men were commemorated by a service in Westminster Abbey. There was a widespread feeling that the ground was shifting underfoot and that a stable and settled society was in the midst of uncertainty and confusion.

The police faced serious recruiting problems because of the high wages being offered to unskilled men by expanding production-line industries such as car manufacturing. This was still the era of 'You've never had it so good', when the old attractions of police work – including steady, guaranteed employment – no longer counted for much. Few young men used to a more relaxed world were now prepared to face the discipline and tedium of life on the beat. For every ten men who joined the police in 1964, nine left; 5512 joined and 4888 left during the first eleven months of the year. In early 1965 the government admitted that the police force was 15,000 under strength. George Thomas, then a junior Home Office minister, promised that the gap would be filled with up-to-date equipment and other measures. Such was the crisis that even the Monday Club was urging the recruitment of 'coloured' policemen, then the politically-correct term. This was widely seen as an outlandish and impractical notion. *The Times* quoted an unnamed officer as saying that this had not happened because 'the British public would not tolerate being arrested by coloured men'.

The problem was exercising many minds even before Roy Jenkins came to the Home Office. In May 1965 his forerunner, Sir Frank Soskice, told the Police Federation at Llandudno that he hoped the day would soon come when there would be 'coloured' policemen. Reg Webb, chairman of the Police Federation, responded by warning that every chief constable would have to ask 'will this man be able to fit into the force and be accepted by the general public... I wonder if the country has yet grown sufficiently used to the idea of being a multiracial society to accept the idea of coloured policemen'. The Federation's preferred solution was better pay, not a welcome idea to a Labour government wading through a severe economic crisis which would end in the humiliating devaluation of sterling.

Another enormous change was about to begin. The 1962 Royal Commission on the Police had urged, in the fashion of the times, that larger organizations were better than small ones. It proposed that the 127 English and Welsh police forces should be amalgamated into fewer larger ones. Nothing had been done about this at the time, but Roy Jenkins demanded action as soon as he took over from Sir Frank Soskice in 1966. Labour's general election manifesto in March of that year had been vocal on crime and policing, complaining of a rising crime rate, overcrowded prisons and many seriously undermanned police forces, all supposedly legacies of thirteen wasted years of Tory government from 1951 to 1964. It boasted: 'The slide in numbers has already been checked. Energetic action will now be taken to build up police strength.'

It promised the 'most modern scientific and technological equipment', and declared, without feeling the need to explain, that 'there is also an urgent need for fewer – and larger – police forces... we shall therefore press ahead with a vigorous programme of amalgamations.' It claimed, without evidence, that this was 'the form of organisation best suited to the battle against crime'.

Britain at this time was richer than it had ever been before, but it was also more uncertain and rackety. Trade union militancy was epidemic. Large-scale immigration was transforming many cities and, with a mixture of crude prejudice and baffled politeness, English people were adapting with various degrees of success to a multiracial society. Television and 'beat music' were creating a new youth culture. The comprehensive school revolution was beginning and the first new universities were opening. Millions of families were moving into new housing estates, council and private.

Taboo subjects, such as abortion and homosexuality, were being openly debated on TV and in the newspapers as well as in Parliament, in an age when many married couples had never even seen each other naked. Divorce had begun its sharp upward curve. The Shepherd's Bush police murders revealed a dangerous mood among the police themselves. It also widened the gulf of misunderstanding between the police and the new liberal elite, which many traditional officers saw as condescending and cut off from reality. The public clashes between Roy Jenkins and police officers were the first instance of open police militancy since the unstable years at the end of the First World War. In the midst of all this, reform seemed only natural and did not require much in the way of argument to support it. Change was generally seen as good in itself, new automatically better than old.

In May 1966 the government began the long task, the goal of which is only now becoming completely clear, of nationalizing the police under central control. Roy Jenkins brusquely told the 127 police forces of England and Wales that many of them were to disappear in a matter of months in forced mergers. The 1962 Royal Commission had said that the optimum size for a police force was probably five hundred or a little more, but Jenkins went even further. His plans meant that the smallest force would be almost seven hundred strong. He also struck hard and fast to make sure that any small forces that wanted to keep their independence were cowed in advance. He threatened to use his powers under the Police Act 1964 to force mergers where there was resistance.

The parliamentary opposition did not appear to see any difficulties in a plan that blatantly undermined the independence of the police force. Their complacency might seem astonishing, given the huge debates that had preceded the initial founding of the police. They seem not to have been aware of the historic English opposition to the state gathering too much power into its hands. However, the Conservative Party of the day had decided to be more revolutionary than the revolutionaries. Many Tory lawyers, especially the Inns of Court Conservative Association, actually favoured a national police force at this time. So perhaps it ought not to be shocking that the shadow Home Secretary, Quintin Hogg, 'in principle gave general support' to a plan that was to break the century-old links between the police and their localities. In effect, the policy turned them into little more than branch organizations of the Home Office. Only the Metropolitan force came under the direct control of Whitehall. Until the mergers, most forces outside London were based on counties or the 'county boroughs' – towns or cities so self-contained that they were given their own independent local government, a simple and workable system which was, inexplicably, to be abolished in local government reforms at about the same time.

County forces were often controlled by chief constables from the local landowning gentry, often with military backgrounds. Borough forces were frequently run by long-serving chief constables, who had risen through the ranks. When the forces outside London were established, their chief constables had been made answerable to the Justices of the Peace, then much more powerful and independent figures than now. As the Justices' powers declined, the chiefs reported to local government 'watch committees' which gave them much freedom of action. Thus they had enormous independent powers of decision, powers of which the Home Office was obviously jealous. The mergers, by creating regional forces such as Thames Valley or Humberside put paid to that independence in several ways. They snapped the links between chiefs and their localities, not least because English people did not and do not have regional loyalties. What does Oxford have in common with Reading, or vice versa? They would now be rivals for resources within the new force, whereas previously they had had their own concerns and their own ways of meeting them.

The new enlarged forces – and their ambitious chiefs – were much more likely to look to London for guidance. They would naturally seek the favour of the Home Office and the national press and TV rather than that of local councillors or newspapers. Any chief of a major force knew that he might rise to become the Commissioner of the Metropolitan Police – a remote chance for most of them in the days before amalgamation. Technically, they were responsible to shapeless police authorities made up of local authority appointees and magistrates. In practice, the 'regional' character of the new forces, devoid in most cases of any recognizable common sense of place, made their chief constables more likely to follow national trends and respond to national pressures. Mr Jenkins explained that he had not chosen to create a national force because he valued the local connections and the relationship with the public formed by smaller units, but he also said that he hoped that by April 1967 there would be only forty-nine forces and stated that the changes did not exclude the possibility of a national force in the future. An interesting consequence has been that responsibility for the Metropolitan Police was later 'devolved' to the Greater London Authority and the Metropolitan Police Authority, without any real loss of central control. The Home Office would simply not have permitted this handover if it had had any serious fears that central government might lose real control of the policing of the capital.

The first steps were also being taken towards the creation of a new police elite, selected from the most able mid-ranking officers and then imbued with the Home Office ethos at the Bramshill college. Soon, promotion to the higher ranks would be almost impossible without a spell at Bramshill, establishing an old-boy network of great influence which would come to dominate the Association of Chief Police Officers (ACPO)and create a national police officer class which was far closer to Whitehall than the retired military men, local squirearchy and experienced beat officers who had previously been in charge of operational policing. There was also a steady, increasing pressure on the police to recruit university graduates or to send their promising officers to university. This may have been meant to raise their educational level. It also meant that politically, socially and culturally conservative attitudes became confined to the lower ranks of the force. This has led to tension between the instincts of the rank and file and those of the officer class. The centralizing, socially-concerned ideology of Bramshill and ACPO has since become a potent, ever-present influence throughout the entire police service.

There was almost no open dissent from the view that the massacre of small independent forces was necessary and justified. Displaced chief constables were generally offered senior posts in the new merged forces. Only a Mr R. McCartney, Chief Constable of Hertfordshire, stood out in public against the change, arguing that there was 'still a lot of evidence' that small units were as efficient as, and sometimes more efficient than, larger units. He said, with some justice, that there was no guarantee that the proposals would achieve their aims. In the 1960s it was not yet fashionable for governments and officials to believe that small was beautiful. *The Times* said it was 'the greatest upheaval in policing since the time of Peel', which, in conjunction with the abolition of regular foot patrols, it certainly was. As with so many of the changes of that era, it was achieved mainly by elite action and never became an election issue or a subject of partisan debate in Parliament. Nobody mentioned the original constitutional objections to having the police under the control of central government.

By the time Roy Jenkins had left the Home Office to become Chancellor of the Exchequer in November 1967, the whole face and shape of the police in England had changed for good. A junior minister, Lord Stonham, told the House of Lords that month that half the programme of force mergers was already complete. After April 1968 there would be only forty-one police forces. For unit beat policing the Home Secretary had authorized the spending of an additional two million pounds (then a considerable sum) on small cars. By early in the next year two-thirds of the population would be covered by unit beat policing. By the end of the next year 80 per cent of the country and 90 per cent of the Metropolitan police area would have lost their foot patrols, although the minister did not put it like that. Lord Stonham also paused to praise the TV programme *Softly Softly* and to reveal that six hundred detectives were now working in regional crime squads like the one portrayed in *Softly Softly*. As politicians so often do, he spoke as if the main concern of the police was major crime and organized dishonesty, rather than small and unbearable losses, insults, threats and slights. He announced proudly that there was at last to be a police national computer, with that touching faith in the magic of electronics that had by then infected industry, commerce and politics and which survives despite all the evidence that circuitry cannot replace human ingenuity or effort, let alone initiative and personal knowledge.

In general, Lord Stonham's speech bulged with optimism and the fashionable love of technology as the solution to all ills. He declared that the use of helicopters, computers, regional crime squads, amalgamations and the system of unit beat policing were keeping ahead of the criminal. And he claimed that any young man considering a life of crime would do well to think again. In words typical of the times, he said: 'Out-thinking a policeman is one thing but even an Al Capone might have had trouble with a helicopter-backed computer.' On the contrary, Al Capone would probably have made far more effective use of helicopters and computers than any police force ever has done or ever could do.

There were dark undercurrents in the debate hinting at the truth – that crime for most people does not take the form of Al Capone but of a slight, nimble and ruthless young man breaking into their house or snatching their wallet in a dark street. As if puzzled by his own hopefulness, Lord Stonham admitted that while under the welfare state there were thirty-five thousand people in prison, in the 1930s, when life had been much harder, there had been only eleven thousand. His fellow Labour peer, Lord Rowley, also mentioned the uncomfortable fact that while in 1937 there had been only 209 cases of robbery with violence in England and Wales, in 1966 there were 4474. The comparable figures for indictable offences were 216,000 in 1937 compared with 1,119,000 in 1966. Something had gone wrong out in the dark streets despite the radios, cars, helicopters, computers and modern, efficient management – but nobody seemed to know what it was. Even so, everyone seemed to think it was safe to retire Dixon of Dock Green and move into the age of *Z Cars*.

III

The slow, bureaucratic death of George Dixon

The real significance of the unit beat system was that it ended the old foot patrols and undermined the idea that the main purpose of the force was to *prevent* crime from taking place. Thanks to unit beat, the constable ceased to be the embodiment of the notion that the law belonged to the people of England – one of the very few examples of a real 'People's Police' ever to have existed. As the police manpower working party had rightly said, the old method gave solid expression to the concept of the policeman as a citizen in uniform, freedom under the law made flesh. Had unit beat been applied as it was originally designed, it might well have worked in some areas as a preventive and a reactive system at the same time, preserving just enough of the old beat method to retain public confidence. As we shall see, things did not happen quite like that. For it arrived at the same time as the new merged forces and together with a shiny new set of mechanical toys. It came just as American law-and-order culture was gaining a grip on the public (and the police) through television.

Many of Eric St Johnston's innovations were American-influenced. Both the radio and the car were well suited to the enormous American cities where they were first used for police work in a completely different tradition from that of Britain. To an extent that is still not really understood in Britain, much of America polices itself without much need for men patrolling on foot. Its prosperous suburbs are so distant from those who might want to rob or vandalize them that they are mainly trouble-free. American suburbanites can still leave their cars and houses unlocked in many areas. The USA's country districts are full of self-reliant people who expect to have to defend their homes and property, and are equipped and legally permitted to do so. In such areas the police are so distant that they could take hours to arrive – hours when anything might happen if householders did not hold the law in their own hands, from which it has never been taken. There are other differences, too. America's lawless urban areas, for historic and racial reasons, have seldom been willing to accept policing by consent. Police patrolling in such zones often takes a form alarmingly close to military occupation.

American law in many places permits the armed pursuit of felons by citizens, as well as the use of deadly force in defence of life and property. The patrolling officer on foot did once exist. In some places he still does, but not in the same way or to the same extent. In concentrated cityscapes such as Manhattan he can still be found – and is very effective, not least because he is not restricted by laws such as the Police and Criminal Evidence Act 1984. The Washington, DC Metro is superbly patrolled by officers on mountain bikes ready to pursue malefactors through its majestic vaults, although they rarely have to do so on a system that nowadays feels – and is – much safer than large parts of the London Underground. Manhattan is unique among US cities. Washington, DC is equally exceptional in a different way. All American police forces – big-city, suburban and rural – are armed, so that when they are called on to act they often do so lethally, but their weapons place an unseen barrier between them and those they guard.

So it may not be wise to copy their methods too slavishly in this wholly different country. One of the most striking things about modern English police methods is the way that American techniques are copied, as if directly from the TV screen. The British police car, once a sober and subdued affair with only a bell and a small illuminated sign to identify it, has become a highway patrol cruiser adorned with splendid coats of arms, slogans, reflective stripes, banks of multicoloured strobe lights and sirens which can be heard in the next county. Many are now more spectacular than the relatively modest vehicles used by American suburban forces. Newspaper reporters invited to go out on patrol with the police are almost invariably taken in such cars. It is clear that the officers are longing for the excuse to switch on the lights and sirens and fly to the rescue at speeds way above the legal limit. Who can blame them, with such machinery to play with and such inspiration from the many police programmes they have seen on TV, from the fictional dramas to the factual clips in *Police... Camera... Action*? Yet it is often the case that the crime they have gone to at such speed simply does not justify the effort, or the danger to officers and public of driving at speed through a built-up area.

Here is the problem. The machinery and structure of the English police have been designed since 1966 to react to crime instead of to prevent it before it happens. Its chief constables have become driven by targets, which inevitably concentrate on the major crimes that attract the most media attention. Unit beat patrolling is ineffective against such crimes and poor at preventing more normal crime and disorder. It requires many men and women on duty if it is to work properly, and it has long been regarded with contempt by the new ambitious and star-struck type of policeman and woman. These types also tend to despise the community policemen who have sought to fill the gap left by the vanished beat officers. They are mocked as 'hobby bobbies' by their supposedly tough colleagues on the specialist squads and in the rapid-reaction cars. The real man's work, with status and the hope of promotion, is in those specialist squads, raiding drug-dealers, hunting down bank-robbers, catching paedophiles and tracking down murderers.

No doubt all these things are very necessary and worthwhile –

but the embarrassing truth is that most crime is amazingly trivial unless it happens to affect you personally. Then it is a grief and an outrage which can darken your life permanently or even shorten it with worry and fear. Most crime is the kind of misbehaviour that was never worth prosecuting but that was always worth preventing, and still is. That prevention was, and could again be, achieved by a uniformed police force on foot among us, which shared our fears and hopes, gave us courage to stand up for ourselves and expected support when it stood up for us. This sort of crime consists of smashed windows, footballs kicked against houses, boys churning up pensioners' front gardens, children riding bicycles on the pavement and knocking old ladies to one side, youths spitting on the pavement and swearing at passers-by, the dropping of litter and the scrawling of graffiti. It consists of shoplifting, bag-snatching, bicycle theft, urinating in public, making unnecessary noise late at night. Leave these things unattended, as a famous American study – 'Broken Windows', the seminal article in *Atlantic Monthly* of March 1982, by James Q. Wilson and George L. Kelling – showed, and you move down to the next bitter stage of burglary, muggings, car-theft and open drug-dealing on the street.

Much of this crime cannot by its nature be reported or recorded. Much of it is not worth reporting, because in some areas insurance rapidly ceases to pay out and even speaking to the police can become a good way of bringing trouble to your home and misery to your life. So while this book will mention crime statistics and cite them where they show that the world has changed in important ways, it is written in the belief that no figures yet published have measured the sheer misery that has been caused by the retreat of the police from the streets.

As for that retreat, let us look at some of the many studies of Eric St Johnston's bright idea in action that are to be found in the archives of Bramshill Police College. One of the earliest is 'Unit Beat Policing: Reflections on the experiments and implications of a wide-spread adoption of the system', prepared by Chief Superintendent

E. Gregory in July 1967. Mr Gregory accepted that the Peel system was the foundation stone of the British system. He produced no reason why it should be generally abandoned and his paper did not seek to do so. It assumed that unit beat was going to happen and stated with some frankness who he thought was behind it: 'Beat patrolling is the basis of the British police service. It has generally changed little over the years and, in some forces, beats have remained largely the same for as long as 30 years.'

Although aware of the Kirkby pilot, Chief Superintendent Gregory did not think that it was the true beginning of the new model police. 'Unit Beat Policing (UBP) was first introduced by the Research and Planning Branch in Accrington, Lancashire, on 1st June 1966. Carlisle quickly followed and today there are over 30 schemes operating in the country. Other forces have stated their intention of trying the scheme as soon as the necessary personal radios and cars become available.' He revealed that 'the encouragement of the Police Advisory Board and the Home Secretary have furthermore made it likely that this or similar methods of policing may be used very widely in the near future.' He cited UBP's merits as greater speed of response to complaints and calls for help. It also helped overcome the shortage of officers at the time. Like most of its advocates, he recognized its drawbacks, namely that 'it is widely held that men in vehicles do not cultivate a better understanding with the public nor improve the information flow.' The favoured way of overcoming this was the use of clearly marked vehicles, plus resident foot constables to back up the car patrols. Another issue had already crept into the argument – what to do with the men no longer needed on the beat. There were going to be a lot of them: 'The saving of beat patrol manpower requirements produced by the scheme varies considerably from force to force and even from area to area. It is envisaged, however, that on average at least ten per cent of the men currently used for beat coverage could be saved from that type of work and made available for other duties. The question now arises of how best to use these men.'

Another view came in a study of the first big-city test of unit beat policing. Carried out in March 1968, this was titled 'Unit Beat Policing: Its application to a city of over half a million population (Birmingham)' and was the work of three experienced sergeants from varied forces, M. F. Bennison (York and NE Yorkshire), D. Flanders (Surrey) and J. C. Hoddinott (Metropolitan). The trio found that unit beat policing was not in fact the magic formula that had been suggested. They quickly spotted an obvious fault that would come to bedevil much police work in the years to come: police officers in cars cease to be part of society in general and become part of the traffic stream. The police had not had any cars before 1919, and even afterwards their numbers had grown quite slowly and they were mainly concentrated on patrolling traffic; now they all had to learn to drive – many forces suffered an embarrassing number of accidents during the early learning period – and cars were available to almost any officer with a good excuse. Naturally they begin to take a greater interest in the misdeeds of motorists than in those of pedestrians since they are in constant contact with other drivers. 'It is apparent that Car Beat Patrols and Resident Beat Officers spend a large proportion of their time dealing with traffic problems and accidents, whilst it seems to us that this scheme is essentially designed to deal with crime and public order.' They also spotted the natural tendency of almost every human being, offered the choice of going on foot or driving a car, to take the car. 'There are, however, areas of a city centre which are inaccessible to motor vehicles and require traditional policing on foot. Birmingham have recognised this problem but whether or not they have found the correct balance between UBP and traditional methods will require deeper research. There does however, appear to be a tendency to use available manpower primarily for car duties, rather than foot patrol duties.'

The officers perceptively warned of another difficulty which must have become commonplace over the last thirty years: 'With an increase in the number of arrests made by a force substantially the same in number, it follows that each individual prisoner will have proportionately less time spent on him in interrogation.' There will therefore tend to be a decrease in the number of TICs – previous offences 'taken into consideration', a device allowing criminals to own up to past offences when they are charged so that they cannot be prosecuted twice for them, which also allows officers to claim to have cleared up these crimes (perhaps these are not always wholly honest on either side, but most forces view them as important). 'We see little evidence that UBP will produce a saving in manpower under present conditions. There must be coverage in addition to UBP as we have mentioned. The system at present highlights exist-ing manpower shortages when not enough men are available to fill car beat patrols.'

And they saw very early on that the new kind of policing would have an odd effect on the crime statistics, pointing out that 'Since the introduction of UBP in Birmingham, whilst arrests for crime have increased, so has the amount of reported crime, and the per-centage clear-up rate for crime has slightly decreased.' This makes good sense. The new system encourages arrests rather than preven-tion, because it expects the police to arrive after crime has been committed. It encourages the formal reporting of crime, because citizens can no longer speak informally to a beat officer. It begins the process of turning the police from a preventive agency, linked to the public by friendship, common purpose and familiarity, into a distant bureaucracy whose main purpose is to function as a crime-reporting agency for government statisticians and insurance companies.

Reported crime, much of it impossible to detect or clear up, is bound to pile up on the logs faster than officers can get round to check up on it. So the gap between the reporting and the clearing up of crime is bound to grow. The old arrangement, under which crime was 'reported' by Mrs Robinson to PC Jones, who then went and had a word with somebody, produced almost no statistics. PC Jones, by plodding the streets, prevented a huge amount of criminal and antisocial behaviour but his effect could not possibly be measured in a Whitehall report. Most matters were dealt with informally and sometimes, it is true, quite roughly, without ever troubling the courts or the prisons. Sadly, this effect can only be measured now that it is no longer there, in the colossal differences between the crime figures of forty years ago and those of the present. You might think that these figures come from two different galaxies and that the streets of England are already boiling with disorder and brutality. This is an obvious exaggeration. The two Englands are recognizably the same place and, while conditions have grown a great deal worse, they have not grown *that* much worse. Had they done so, the cities would be smoking ruins.

There were crime and disorder in the past and, although there were significantly less of these scourges than there are now, that past was not a golden age of peace and order. By removing the risk of being disturbed by a patrolling officer, fire-brigade policing has given evildoers a new feeling of freedom from fear and so made the streets less pleasant and less safe. It has done something else too. By compelling the police to respond to incidents after they have occurred and encouraging the public to report them to a central authority, it has created a statistical monster, a demand that can never be met and a problem that cannot be solved, least of all by increasing the numbers of officers doing the wrong thing.

Some more early warnings were to be found in a June 1967 report on the original Accrington scheme, 'Unit Beat Policing: Accrington and a comparison with other schemes', by Sergeants G. W. Jones, (Gloucestershire), Banthorpe (Suffolk), Vine (East Riding) and Fullelove (Metropolitan). They noted that patrolling in cars made it harder to observe areas properly. However, they drew exactly the same wrong conclusion as many police forces since. They suggested that panda cars should have a crew of two, since 'The driver, if on his own, has little time for observation but a companion would remedy this and he would also provide assistance in times of emergency and on everyday police work.' This is perfectly true. But the widespread adoption of the two-in-a-car policy is a major reason why the police came, over the following thirty years, to view themselves as a special corps of men and women separate from the 'civilian' public. Anyone who has ever watched two police officers patrolling together will have noticed that they spend most of the time talking to each other and are, even if on foot, much less approachable than if they were on their own.

The Bramshill quartet obviously believed the current wisdom that the Accrington pilot was a sparkling success. However, their conclusion contained some interesting reservations: 'We realise, however, that the scheme is new, if not in concept then in practice, and there is therefore a tendency for keenness, devotion and persistence to assume a disproportionately high level, only to fall away after some time.' They balanced this sensible caution with words that sound like a Soviet propaganda bulletin from the Stakhanovite shockworker period. The modern reader cannot help wondering if this was not some model project that had been ordered to succeed at all costs. The sergeants said they regarded some decline in its success as inevitable,

> but accept the fact that whatever low level is reached it
> will be higher than it ever was under the traditional
> method of policing. The morale of the men is
> exceedingly high with a correspondingly increased desire
> to work – it is amazing how often the area constables
> volunteer to do night and evening and night as well as
> split tours of duty and overtime. There is no doubt that
> in Accrington and, we feel, in other areas, where the
> scheme is adopted, great advances have been and will be
> made and will continue to be made in the war against
> crime and in all other facets of police work.

More than fifteen years later the optimism had worn off. Eric J. Hewitt, in an MA thesis submitted in 1984 to the University of

Manchester and titled 'Preventive policing: An examination of the effectiveness of a form of directed patrol carried out by Greater Manchester's tactical aid group' took a cooler view. 'The strength of the police in England and Wales has more than doubled during the past thirty years,' he said, 'and yet crime continues to rise at an unprecedented rate. Moreover the number of "civilians" employed by the police in posts previously held by police officers has also grown at a corresponding pace, thereby enabling more and more police officers to return to "operational duties".'

Hewitt thought that the basic premise of patrolling had been adhered to up until the outbreak of the Second World War in 1939, but that it did not survive long into the post-war era. Hewitt blamed the scale of change on greater freedom and mobility of the individual, relief of poverty and ignorance, and extensive urban growth.

> The UB system, however, has not met with anything like the success hoped for it. At the time of its inception there could have been no idea of the extraordinary pressure to which UBP was to be subjected...
>
> Constant pressure on manpower has tended to devalue the role of the area man; he is the first to be pulled off his normal duties if there is a need elsewhere or if there is a man short in the station. Many policemen deride the area man and his job as they feel that 'drinking tea with old ladies' is not 'real police work'.

This scorn for the traditional form of policing was made worse by the separation of constables from their clients by boxes of steel and glass. They never met anybody except villans, strengthening the dangerous idea noted above that the police are a separate elite and everyone else is a civilian: 'The isolation of officers in heated cars with their windows closed was reinforced by the fact that they were limited to conflict situations, encounters with victims or criminals, sealed off from the rest of the community. This leads to insensitive policing and withdrawal of consent.'

Hewitt also noted the important truth, for a force where status is often measured by the number of 'collars', that car-borne officers are more likely to make arrests, so that the identification of area patrolmen as 'hobby bobbies' and car drivers as 'real policemen' is increased. And he quoted from R. Baldwin and R. Kinsey's *Police Powers and Politics* a senior officer who said: 'Unit beat policing was a good idea but it didn't work out because of the rising number of incidents they have to attend. The treble nine calls are stacked up now, three or four at a time, and you have to take the priority calls first. It's unfortunate. The pandas stopped being there to show the flag and went on to "fire brigade" policing just answering calls, one after another.'

Hewitt also highlighted two other fascinating pieces of research. One was a Kansas City experiment in 1974, where different levels of (car only) patrol made no difference to public feelings of safety. The other was J. A. Bright's *Beat Patrol Experiment*, a Police Research and Development Branch report published by HMSO, which found that the 'number of reported crimes on a beat decreased when the officers patrolling it increased from zero to one'. Further increases in numbers made no difference.

A few years earlier (its date is unclear) the Bramshill library received another professional assessment of unit beat policing made by experienced officers. It is strikingly different from the fresh-faced optimism of the early 1960s' studies. This was 'Unit beat policing: An assessment', by Sergeants Watson (Durham), Norris (Hampshire), Crew and Melvin (Metropolitan). They visited Manchester and Salford, which had adopted the system after the great Jenkins mergers took effect in April 1968, as did most forces. They were already concerned by 'The possibility that future young policemen will be car-orientated, having little foot-patrol experience'. In its early stages, unit beat policing in this area seems to have led to a huge increase in car accidents, as officers were forced to learn to drive for a job that had until then been pedestrian. Once again, more crimes were being recorded. Vehicle crime had not been substantially affected. There was one huge and abiding change:

> Because so much time is necessarily spent by police
> officers in panda cars, and the public have less
> opportunity to put their problems to the foot patrolman,
> many more calls are made upon the police by telephone.
> In 1967 there were 52,030 '999' calls made to the
> Manchester and Salford police forces. In 1968 the number
> had increased to 69,971. The number is still increasing...
> The question must be asked: 'are we providing a fire
> brigade service?'

The answer, of course, was 'Yes, we are'. And to provide this service a bulging bureaucracy of telephone answerers, controllers and record-keepers was required: 'One disadvantage has been a necessary increase in the amount of staff, collators and communicators etc., required to service the system.'

The curious thing is that the failure of the system has never prompted any serious attempt to return to the practice that it replaced. If the Peel method had been given the money, equipment, men and women that have been lavished on the failure of unit beat policing, the streets and countryside would be in a very different state. Those who dare to suggest this are told that it is impossible or useless. A recent Audit Commission report, titled 'Streetwise – Effective police patrol' (February 1996), complained about the public's appetite for 'bobbies on the beat', claiming that it was unrealistic when set beside their requirement for fast response times. It also revealed the shocking truth that only five per cent of police strength is now out on patrol at any one time. This means that out of the average 2500 strength of a normal English force, only 125 will be on the streets at any time.

Many of these will be in cars. The rest are swallowed up in the ever-expanding number of specialist squads, the shift system, leave, waiting to give evidence in courts, sickness (now a serious problem, quite probably connected with declining morale and discipline), training (much of which will be of the racial-awareness, sexual-equality or other politically-correct types, rather than aimed at making the police better at policing as such) and the activity known as 'need to spend time in the police station'. This is mainly a creation of the Police and Criminal Evidence Act 1984, a sort of legal tombstone placed on top of old-fashioned policing to make sure it can never rise again.

James Bartholomew, writing in the *Daily Telegraph* in July 2001, described the bureaucratic cobweb through which an officer must struggle if he dares to do so much as issue a caution to a suspect. After making the arrest, he must 'call up transport', then queue for space in the station 'custody suite', with an average wait of twenty-five minutes. Then there is 'booking in', the reading of rights, and logging of possessions – another twenty minutes. Then a solicitor must be found, a process that can take hours. If the suspect is drunk or injured, he must be seen by a 'forensic medical examiner'. These are not instantly available. If the suspect is a juvenile, an adult must be found who can accompany him. The suspect must be read his rights again in the presence of this 'appropriate adult'. No medical examination or interview can take place until the adult is there.

The constable must also write up the arrest according to the elaborate codes of practice in the Police and Criminal Evidence Act 1984, knowing that any error could rebound on him in a career-wrecking complaint. The process is still not over. The case must again be referred to senior officers for their judgement on whether a caution is appropriate. Bartholomew concluded:

> the police officer, knowing that five hours of his time
> could be taken up with bureaucracy if he makes an arrest,
> has a strong incentive to ignore minor crimes. That
> means that there is no chance of getting the much touted
> 'zero tolerance' policing in Britain. The police just have

not got enough five hours to arrest people who write
graffiti, vandalise telephone booths, cycle on the
pavement and so on. They have only got time for the big
stuff. The small stuff is 'completely tolerated'.

This is one of the reasons why, as the Audit Commission concluded, working a beat of any kind is 'close to the bottom rung of the police status ladder'.

'Unrealistic public expectations and rising demands mean that the police are at a crossroads; they will have little time for foot patrol unless they match their responses more closely to the seriousness of incidents,' the Audit Commission said. Its argument that you cannot have Peel's police and *Z Cars* at the same time is perfectly true. But they did not see where this leads. Like almost everyone in the police business since the introduction of unit beat policing, they did not grasp that preventive patrolling and response policing are two different and mutually exclusive systems, based on different views of human nature, law and crime.

Even so, they knew which side they were not on. They favoured what they called 'well-directed patrolling', the special concentration of police on areas where trouble is likely and concern is high. Such 'well-directed patrolling' is used in busy city centres and on estates where order has broken down. It is mistaken by the public for a return to the beat. Perhaps it is meant to be mistaken for it. The officers involved are dressed in reflective yellow jackets to make them stand out, presumably as a counter to claims that the police have become invisible. However, like 'fire-brigade' policing, it is deployed in response to crime and disorder, not in an effort to stop these happening in the first place. And it is seldom if ever permanent, being withdrawn once the crisis has past as resources are shifted to new fronts.

The enforcement of the law has become a concession granted by the authorities from time to time, not a right enjoyed equally by all. The Audit Commission's strictures also revealed that it shared the politicians' and chief constables' obsession with 'major' crime. It also shared their lack of interest in the small-scale wrongdoing that really blights lives. Its original version, leaked to the *Guardian* newspaper, was even more critical of foot patrols than the published text, which appeared to have been toned down as a result of public criticism. Modern chief constables, too, often argue that patrolling officers almost never interrupt a crime in progress. This assertion reveals a complete failure to grasp the beat's deterrent purpose. You might as well criticize the British nuclear submarine fleet for never having fired its missiles. It is just a variant on the more usual claim that there are simply not enough officers to provide the sort of cover that was available in the 1950s when, according to the great man-power falsehood, there were so many more officers available for a smaller population.

A similar failure to grasp the reality of life was shown in the Commission's attitude towards 999 calls. It pointed out that they had risen by 150 per cent between 1980 and 1996 but that only 30 per cent of such calls were about what it considered to be crime. Many, it declared, concerned 'nuisance or anti-social behaviour'. Others were inquiries about late-night chemists and football scores. It is perfectly true that some 999 calls are trivial, stupid and wasteful. Similarly, doctors and nurses in hospital casualty departments are sometimes asked to examine cases of dandruff. Other calls are an effect of the mass slaughter of police stations or the fact that it is difficult to reach the police on their normal phone numbers and all but impossible to speak to an individual officer. However, 'nuisance or anti-social behaviour' is a source of grave unhappiness to millions. It is also the very thing that the old Dixonian police force was very good at controlling, discouraging and preventing.

So why, given all the problems that have followed, has there never been a counter-revolution to restore the Peel system, which, for all its faults, appears to have worked much better than the unit beat? There seems to be some sort of psychological block. 'We can't go back to the old ways,' say chief constables, as if this were an unalterable truth. But why ever not? And why is the argument conducted with such dishonesty and ignorance?

The manpower shortage theory – demolished above – is so widely accepted and so wholly untrue that its constant use is itself part of the mystery. It requires an explanation. There must be another reason for the obstinate clinging to 'fire-brigade' policing and to the Kafka-in-reverse rules that ensure that the individual constable is actually afraid to arrest anyone because to do so will spoil his, the constable's, whole day.

Of course, there was a desire to cut costs, and especially wage bills, but this cannot possibly still be the problem that it was in the thin days of 1966. Police equipment, spending and manpower are all financed by rivers of public gold beyond the dreams of the 1960s. The Britain of the mid-1960s was sunk in economic failure and pessimism. There was a prevalent belief that we simply could not afford to be what we had once been – which now looks remarkably foolish given the huge mountain ranges of money we were to spend on new schools that could not teach, new local authorities whose names nobody could remember, new courts that could not cope with crime and new roads that swiftly became more clogged than the ones that had gone before. However, it was what people thought at the time. The affluence of the Macmillan era was beginning to fade and the shadow of the coming devaluation of sterling lay across the country. Wages and salaries are always the most expensive part of any public service. It made sense of a sort to paper over manpower shortages with capital spending on cars and radios. Unit beat policing was policing on the cheap. Then there was the 1960s' mania for gigantism. Big companies, big factories, big hospitals, big schools, big local authorities and big government all came into fashion then. Most have since fallen out of fashion, especially in the private sector, as their boasted 'economies of scale' have turned out to be illusory. These changes can be explained by the pressures of the day. When they have obviously failed, why not change back, now that we are in an age of vastly greater wealth?

Other interesting questions demand an answer. Why was Roy Jenkins so keen to merge smaller police forces into bigger ones? Why did his Home Office encourage Eric St Johnston, with the fervent support of Harold Wilson's Downing Street? Why was unit beat policing adopted so swiftly and without being given time to reveal its failings? How was it that so many innovations, from police helicopters to crown courts, majority verdicts and suspended sentences, came under his stewardship? Regrettably Lord Jenkins can never answer these questions more fully than he did at the time in his Commons speeches or later in his charming and fascinating autobiography. Even so, it is not unreasonable to seek for some sort of pattern. A different sort of society came into being after these changes. It could be said to have resulted from them. Was it the sort of society that Mr Jenkins intended? Consciously, subconsciously or even unconsciously, could he have seen in the Peel system of policing an important pillar of the old conservative state?

There is something worthy of Edmund Burke in the method of policing adopted by the Victorians. They were reluctant to have a police force of any kind on English soil. Peel's 'Blue Locusts' were initially denounced as 'an insidious attempt to enslave the people by arbitrary and tyrannical methods.' The police were to be employed, it was said, as the instruments of a new despotism, the enlisted members of a new standing army. English conservative thinkers at the end of the eighteenth century hated the idea of a Continental type of force, originally proposed in the days of Pitt the Younger. T. A. Critchley, in his *History of Police in England and Wales*, details the difficulties the reformers had in getting the idea past a hostile Parliament, which viewed the very concept as foreign and repressive, despite the very high levels of disorder in the England of those days. William Shenstone had complained in 1743: 'Pickpockets, formerly content with mere filching, make no scruple to knock people down with bludgeons in Fleet Street and the Strand.'

The terrifying Gordon Riots of 1780 caused William Shelburne, who was to become the first Home Secretary, to praise the French police system and recommend something of the kind in lawless London. William Pitt's Solicitor-General, Archibald Macdonald, introduced a radical Police Bill, anticipating Peel by thirty years. The City of London saw its provisions as a threat to its ancient liberties and the bill was withdrawn, not to be discussed again for decades. Like many other radical ideas, it became unacceptable because it was associated in the national mind with the enemy. The French revolutionary tyranny, by making everything French stink in the nostrils of freedom-loving Englishmen, closed all such discussions for years to come. Parliamentary committees in 1816, 1818 and 1822 rejected police proposals as incompatible with British liberty. The very word 'police' had a sinister ring to most English people then and for long afterwards, and even a hundred years later there were many who remained suspicious of the idea and the practice. The 1818 parliamentary committee said that a Continental type of police would be 'odious and repulsive, and one which no government would be able to carry into execution. It would be a plan which would make every servant of every house a spy on his master, and all classes of society spies on each other.' The 1822 committee said:

> It is difficult to reconcile an effective system of police,
> with that perfect freedom of action and exemption from
> interference which are the great privileges and blessings
> of society in this country; and your committee think that
> the forfeiture or curtailment of such advantages would be
> too great a sacrifice for improvements in the police, or
> facilities in the detection of crime, however desirable
> themselves if abstractedly considered.

The chairman of that committee was Sir Robert Peel.

Eventually, Peel and the Duke of Wellington came to believe that there had to be some sort of police system controlled by the government. The 'Peterloo Massacre', the disastrous use of mounted troops against a peaceful crowd in Manchester, helped convince the Duke that it was foolish to rely on soldiers to support the civil power in time of trouble. Their own doubts, together with the long hostility of the political class to such a foreign idea, meant that they introduced something unique.

The Peel police force was deeply influenced by the English past, restrained by law and custom. The unadorned, far from majestic or overbearing constable, patrolling alone and on foot, was the outcome of the struggle between the need for some sort of force and the wise mistrust of a Continental gendarmerie. It was a cunning compromise, imposed by men who did not really want a police force at all and suspected that it would become a monstrous tyranny if not closely watched and constantly restrained.

That suspicion was still alive in the early twentieth century, as revealed in the entry on 'police' in the eleventh edition (1911) of the *Encyclopaedia Britannica*. While most modern reference books rejoice at the technical prowess and efficiency of various police departments, the *Britannica* at that time was still able to envisage a society without any police at all and to doubt whether the idea of a police force was a wise one. It noted that Charles V of France is said to have been the first king to invent a police force in order to increase the happiness and security of his people, but that it had developed into 'a horrible engine of repression'. This is not because the *Encyclopaedia*'s authors were complacent about the levels of crime in the years before Peel's Metropolitan Police Act. They wrote:

> ...crime was rampant, highwaymen terrorized the roads, footpads infested the streets, burglaries were of constant occurrence... the watchmen appointed by parishes were useless, inadequate, inefficient and untrustworthy, acting often as accessories in aiding and abetting crime...
>
> At the commencement of the 19th century it was computed that there was one criminal to every 22 of the population...

> In those days victims of robberies constantly compounded with felonies and paid blackmail to thieves, promising not to prosecute on the restitution of a portion of the stolen property.

Despite all this there was much opposition to a police force. This hostility was based on the idea that the price being asked for controlling crime was higher than any free Englishman ought to be willing to pay. It would place in the hands of the state a power it had not had since the hated days of Cromwell's Major-Generals. Peel's scheme was denounced as 'an insidious attempt to enslave the people by arbitrary and tyrannical methods'. The police were to be employed, it was said, as 'the instruments of a new despotism, the enlisted members of a new standing army'. Fear of such a standing army was still alive and dangerous in English politics less than two hundred years after Cromwell's death.

Huge care was taken to limit the powers of the police, to prevent them from acting too haughtily or arrogantly or becoming the state's private army. As a result of that care, they came to symbolize in practice the Englishman's belief that the state was beneath his feet, supporting him, not above his head, oppressing him. The early police also had the good luck to arrive at a moment when the remoralization of society was well under way, and to spread across the country at the same time as Victorian morality and Christian self-restraint. Even when, in later years, the police were sometimes used as strike-breakers or to restrain legitimate demonstrations, these actions were seen as exceptional. Their powers remained strictly limited, and it is nowadays astonishing to read official reports, such as the 1929 Royal Commission on Police Powers, which make this plain. It declared that 'It is desirable to avoid any questioning at all of persons in custody', and it dwelt at length on whether the police had any right to question anyone at all, although the semi-official 'Judges' Rules' of 1912 implied that some sort of right to do so did exist. The Commission quoted Mr Justice Hawkins, who said in 1892, 'Neither Judge, magistrate, nor juryman can interrogate an accused person. Much less then ought a constable to do so.' Hawkins was also the author of the once-famous maxim that a constable 'ought to keep his eyes and ears open and his mouth shut'.

The 1929 Royal Commission also reasserted Peel's principle that a policeman is not a special official but 'a person paid to perform, as a matter of duty, acts which if he were so minded he might have done voluntarily'. A policeman, it believed, possessed few powers not enjoyed by the ordinary citizen, and 'public opinion has shown great jealousy of any attempts to give increased authority to the police.' These pieces of conventional wisdom from the Victorian era would have made sense to a 1950s' officer. They are outlandish to anyone used to the vastly increased powers of the modern English police. A police veteran or lawyer from that era would be shocked by the change in character the police have since undergone. They have developed into something much more like examining magistrates, who can grant bail and are permitted to interrogate, unrestrained by a full right of silence. To confuse things further, they must do so under rules that seem designed to aid the unscrupulous, who can all too easily use the complex rules of procedure to avoid prosecution.

Police forces, too, were highly independent of central government as late as the 1962 Royal Commission. While admitting that Whitehall was now interfering more than before, it could still say of the individual chief constable:

> [He] is accountable to no-one and subject to no-one's
> orders for the way in which, for example, he settles his
> general policies in regard to law enforcement over the
> area covered by his force, the disposition of his force,
> the concentration of his resources on any particular
> crime or area, the way in which he handles political
> demonstrations or processions and allocates and instructs
> his men when preventing breaches of the peace arising

from industrial disputes, the methods he employs in
dealing with an outbreak of violence or of passive
resistance to authority, his policy in enforcing the traffic
laws and in dealing with parked vehicles, and so on.

Arthur Scargill's unprecedented use of mass pickets in an effort to thwart an elected government through industrial power was mainly approved of by the supposedly democratic political left. The equally unprecedented government response to it, restricting the picketing miners' freedom to travel, was a dubious and possibly unlawful extension of police powers and of government powers over the police. There may have been a good excuse for it, but it did permanent damage to the neutrality of the police. It also provided an excuse to withdraw officers from many duties to which they seem never to have returned. Given this bending of the rules of democratic behaviour by both sides, and the New Labour assault on the constitution that followed it, the views on the certainty of liberty expressed by the 1962 Royal Commission seem complacent. However, they were the views of most at the time. It is hard for those born later to realize how secure England felt before 1965. 'British liberty,' the Commission proclaimed, 'does not depend and never has depended, upon the dispersal of police power. It depends on the supremacy of Parliament and on the rule of law. We do not accept that the criterion of a police state is whether a country's police force is local rather than national.' But immediately afterwards they thought it wise to add that there was 'a fundamental contrast: between the continental principle of placing responsibility for the maintenance of law and order upon the executive government, and arming it with powers of direct enforcement; and the British principle that it is the right and duty of each citizen to preserve the peace and bring malefactors to justice, with its corollary that the police are merely paid to act on the citizens' behalf'.

Reading these words in the age of David Blunkett and Alastair Campbell, it is necessary to wonder how important might be the dispersal of police power if the supremacy of Parliament were to dwindle and the rule of law be called into question. In such circumstances, the dispersal of police power might become considerably more important. The wise lawmaker, like the drafters of the American Bill of Rights, takes precautions against the apparently unlikely as well as the obvious. The Victorians, who ensured that no national police force was created, seem to have taken the view that there might one day be circumstances in which this would matter. They also thought that nothing important would be gained by having a single force. At the back of their minds was the completely different character of the English state from those on the Continent. The 1962 Royal Commission again expressed this point with great clarity. For its members, the new post-war democracies of Western Europe were young and untried. Their historical memories stretched back to earlier eras when the difference between the two sides of the Channel was more marked: 'The contrast, in this view, is seen in the big things and small things alike: the British police are unarmed but most policemen on the continent carry arms; and political and secret police appear to flourish on the continent, for their role as agents of the state leaves them a prey to political extremists.'

They were unimpressed by the arguments of those who sought a national force on the grounds of greater efficiency against that useful bogey, organized crime. Speaking of the 'basic soundness' of the existing system they concluded: 'the police forces of this country should not be brought under the direct central control of the government.' Some members even argued that higher efficiency, as well as more scope for the exercise of initiative, was attainable within a system of local forces. As for the 'serious and growing problem of organised crime', they accepted that reported cases of robbery with violence more than doubled between 1950 and 1960. They noted that a high proportion of these robberies occurred in London which already had a large-scale police force – but in reply to those who argued that big was better, they pointed out that the

Metropolitan Police CID had a detection rate lower than almost anywhere else in the country. They concluded: 'The great bulk of crime is still local, in the sense that it is committed by local people operating near their homes. We have no doubt that crime of this kind is best tackled by detectives who form part of the local force, enjoying the continuous interchange of information with the uniformed branch which daily association affords.'

Once again, all the arguments were on the side of small forces – just as they had been on the side of the beat system. Yet the Jenkins era chose to ignore the fears and experiences of the past and press ahead with changes that reduced police independence, strengthened the power of central government and gave no obvious benefits in return. Public dissatisfaction with remote forces has grown every year since they began, and a dwindling number of people now even know that things were ever done differently or that the arguments for change were feeble and have not been borne out in practice.

Actually, there are several reasons for the obstinate refusal of government and police to consider that they may possibly have been mistaken. Some of them will be dealt with elsewhere at more length. One is simple: in the age of Railtrack, one should never rule out stupidity as an explanation for anything in modern English government and administration. There is no doubt that some foolish things have been done by a Parliament that was not paying attention. Many of them have been the work of the 'Conservative' Party, which was supposed to be protecting us against the more adventurous elements of the liberal elite. However, it is not the only explanation, or a complete one.

The Police and Criminal Evidence Act 1984, the establishment of the Police Complaints Authority and the setting up of the Crown Prosecution Service (created by the Prosecution of Offences Act 1985) might have made sense in some Arcadian society of well-behaved and self-effacing folk who also happened to be extremely rich. These measures effectively destroyed individual initiative in the police force and demanded a perfection in action that few could attain. They bore no relation to the reality of crime and disorder, or to human nature as displayed in twenty-first-century Europe. They also ignored the social breakdown caused by the cultural revolution, the permissive society, the abolition of the married family, the abandonment of corporal punishment in schools, the dropping of the principle of any punishment at all in prisons and the scrapping of the death penalty. Our leaders seem to have believed that modern English society would just stay up by itself once all its foundations, props, guy-ropes and buttresses had been removed. More unworldly still, they seem to have decided that one of the few forces in society that still stood for conservative morality and discipline should be systematically transformed into the uniformed army of social liberalism. Yet their actions were in tune with most of the legislation and reform of the last half-century, based on the idea that government has supplanted God and can solve all dissensions, bind up all wounds and wipe away every tear from every eye. There is a utopian pattern here: the modern secular belief that if society is run by an elite of perfect, civilized and brilliantly able mandarins, people will no longer have to be good, because the machine will compel them to be.

The plodding, unarmed constable in his dull blue tunic and helmet, proceeding slowly through the night streets with his lantern, was the creation of sceptics who mistrusted human nature and suspected that men would behave badly if not watched and restrained. They applied this rule to governments as well as to criminals, by making sure that this mild police force could not be turned into a tool of tyranny. They had the great good fortune to inherit very ancient and beloved Anglo-Saxon ideas of 'every man his own constable' and of the law as the treasured possession of the common people. They trusted the constable to kick the right backside, apply fist and truncheon where necessary to the right suspect and to show respect to the respectable of all classes.

Let us not be in any doubt that the old police force was the army of the respectable (though *not* the army of the wealthy) and that it was often unscrupulous in its methods. All societies are imperfect. Most people, asked to make the choice, would choose this imperfection rather than the one we currently suffer from – that the police are almost entirely powerless against wrongdoers. Yet although our grandfathers trusted the constable to fight rough battles with the criminal classes, they did not trust him with powers of forced entry or interrogation, or unlimited detention. Almost by accident they conceived a scheme of great brilliance, which defended and enforced the law, and contained crime and disorder without threatening liberty in general. This, the original English police force, embodied morally conservative notions of right and wrong. It therefore offended the new liberal religion of benevolent government, welfare state and human rights. Instinctively, the new elite knew that the 1829 police system was an obstacle to what they wanted. Without really knowing why, they knew the bobby on the beat was the enemy of what they stood for and what they wanted. He had to go – and they got rid of him.

IV

Making bad people worse

Modern prisons are the result of idealist projects to improve the world, like most other human mistakes and disasters. Those forbidding towers and walls are in fact temples of the Enlightenment. This truth is largely ignored because most people prefer to forget that such horrible places exist at all. Yet for much of the last two centuries prisons and penitentiaries have striven incessantly to improve those who were sent to them. No matter how many times they failed in this task, the utopians tried and tried again. Solitary confinement, ludicrous as it seems now, was supposed to save the prisoner from contamination by his fellows. A Tory Home Secretary, David Waddington, delighted the penal reformers by remarking in a 1990 White Paper that prison was 'an expensive way of making bad people worse'. How this would have shocked the French revolutionary Mirabeau, who was fond of describing prisons as 'Houses of Improvement' (Maisons d'Amélioration) and pioneered the ideas of labour, separation of prisoners from each other to curb bad influences, rewards for good behaviour and aid to discharged convicts.

Prison had been formally introduced as a punishment, rather than simply as a place where punishment happened or where people were held while they waited to be punished, in the French penal code of 1791, which had itself been inspired by the Declaration of the Rights of Man of 1789. This distinction – between detention and reformation – is still made in the American system, where a jail is simply a place where the accused are held. The word is never used to describe a penitentiary, where inmates are supposedly punished or reformed after the courts have convicted them. The first American colonies did not, to begin with, use imprisonment as a punishment at all.

In England, where the prisons were stinking and diseased dungeons mainly used for holding people on their way to transportation or the noose, the idea of prison as reformatory had its first flowering remarkably early. The original Millbank Penitentiary, built in London after the Napoleonic Wars, was intended to reform its inmates. Fully operational by 1817, it was initially dedicated to rehabilitation. Its inmates were carefully chosen as being the most likely to respond to such generous treatment. The work they were to do was intended to be useful in the world outside – tailoring and weaving for men, sewing and laundering for women. While the punishment cells were subterranean and lightless, the normal accommodation was, by the standards of the time, comfortable. The cells had glazed windows, were furnished with a bed, table and stool and were warmed by flues. All went badly. Within a few years the model gaol suffered from disease caused by its poor site on low-lying land near the Thames. It also experienced malnutrition and full-scale riots. Flogging was introduced to keep control of increasingly riotous prisoners, and the reconviction rate for ex-inmates was found to be over 50 per cent. In 1844 the whole experiment was written off as a failure and Millbank became a reception centre for the hulks and the new youth training centre that had just opened at Parkhurst.

The hulks, dismasted former warships moored permanently in dreary locations such as the Medway, and familiar from the opening scenes of *Great Expectations*, were disgusting hellholes with no social purpose. They were miserable beyond belief for the poor and weak but tolerable for the richest, hardest and most lawless. To that extent, they bear a disturbing resemblance to the pointless, anarchic warehouses we have today. They had bribable officers. Prisoners who knew the ropes were able to get hold of pornography, drink and tobacco, and had free association up until 10 p.m. In another curious prefiguring of our times, it was the mentally ill who suffered most in these places. Conditions for them were especially savage, squalid and unspeakably cruel. There are fearful accounts of men in chains literally rotting in puddles of their own urine.

Of course, it was not officially meant to be so. Sir Samuel Hoare, great-great-nephew of Elizabeth Fry, would in 1938 praise the early nineteenth-century reformers, especially Robert Peel, for their revolutionary act in bringing to an end the medieval conception of punishment – that is, 'the system under which imprisonment played a very small part and in which punishment depended almost entirely upon sentences of death', or mutilation or confiscation. The old dungeons had been places of abandonment, disease, chaos and lawlessness while the accused or condemned waited for trial and execution. In the hulks, where the law was supposed to prevail, the government's rules stated: 'Every person belonging to the Convict Hulk establishment is on all occasions to treat the convicts with humanity and to lend a willing ear to their complaints and grievances, whether real or imaginary.' English prisons, it seems, have always been fond of notices exhorting everyone to behave well. Judged by the end results, the cynics and brutes had not done all that much worse than the enlightened reformers.

The next experiment was at Pentonville, which was at first intended to fit convicts for freedom in the colonies, by subjecting them to a long period of solitary confinement. It was built after William Crawford, a Home Office delegate, had visited the then-famous Eastern Penitentiary in Philadelphia, which was seen as the most advanced prison of the day. The plan was for eighteen months of complete seclusion before transportation. There was to be no contact whatsoever with other prisoners. Each convict's cap had, grotesquely, to be pulled down over his face if he met another prisoner in case they should communicate or recognize each other. This experiment, too, was abandoned gradually in the 1850s, thanks to its failure as much as to its inhumanity. Although the idea of reform never entirely died, the Victorians eventually settled on something much less ambitious and, as it turned out, much more successful. Robert Peel, when not creating the police, developed the first modern English penal code, which replaced barbarities such as the gibbet (unpopular with the middle classes because they did not like rotting corpses being displayed in cages near their homes) with graduated prison terms. Great victories were won against physical and moral squalor.

The notable humanitarians, Elizabeth Fry and John Howard, fought with courage and ferocity against the cruelty, filth and moral depravity of the eighteenth-century system and the hulks, and they are strikingly commemorated in bas-relief sculptures on either side of the gates of Wormwood Scrubs prison in London – a startling reminder that this place, when it was built, was a triumph of the most modern and advanced penal thinking. Every cell had its own plumbing, the cell-blocks were light and airy and easy to keep clean. Pass through the gates and the ugly new fencing that bounds the secure interior and you will find a majestic Victorian chapel which would grace a fair-sized town, its chancel decorated with accomplished paintings done on old mailbags, symbolizing the moral improvement the Victorians hoped to achieve among prisoners.

The faces of Fry and Howard are the only comforting things about the exterior view. As Giles Playfair wrote in his *The Punitive Obsession*, the Victorians thought that prison architecture should make the beholder afraid: '[Jeremy] Bentham believed that the very sight of a penitentiary from outside should fill all who beheld it with such dread of what might await them inside that they would never dare take the risk of being put there.' The government architects listened to this view and did their worst. Castles of doom sprang up in prominent sites across the country, although, as it turned out, none of them ever quite matched the sheer raw, stark representation of penal servitude achieved by the dismal cell-blocks of Dartmoor Prison at Princetown, which were originally put up to house French prisoners of war in Napoleonic times. Even so, they left a lasting and permanent impression and it was a deliberate one. As Major H. S. Rogers, the Surveyor of Prisons, remarked in 1910: 'It appears that a prevailing view on prison construction was to provide heavy, massive and gloomy structures, giving an impression of donjons, bars and chains; small, heavily-barred windows, with obscure glass, dark passages etc.'

English prisons, like English policemen, still look much the same from the outside as they did in a previous age. There are many new jails (though nothing like enough of them) mostly buried in the countryside or remote suburbs where few see them. However, it is hard to miss Pentonville, Armley, Leicester and many other nineteenth-century monuments to stern retribution, hard labour and penal servitude, glowering over the Victorian cityscape. You might even think that Victorian ideas still survived within. However, the paradox of English prisons today is that these imposing outsides hide a rather pathetic secret on the inside. Perhaps that is the way the government wants it to be. We, the public – victims and potential victims – can deceive ourselves that there is still a penal system of grim fortresses where cowed convicts in arrow-flecked suits live on porridge and do hard labour. Meanwhile our rulers, weakened by generous social consciences, know the truth – that the nineteenth-century battlements conceal well-intentioned warehouses of futility where a little social work is attempted but not zealously pursued.

There are powerful national myths about prison. In newspaper cartoons convicts still wear arrowed uniforms and are often depicted in chains or even shown breaking rocks. Their heads are shaved. They can see visitors only through wire-netting. They eat porridge. It is entirely false. There is also an opposite myth, with some truth in it, that of the pampered prisoner, allowed out to go to the pub or the shops, or even home for the weekend, playing snooker, watching TV, bribing the warders to bring him gourmet food and wine, taking and dealing in drugs which are passed to him by mouth-to-mouth contact during poorly supervised visits. And there is a third myth, a dark one of prisoners beaten up, stabbed, forced to smuggle drugs and robbed by fellow inmates, of gangs running whole wings after dark. This is, regrettably, the closest to the truth, although the Inspectors of Prisons do not often dwell on it. They see it as their job to criticize the official running of the prisons, not the unofficial regimes.

One rare exception to this rule was the investigation into Wymott Prison in Lancashire before and after a disastrous riot there in 1993. The then Chief Inspector of Prisons, Judge Stephen Tumim, had found that the jail had been subject to 'a reign of terror by prison gang leaders' which 'reduced a model jail to a burnt-out shell'. Staff as well as inmates were intimidated by drug barons who ruthlessly exerted control similar to the 'paramilitary influence in Northern Ireland prisons'.

> In the run-up to September's riot [in 1993], Wymott was 'close to anarchy'. Prisoners, who lived in student-style rooms rather than cells, had their own keys and did as they pleased, within their locked wings, for hours at a time, particularly at weekends. Judge Tumim believes that the free-and-easy, university-style regime was one of the main reasons for the troubles. However, it was the drugs rackets that gave the gangsters so much power. Inmates returning from home leave were forced to strip by racketeers and searched for narcotics, the main currency inside. The judge criticised Wymott as 'no more than an open prison with a fence around it and wholly inadequate for the majority of young and volatile inner city men it was receiving'. About 100 inmates were actively involved in the riot, which caused at least £20 million worth of damage.

Judge Tumim was reported as saying: 'The majority of prisoners were left to the mercy of the activists. They were placed in a vulnerable position which could have resulted in death or serious injury.'

Less than a year before the riots, the Prison Inspectorate had produced a report that uncovered drug dealing, violence and evidence of no-go areas at Wymott. They said that Manchester's gangland culture had been re-created inside the jail and that drugs, including heroin, were easier to obtain inside the prison than outside. Staff were said to be unable to reimpose order. Wymott had been built in 1979, optimistically intended to hold more than eight hundred low-security prisoners on short sentences. It quickly filled up with far more serious criminals than had at first been intended, making a nonsense of its idealistic buildings and regime. There were riots in 1986 and claims of reform and improvement in 1990. By 1992 the inspectors were warning: 'It is hard to imagine a more corrupting environment in which to place an offender.' Inspectors on a night visit 'confirmed that inmates appeared to be completely in control behind secure gates'. Prisoners were said to have appeared amazed that anyone should trespass on 'their' territory. During the visit, heroin worth £2000 was thrown over the wall. After the report the Home Office said security had been strengthened. Judging from what was to happen there later, they either strengthened it too much, or not enough – in the prevailing atmosphere it is hard to know which is which.

So what does actually go on in English prisons, places where the inmates can actually be allowed to take over the buildings at night? What does not go on is punishment. The official view, repeatedly expressed, is that being locked up is punishment enough, that convicted criminals are locked up *as* punishment, not *for* punishment. While they are inside, which is often not for very long, some sort of attempt is made to turn the criminals into good citizens. It does not seem to be very successful. All figures agree that huge numbers of ex-prisoners rapidly reoffend.

At a time when violent crime is at its worst in living memory, when no property is safe from the thief or the vandal, you might think that the unfashionable idea of punishment might be reconsidered. You might think that the social-work approach would at least be questioned, since its results have been so bad. At the very least, you might think that there are many people now on our streets who ought to be locked up for the good of the rest of us. You might think that our experts would look enviously at America's achievement – serious crime down 16 per cent in four years, violent crime down 20 per cent in the same period. They might be interested, too, to know that this achievement followed the building of nearly five hundred new prisons and a general ban on light sentences and early releases. There is no sign of it, though. Lord Woolf, the Lord Chief Justice, said in January 2001 that judges should send far more criminals on 'vigorous' community projects instead of locking them up, although not long afterwards he started demanding long sentences for people who stole mobile telephones. The Home Office has let thousands of prisoners out early with tags on their ankles. By contrast, the US prison system has vacuumed the wicked and the ill-behaved off the streets, so that two million now languish behind American razor-wire.

However, among the narrow-minded elitists who take the real decisions on criminal justice in this country, the only prison debate is about the conditions inside. Almost monthly some new Chief Inspector of Prisons denounces one jail or another for its squalor, hopelessness or failure of management and discipline. There is a fuss, the Chief Inspector demands action, the Home Office promises action and the same problems then happen again elsewhere soon afterwards. A new, still more liberal, Inspector of Prisons is appointed, who begins the same cycle of frustration. Nobody ever adds up these reports and wonders if prisons, as they are currently run, are as certain to be nasty as the sea is to be wet. Of course we should be concerned about prison conditions. But are we concerned in the right way? Squalor, neglect and casual cruelty are signs of barbarism. They are also signs of a complete lack of serious purpose in buildings intended for one thing and now used for an utterly different aim.

In 1910, Winston Churchill, then Home Secretary, urged 'a constant heart-searching by all charged with the duty of punishment, a desire and eagerness to rehabilitate in the world of industry all those who have paid their dues in the hard coinage of punishment, tireless efforts towards the discovery of curative and regenerating processes and an unfaltering faith that there is a treasure, if you can only find it, in the heart of every man'. Churchill's words are often quoted by modern prison reformers. However, they usually omit the vital words 'the hard coinage of punishment'. While deprivation of liberty is nowadays considered to be punishment in itself, it was not so when Churchill was Home Secretary. Ninety years ago the English Prison Commissioners described their task as 'the due punishment of fully responsible persons', a mixture of retribution, deterrence and reformation, in that order. They explained that 'the penalty of crime is in the dishonouring circumstances which must accompany loss of liberty; in the deprivation of what liberty permits in the way of indulgence and self-gratification; in compulsory labour; in the loss of self-respect'. Even then, the Commissioners already sensed that the elite's resolve was weakening. They criticized 'loose thinkers and loose writers' for reversing the order of things so that prison would be 'altogether reformatory, as little as possible deterrent and not at all retributory'. They might also have said that, if there is no punishment, there will be no reform either.

Early in the year 2000, I visited Her Majesty's Prison at Wormwood Scrubs in London to see what the Home Office hoped for in a modern prison and to write about it for the *Mail on Sunday*. Unlike Her Majesty's Inspectors, I was not able to choose the prison I wished to see, nor the time at which I saw it. They told me when I could go and they chose it for me – from a list of current and former 'hellholes' named in a recently-delivered speech by Martin Narey, the director general of the prison service in England and Wales – so it is reasonable to assume that they are fairly happy with the way it is.

I was puzzled. It seemed odd that the man in charge of the prison system should be able to criticize his own empire in public in such terms. Was this bravery, or a public refusal to accept responsibility for a system imposed on an enlightened elite by the crude punitive demands of a supposedly stone-age electorate?

As soon as I stepped through the gates of the prison I struggled to discover what its true purpose might be. It was plainly more civilized, in simple physical terms, than it used to be. Criticisms of dirt and crude discipline made by the inspectors had been heeded. But were they the right criticisms? Was it better in the right way? Behind the great, gloomy gate, the stern, overbearing towers and the tall, thick walls that the Victorians built, you might almost be in a university hall of residence. Everywhere there were politically-correct notices denouncing discrimination of the usual forbidden kinds. There were table-football sets, payphones, showers, the everyday echoing noise of pop music. The cells, each with its own TV and en suite lavatory, might almost have been study bedrooms. Even the bars were disguised by window frames in a cheery blue, the panes of which could be opened. Most people were in tracksuits or jeans, trainers or slippers. The only inhabitants in a recognizable uniform were the warders but, without tunics or peaked caps, they had less physical menace than the average parking warden. Nobody really had to work, although they could earn up to £30 a week in some jobs and spend as much as £15 of that on little luxuries in the prison shop.

No one sewed mailbags any more. A typical job was repacking headphones for airlines. There was even 'unemployment pay' of £2.50 per week for those who did nothing at all. Those who could not read – and many prisoners were very bad at it – got a chance of a proper education. Here, thanks to the threat of losing pay, there was some of the discipline they never experienced at school, and they were taught to read by traditional methods which are seldom used in the sort of schools they attended. It is odd that you have to commit a serious crime before the British state is prepared to grant you the boon of a disciplined education at the taxpayer's expense.

Wormwood Scrubs had its own branch of the Citizens' Advice Bureau. Copies of the European Charter of Human Rights are everywhere. Perhaps somewhere in a cell nearby was the prisoner who would take the government to court and win the cases that everyone knows are inevitable under our new law – conjugal rights for the married and unmarried prisoner, clean needles for heroin addicts and, almost certainly, the right for transsexuals to dress as women. No doubt the modern prison service will learn to cope with convicts in tights. The kitchens had already adapted to the twenty-first century's fads and necessities, with two kinds of vegetarian and one vegan menu, and rice for those who would not eat potatoes. Islam was catered for with both halal meat and Friday prayers.

Even so, it would have been foolish to describe this place as any kind of holiday camp. There was an air of unstated, intangible menace and a feeling that, after dark, this is no place for a weak or gentle man. The pastel-painted walls are plastered with warnings against 'bullying', as if this were Wormwood Lane Comprehensive. However, bullying in a place like this, where you cannot go home, has a much more sinister meaning. 'Are you a bully?' asked one such placard, giving away more than it intended to about the real nature of the establishment:

> Do you intimidate or threaten prisoners who are weaker than you? Do you force others to join you in drug taking or other subversive activities and make them feel weak if they don't? Do you persuade other prisoners to smuggle contraband through visits? Do you think it's OK to intimidate or assault sex offenders? Do you think it's OK to intimidate or assault other prisoners who have been labelled as 'grasses'?
> If you do any of these things then you are a bully. Bullying is antisocial and destructive. It destroys lives and can lead to self-harm and suicide. So don't do it!

This all seems terribly worthy, like an appeal for subscriptions in a youth club. However, in a prison apparently run by an unofficial consensus between officers and inmates, calls to 'Stop it!' are unlikely to have much effect. Authority seems to rule with a deliberately light hand, not wanting to provoke trouble from fit young men in a confined space where the guards are usually outnumbered. There were still plenty of places where a vulnerable prisoner might have been pushed into an unseen corner and threatened. Who would take the risk of reporting this and being denounced as a grass, a marked man for the rest of his time inside? (Judging by private telephone calls I received from former inmates and officers after the *Mail on Sunday* article was published, my suspicions are justified.) But officially all is relatively well.

It is even more difficult to tell how much drug abuse goes on here. The men are locked away for nearly twelve hours each night. There is drug testing but it is not frequent. Physical contact at visiting times (not allowed in the American prison system) means that parcels of dope and heroin can be – and certainly are – exchanged while kissing. Prisoners asked about this do not even try to pretend that there are no drugs available. Sometimes outsiders throw packages of narcotics over the walls in tennis balls, hoping or knowing that the delivery will be passed on.

Drugs or no, a fortune has obviously been spent on rebuilding, redecorating and civilizing the 114-year-old cell-blocks. A lot of trouble has been taken to keep them clean. There is no stink of sewage, not even the normal jailhouse aroma of stale food and dried sweat. Fresh paint and bright lights make the fortified walls and armoured doors seem almost picturesque, their original hard intention obsolete. However, the yards outside are scattered with litter flung needlessly from the windows, a warning that spiteful, damaging anarchy is never far away and that improving conditions does not necessarily win either appreciation or co-operation. Until recently it was undoubtedly a place of ill-repute, neither Victorian jail nor twentieth-century penal laboratory, just a slum. When the then governor, Stephen Moore, first arrived in 1998, it was so squalid, overcrowded and dismal that, as he put it to me, he wondered if he had been put in charge of a prison in Romania or Albania. No civilized person could want that. However, should a civilized person want the sort of place Mr Moore then created, a kind of ideal, liberal prison where everything flows smoothly and nobody is made to do anything much, except be locked up? Here is the problem: Mr Moore had no official duty to punish those he was guarding. 'The courts punish people by depriving them of their liberty for some time. We are in the business of using that time as constructively as possible.'

How constructively is that? In a special unit I met a well-spoken and personable young murderer who, while high on heroin, had knifed his victim to death. With every appearance of sincerity, he said he was determined to stay off drugs. He had good reason to do this since, if he did not, he would never get out. In the modern fashion of 'confronting your crime', he had been persuaded to re-enact his deed, to imagine himself the victim, to realize what he had done. Does he really? A murderer who really knew what he had done might not think it was right that he should be released, ever.

In another special unit were the miserable figures of the mentally ill, moaning and slumped in their cells, bewildered, pitiful yet probably dangerous. It is likely that many of these people had come to this state because they had taken illegal drugs and permanently damaged their minds. The prisons have become the final destination for many such people because of the demolition of the mental hospitals under the shameful Care in the Community programme. Their presence is a terrible burden on prison staff, who ought not to be asked to do this. These people are dangerous to themselves and to others and should not be in prisons at all. Their presence is undoubtedly the cause of much grief and trouble, and, like all aspects of Care in the Community, it is a national disgrace that ought to be reversed and whose advocates should in some way be punished for what they have done.

Inside this place it was easy to see why staff thought that their main job was to help the prisoners become better people. When you see only the criminal, never the victim, it is easy to forget that at least part of your job is the reassurance of the wounded and the robbed, and the discouragement of wickedness. You may be inclined to become confused about which one you are supposed to be helping. Common humanity, where it can, seeks to avoid cruelty and assuage misery, and it is right that it should be so. Dirt, brutality and gloom are never good. But much of what passes for kindness is also a form of appeasement, driven by the permanent fear of a new outbreak of prison riots, cell-blocks ablaze, warders perhaps kidnapped or worse, TV cameras camped outside as the government hesitates between negotiation and a SWAT team.

It is certain that the TVs in the cells – something that most victims of crime and many others besides think is quite wrong – are there as an electronic cosh to keep the prisoners quiet and contented. It is also possible to wonder if authority's blurred, if not quite blind, eye to the flow of drugs has something to do with the same fear of trouble. If dope helps to keep the cell-blocks quiet, then it is easy to see why the authorities might be tempted be relaxed about its supply and use. Then there is the way in which warders have been turned into social workers, sticking up notices telling everyone to be good. Warders do not need to act like prison-camp guards. Many have distinguished themselves over the years with a wise mixture of humanity and firmness. But the relationship between them and the prisoners is now strangely equal, symbolizing the elite state's neutrality between victim and offender.

The idea of private prisons is repellent to many because of the total absence of moral disapproval from the commercial contract. Imprisonment is not a business. It is a stern public obligation. However, such morality is now just as absent from the state sector. Most people who have suffered at the hands of criminals would think that mere deprivation of liberty was not punishment enough. Nor would they want those criminals to be able to use the telephone or play pool, to wear an outfit designed not to look like a uniform or to choose what they eat from seven different menus. And no one in his right mind would think it acceptable that illegal drugs, the cause of so much crime in the first place, should circulate in places supposed to be completely under the control of the state.

There is another aspect of this new regime that ought to worry the gentle and thoughtful. As the authorities have relaxed control of the prisons, the inmates have not become any more free. They have swapped one oppressor for another. Where governors and warders no longer rule, the hierarchy of criminals asserts itself. A violent, ruthless, strong and selfish person has little to fear in this sort of jungle. The weak and non-violent, who do most certainly end up in our prisons, have much of which to be frightened. Most unbearable of all is the likely fate of any innocent person locked up and abandoned in a snakepit of tattooed career criminals. As the prison doctor, Theodore Dalrymple, has written, we owe a great deal to the prison officers who are prepared to offer at least some protection to the vulnerable in prison. It is wrong in principle that a man in prison should be more afraid of his fellow prisoners than he is of the law.

Once, long ago, when Wormwood Scrubs was new, it had a clear, hard and frighteningly grim idea of its purpose which prevented many of the abuses we see today, even if it had abuses of its own. Realistically, we cannot go all the way back to that time. We would find it hard enough to cope with the lives lived by free and prosperous Englishmen of a hundred years ago, let alone the Edwardian prison regime. As the violent and the dishonest laugh and sneer at a criminal justice system that holds no fear for them, vegetarian diets, anti-bullying campaigns and therapy cannot be the right answer. As the old and the weak and the vulnerable live in growing fear, their lives in many cases more confined, dangerous and restricted than those of convicts, has the government forgotten its first duty to defend the gentle and punish the wrongdoer? If so, the process has been a long, slow one, winding along that primrose path, paved with good intentions, which always leads to the same place. How did we get from there to here?

The most explosive event in the history of modern British prisons was the publication in 1922 of *English Prisons Today*, edited by the prominent and clever liberal reformers, Stephen Hobhouse and Fenner Brockway. This book, a respectable middle-class person's view of the penal system, was the consequence of two foolish mistakes by the government. The authorities used prisons designed for transgressors to attempt to crush women and men who were essentially political offenders. They persecuted the suffragettes and then soon afterwards imprisoned those who refused to serve in the trenches after conscription was introduced in 1916. They exposed educated, articulate and normally law-abiding people to the harshness of a world they had not even known existed. (There would be a faint echo of this in the 1960s, when rough police treatment of left-wing protestors – especially the Challenor case where an unhinged detective planted a brick in the pocket of a pacifist cartoonist – was to turn the radical middle class of the day against the police. This had grave and lasting consequences on relations between the thinking classes and the police, still felt to this day.)

Brockway was one of those imprisoned for refusing to serve in the trenches. His experiences allowed him to write with authority on the hitherto undiscovered territory behind the thick high walls. He was no crude propagandist. He and Hobhouse produced a book that had the scope and authority of a Royal Commission, and which influenced prison policy for years to come. It must have been welcomed by at least some of the Prison Commissioners themselves, who were already trying to lessen the rigour of the regime. It was and remains an impressive piece of work, a fascinating description of things as they were as well as a coherent plan of reform.

They quoted what would now be called the 'policy' or 'mission statement' issued by the English Prison Commissioners in 1900: 'the principle of the English system is to deter by an exact though not a severe discipline, inculcating habits of obedience and order, and at the same time to reform by labour, education, and religious ministration.' The Commissioners were also clear that at least part of the point of the prison system was the effect that it had on those who had not yet offended, a point nowadays almost completely forgotten. Prisoners must suffer not only for their own good but also so that others would seek to avoid the same suffering. The Report of the Directors of Convict Prisons 1873 had proclaimed: 'When everything has been done to deter from crime or reform the criminal there will still remain a certain class whom it is hopeless to influence and who must be dealt with in course of law, not for much result on themselves but to carry out the principle of justice and mainly to deter others.'

This was a modernized version of the early nineteenth-century remark by a judge who told a condemned man: 'You are sentenced to be hanged not because you stole the horse but in order to prevent others from stealing horses.' Halsbury's *Laws of England* similarly stated: 'The object of punishment is the prevention of crime, and every punishment should have a double effect, namely to prevent the person who has committed a crime from repeating the act or omission, and to prevent other members of the community from committing similar crimes.' Few would have dissented from what would have seemed at the time to be a rather obvious statement.

Hobhouse and Brockway describe in gloomy detail what this policy involved for those who were convicted. The facts they revealed to a surprised and disquieted middle class were of course well known to the criminals of England, who had for decades seen such things as the risks of their profession. They were also known, by rumour and repute, to the classes most likely to turn to crime. Cells, all for individual occupation, varied from ten feet by seven, by nine feet high, to thirteen by seven by nine where they were supposed to be used for labour. Windows varied from fourteen to twenty-one panes measuring eighteen inches by four, with one or two panes designed to be opened. Winter temperatures were fifty degrees Fahrenheit (ten degrees Celsius) or lower, so that in the coldest weather inmates were only able to keep warm by walking around or wrapping themselves in blankets. The floors were of stone, tile, concrete or asphalt. 'It is difficult to convey an impression of the hope-destroying, forbidding aspect of prison buildings,' they wrote. 'They embody architecturally the repressive characteristics of the prison system. Many of our witnesses, drawn from both officials and ex-prisoners, express the view that the only reform to which the buildings can be usefully subjected is dynamite.'

They set out the reception procedure and prison life for a man sentenced to the 'Third Division', then the commonest type of sentence. Those who have read the description of the arrival of Paul Pennyfeather in prison in Evelyn Waugh's *Decline and Fall* will be familiar with much of it, although it must often have lacked the humour that Waugh managed to give it. The new arrival's name was entered in the 'body-receipt book', presumably a reference to the law of habeas corpus ('habeas corpus' translates literally as 'you have the body...'). He was then locked up in a reception cubicle (often dirty), ordered to strip and examined nude, a shocking and degrading experience for men of the period. He was made to wash in nine inches of warm water in a compulsory bath. Then he was ordered to dress in the prison uniform of collarless coat, waistcoat and buckled trousers stamped with the broad arrow marking them as 'government property', a cap of the same material, heavy shoes, socks, cotton shirt, a coarse handkerchief, pants and flannel vest. Clothes were allocated with 'little regard for height and girth'.

The convict was given a Bible, Prayer Book, small towel, brush and comb. During this procedure conversation was forbidden. He was handed the prison rules on a printed card with 'a formidable list of possible offences'. After buttoning on an unsightly yellow badge giving his cell number, he was conducted to the cell, the furniture of which was a wooden table, a small backless stool and a bed-board. The window was 'so high up that it is necessary to stand on the stool to look out of it', which was probably a punishable offence. What view there was, was reduced by several heavy iron bars fixed from outside. The cell light was often not switched on until after darkness fell. The whitewashed walls did not hide 'pathetic and often objectionable inscriptions'.

The description continues with details of the sparse and dispiriting furnishings. The bed-board was two or three planks fixed on a low support, six feet wide by thirty inches broad. During the day it had to be leant against the wall along with the thin mattress (hard labour prisoners had to sleep without a mattress for the first fourteen days of their sentence) and the hard stuffed pillow. A little shelf contained a white, glazed pint pot, salt jar, knife and spoon; soap and lavatory paper; slate and slate pencil; religious books, a wooden rack (permitted only after the first eight weeks) to hold monthly letters from home, and three or four pictures of relatives. A collection of printed cards hung on a nail, including some prayers and a notice threatening the prisoner with punishments for 'a number of activities that would be quite innocent in normal life'.

There are also details of the 'system of progressive stages' through which a prisoner might obtain privileges and some remission. He could earn a target of fifty-six marks for labour and good conduct, which led to 'associated labour' in the workshop, more frequent books, letters or visits. Visits took place through a wire grille or double row of bars, without physical contact. Some prisons were also equipped with an arrangement known as the 'meat-safe', two small compartments similar in size to phone boxes, separated by two screens of wire-gauze about a foot apart. Visits were not permitted more often than every four weeks and lasted no longer than half an hour (modern prisons generally allow weekly visits, where physical contact is allowed, and these can last for some time, since many governors do not believe in strictly enforcing time limits). A letter was often an alternative to a visit. Remission of up to one sixth of the sentence was possible if conduct was good enough (compare this with the automatic remission of half the sentence granted today).

Looking round his cell, the newly arrived convict would see a number of dreary and dutiful objects. On the floor was a metal water can covered by an enamel plate, an earthenware chamber pot (much of the original nineteenth-century plumbing had been removed because the piping was used by prisoners to tap out messages between cells) with a metal top, and a small tin basin. There was also a dustpan and brush, a scrubbing brush, some cleaning rags and a box containing brick dust and whitening for scouring. Each prisoner had a small towel and a dishcloth. Each cell contained a bell handle for emergencies. There were sewing or other implements for his work.

The daily routine of prison life was as follows:

Rising bell at 6.30. Dress, clean and tidy cell and make requests or complaints.

Stitching mailbags.

After an hour pint pot filled with porridge, plus six oz of bread.

Three times a week given bucket of cold water to scrub floor. Must polish tins.

At nine bell rings for chapel.

15–20 minute service, go to and from in silence, under watchful eyes of warders.

Hour's exercise on concentric tracks. Warders watch from raised platforms.

10.15, march back to cells, mailbag sewing until noon, or to workshop.

At noon dinner trays, 40 minutes allowed, work until 4.15, followed by delivery of cocoa and bread and two to three ounces of 'some relish'. Door does not open again for 14 hours. Lights went out at nine.

Hobhouse and Brockway note: 'The man who is expert and diligent enough to complete his task by supper-time can, in some prisons at any rate, spend most of the evening hours in reading his Bible or other book, in pacing round his cell, writing rhymes or blasphemies upon his slate, or occupying his vacancy in any other of the very limited means that a cell affords.' They quote E. W. Mason's gloomy description, from his 1918 book *Free in Prison*, of the night hours within prison walls: 'Outside the prison wards are bare and silent and dark except for a beam of light at every cell lamp hole. They are unfrequented, save for the night-warder, who moves in felt slippers and peers in at the cell spyhole as he works his way up the long landings from cell to cell. From the inside of the cell one hears nothing of him except a click of the spyhole shutter and the dry dragging sound of the slippers.' There were very few solaces. Tobacco was strictly forbidden, although plans to allow its limited use by privileged prisoners were under discussion.

Many things were to change as a result of the Hobhouse and Brockway report. Even so, more than ten years later prison life was still austere and hard. In *The Modern English Prison*, published in 1934, L. W. Fox detailed the daily diet for a man in the punishment cells: 'No. 1 diet is 1 lb of bread per day with water (which could be imposed for a maximum of three days at a time).' By this time, prisoners held for four years or more had facilities for smoking, which was allowed at set times in a prescribed room. Women, for whom smoking was still banned, were allowed to make tea. The close cropping of prisoners' heads had been abolished and the use of broad arrows to mark their uniforms seems to have disappeared in the late 1920s, although W. F. McCartney's prison memoir *Walls Have Mouths*, which deals with the late 1920s and early 1930s, records their use at Parkhurst. With or without these unpleasant and humiliating features, there was little sign that the prisons were deterring those already used to them.

The report of the Persistent Offenders Committee recorded that of the 39,000 sentences of imprisonment in 1930, 28,000 were imposed on culprits who had previously been found guilty of offences. Many had been dealt with through the fines and probation introduced by Winston Churchill before the First World War, which drastically reduced the numbers in prison and eventually ended the era of strictness recorded by Jose Harris. In 20,384 cases the offenders had already been in prison and plenty of them had served repeated sentences, as is shown by the following list:

4740 had served 1 previous sentence.

1949 had served 3 previous sentences.

1499 had served 4 previous sentences.

1115 had served 5 previous sentences.

3382 had served 6–10 previous sentences.

2622 had served 11–20 previous sentences.

2125 had served over 20 previous sentences.

These figures create a picture of a small, slowly circulating group of more or less incorrigible crooks and troublemakers, going in and out of prison despite its dismal conditions. Undoubtedly, among them were a small number of vagrants who committed minor crimes at the beginning of winter so as to have food and shelter during the cold months.

The important figures, however, are the unrecorded ones for people who might have committed crimes but chose not to because they knew what to expect if they did. These, it is reasonable to guess, are the people who have since swelled the prison population, despite the determination of the authorities not to send them there if they can possibly help it.

Another weapon still in the hands of the authorities at the time was flogging, the subject of relentless campaigns for abolition by penal reformers. It was not to be formally abolished until the Roy Jenkins years. The courts still felt able to use it despite growing public disapproval. Leo Page in his 1937 book, *Crime and the*

Prison population of England and Wales (ten-year intervals)

1900–01	17,435
1911–12*	19,797
1920–21	11,000**
1930–31	11,346
1940–41	9377
1950–51	20,474
1960–61	27,099
1970	39,028
1980	42,300
1990	45,636
1999	64,770

During 2002 the total passed 70,000 for the first time.

* Figure for 1910–11 not available.
**Strict liquor laws and conscription are thought to be the reasons for the sharp drop in prison population during and following the 1914–18 war.

Community, examined the use of the birch and the cat-o'-nine-tails during the years 1926 to 1935. He found that it was used mainly to punish robbery with violence – a total of 235 sentences. Its other uses in this period are curious and interesting for what they tell us about the attitudes of a past era:

other offences of violence   1

living on earnings of prostitute   1

male soliciting   2

indecent exposure   4

malicious damage, arson and larceny
by boys of fourteen and fifteen   10

Total   253

133

Page felt that this made a strong case for using it more often, again for the effect it had on others rather than for any good it might have done the flogged robbers. 'In the ten years before the war [corporal punishment] was not used with any freedom (61 times 1904 to 1913) as a penalty for this offence, and there were 1,414 convictions for this crime (robbery with violence); in the last period of the same number of years it has been used with far greater frequency (235 times 1926 to 1935) and the number of convictions has fallen to less than half (656).'

A rather different view of inter-war crime problems is found in *The Lawbreaker*, published in 1933 by Roy and Theodora Calvert. They opposed flogging and attacked as a myth the idea that the nineteenth-century epidemic of garrotting had been stamped out by the introduction of flogging to deal with it. Believably, they said that garrotting had actually ceased before the 'Garrotters' Act' was passed in a parliamentary panic by the Commons after an MP was a victim. They also produce this interesting account of crime for the year 1930: that year there were 122 murders; ninety-one attempts, threats or conspiracies to murder; 178 manslaughters or infanticides; 178 woundings; 289 other offences of violence; 648 'unnatural offences or attempts'; 2524 sex offences; 374 bigamies; 25,937 burglaries or housebreakings; 311 robberies or extortions; 10,019 aggravated larcenies; 84,697 simple and minor larcenies; 11,296 obtaining by false pretences; 2045 other frauds; 2102 receiving stolen goods; 185 arsons; 166 other offences against property; 857 forgeries; 215 coinings; 168 perjuries; 3053 attempted suicides; 311 other indictable offences.

Most of these figures would represent a huge improvement on those of today. At the time, there was some disquiet about them. The Calverts claimed it was unjustified. 'The impression, widely fostered by the sensational press, that violent crimes against the person have increased to an alarming extent, is quite erroneous,' they said. 'There has actually been a steady decrease in murder from 4.7 per million during the five years 1900–4 to 3.7 during 1925–9 and 3.1 in 1930.' Attempted murder was also down and the increase in manslaughter cases was a by-product of the bloodshed on the roads as motoring offences began to climb. 'The highest published figure [for robbery] since the war, viz. 7.8 per million in 1930, is lower than the average figure for the ten pre-war years 1900–9, when the country was not confronted with an unemployment problem comparable with that of the last few years.'

They also recorded a reduction in assaults, cruelty to children, liquor law breaches, prostitution, begging, cruelty to animals and truancy. Their most fascinating finding, for those who believe in a crude link between poverty and crime, was that crime did rise with unemployment. It did so, however, in a complicated pattern which cuts to ribbons the crude 'poverty = crime' equation. In the North, it was true that theft offences had risen (though to nothing like as much as in the period of full employment thirty years later). What they called 'downright lawlessness' was more common in the South, where unemployment was much less of a problem. They wrote: 'The ordinary unemployed man does not drift into crime; he has generations of moral principle behind him and stands with his back to the wall fighting the demoralizing influence of enforced idleness year after year without resorting to crime.' And while they accepted that the great majority appearing before the courts were poor, they rightly added that so were the great majority of those who did not appear before the courts.

Seen from the early years of the twenty-first century, this era of the broad arrow and the exercise yard may seem like one long, chilly epoch of harshness. In fact, it was under constant pressure to change from within and without and was frequently reformed and humanized from mid-Victorian times onwards. One of those pressing for change was Sir Evelyn Ruggles-Brise KCB, who became chairman of the English Prison Commission and set down his thoughts in his 1921 book, *The English Prison System*. He is mocked as Lucas-Dockery, a gullible and well-meaning sort, in Waugh's *Decline and Fall*. But in fact he was no fool. He believed that the imprisonment of suffragettes and conscientious objectors had helped to weaken discipline and undermine the entire penal structure. He wrote:

> Our prison system has, in recent years, been subjected
> to a very severe test by the fact that, of necessity, penal
> treatment in prison, primarily designed for the criminal
> class, has been applied to thousands of individuals in no
> way belonging to that class, whom it has been necessary
> to commit to prison under the Defence of the Realm
> Acts, either as conscientious objectors to military service,
> or otherwise, for the safety of the realm.
>
> Prison rules and regulations press hardly on men and
> women who, under normal circumstances, would never
> have become the subject of those punitive and repressive
> conditions which are inseparable from the deprivation
> of liberty by the State... To persons of refinement and
> education (as many were), the many restrictions
> necessary for the safe custody of criminals would
> naturally seem harsh, unnecessary and even unnatural.
> No doubt their experience has given an impulse to the
> prison reformer who, in his honourable zeal to soften the
> lot of the unfortunate captive, is apt to overlook the
> necessity for strict rules and regulations in dealing with
> a class to whose habits and instincts he is himself a
> total stranger.

He was right. The law was unleashed with fury and without mercy on the middle-class protestors. Despite the great issues involved and the undoubted courage of the far greater numbers who went to the front, the government's zeal against the pacifists now looks like a serious error of judgement and failure of justice. We are paying for it still in the lasting effect it had on prison discipline. More than six thousand men were arrested after refusing to be conscripted. Of these, seventy-one died in prison or after release on medical grounds. 'The imposition of solitary confinement, bread-and-water punishment and the silence rule were commonplace.' Among those imprisoned was the philosopher Bertrand Russell, who was convicted after writing a pamphlet condemning the treatment of a conscientious objector. The outcome of all this was the Hobhouse and Brockway report and a growing, and mainly misconceived, demand for reforms from the post-war left where many of the objectors had become prominent and respected figures (Brockway and Russell would both end their days, full of years and garlanded with honours, in the House of Lords, one by hereditary right and the other by political favour).

Much had already been done to lessen the nineteenth-century harshness of the system, mainly by trying to keep harmless people out of it if possible rather than by making the experience any pleasanter. Churchill's introduction in 1908 of probation and fines for many offences that would otherwise have ended in imprisonment was then considered bold and enlightened. Few had time for social explanations of wrongdoing, since this was an age of falling crime despite social provisions that were minimal by the standards of today. In his book *Criminals and Crime, Some Facts and Suggestions*, Sir Robert Anderson (barrister, JP, Home Office adviser, Assistant Commissioner of the Metropolitan Police and head of CID 1888–1901) urged an attack on professional crime, which he thought could then be utterly defeated. He pointed out that in 1868, the year after transportation had been abandoned, London property felonies had totalled 22,083. In 1905, they were significantly lower, at 18,515, a drop that was even more significant when set beside the fact that over the same period the city's population had risen from 3.5 million to just over seven million.

However, while ordinary crimes against property were decreasing, professional burglary was increasing. Anderson urged a pitiless response: 'The true professional is an advanced disciple of Hobbes. He is not embarrassed by either twinges of conscience or a sense of shame...' He added: 'The humanity-mongers are so lavish in their pity for the criminal that they have none left for their victims.' Sir Robert also took the view, common at the time, that the prisons had been successfully reformed and were emphatically no longer nurseries of crime. Prison, in short, worked and was widely believed to work. The authorities were confident that they had both morality and practicality on their side. Secure in these beliefs, they were happy to allow a surprising amount of reform.

Between 1895 and 1921 Ruggles-Brise made great changes in the local prisons, where most minor offenders then served their terms. When he took charge, convicts still had to turn useless cranks, slowly grinding stone to powder, in their cells. These cranks could be set tighter or looser by a screw on the outside of the cell – hence the name 'screw' still given to prison officers. This practice along with oakum-picking, the pulling to pieces of old rope to form mattress-stuffing fibre (and the origin of the expression 'money for old rope'), was abolished. Ruggles-Brise also scrapped the treadmills, the main purpose of which had been to exhaust the prisoners as they tramped endlessly upstairs. In 1899, the dehumanizing convict crop so much beloved of cartoonists was also dispensed with in local jails, although it would last another two decades in the long-term convict prisons. The rule of total silence was officially abolished in 1898, although talking was still a privilege to be granted by the authorities and withdrawn by them as well.

Ruggles-Brise was followed in the 1920s as 'chief prison reformer' by the energetic Alexander Paterson, a man of great personal courage who had twice been recommended for the Victoria Cross. Paterson was an old-fashioned liberal reformer who believed that unless the wealthy energetically helped the poor, state socialism would follow. He was the force behind many of the softening reforms after the First World War, partly in response to the Hobhouse and Brockway report. He already believed that the regime was too harsh and hopeless. After a visit to Dartmoor as a young man he had written in obvious dismay:

> The drab uniforms of the prisoners were plastered with
> broad arrows… their heads were covered with a sort of
> dirty moss… hair that a pair of clippers could not remove.
> The prison regime, determined to minimize the chances
> of violence or suicide had succeeded in making human
> beings into objects of ugliness and contempt. As they
> saw us coming, each man ran to the nearest wall and put
> his face closely against it, remaining in this servile
> position until we had passed him by.

Like many others who have seen prison in action, he began to feel a keener concern for the piteous object the prisoner had become than for his unseen victims, and to think in terms more of reforming the individual criminal than of deterring crime at large. He wrote: 'If a prison is merely a cloakroom, in which the enemy of society is duly deposited till called for after a fixed period, or a kennel in which he is safely caged until on the appointed day he is let loose on society again, then indeed the protection afforded is of a temporary nature and it may well be that, after the security of a few months or years, society will be at the mercy of an enemy more bitter and implacable than before.' However, he was not blind to the dangers of too much relaxation of discipline, warning presciently that: 'A sloppy and unthinking sentiment may rush us into forms of association far more injurious to those concerned than any evils of solitude.'

In a way, Paterson created the modern English prison system, which would certainly have coped much better with inmates such as Fenner Brockway and Bertrand Russell than what went before. The problem is that, for the most part, its inhabitants were, and always have been, more like Reggie and Ronnie Kray than the great philosopher Russell or the high-principled conscientious objector Brockway. Under Paterson's influence, the total separation of convicts from one another was suspended in 1923 and abolished in 1930. In 1924 compulsory chapel attendance was abolished. Until then, chapel had been one of the few places where news could be passed on, under the cover of hymn-singing or other chants, as wittily described in *Decline and Fall*. This example of a mangled 'Magnificat' is given by W. J. Forsythe in his *Penal Discipline, Reformatory Projects and the English Prison Commission 1895–1939*. The lines on the right are sung to the rhythm of those on the left:

And behold from henceforth	What are you in for?
All generations shall call me blessed	I'm in for shoplifting
For he that is mighty hath magnified me	How long have you got?
And Holy is his name	Six months hard labour

Disciplinary floggings with the cat-o'-nine-tails fell to nil in mid-1920 (although the milder birchings continued). In 1922 raised platforms in chapels to allow officers to keep watch on the praying prisoners were removed. Prisoners could now be released on licence after serving three-quarters of their sentence. In March 1922 conversation was allowed in workshops. From 1924, potential escapers were no longer forced to wear the clownish particoloured uniform and heavy leg chains that had until then been their lot.

In 1921 visiting-boxes were introduced, where husbands and wives could embrace without netting to separate them. From then on, prisoners were transferred between prisons in civilian clothes – to avoid the sort of humiliation bitterly recalled by Oscar Wilde in *De Profundis* where he described the misery of being exposed to public mockery on Clapham Junction station, an experience so foul that he wept every day at the memory of it, at the exact time when it had happened. Paterson was also responsible for the removal of the broad arrows from the prison uniform. Under his influence, earnings were introduced and smoking more generally allowed. Many fictional treatments of prison written much later than this still assume that pre-1914 conditions continued far longer than they actually did. Waugh's *Decline and Fall* was out of date before it was published, and probably when it was written.

Forsythe concludes that this period was a successful one, during which an unloved and unwelcome duty was done remarkably well:

> English prisons were severe, regimented and disciplinary in the early twentieth century. Notwithstanding, provision of the basic necessities of life, freedom from widespread institutionally legitimised violence by staff and an effective recognition that prisoners of the state have the right to some dignity and protection were characteristic of the English prison system between 1895 and 1939. Such features were not typical of many prison systems in the world, then or thereafter.

He also touches on one of the fascinating might-have-beens, had the Second World War not inflicted a vast social revolution on British society which reduced all previous attempts at change to insignificance. He believes that 'overall in England the inter-war years witnessed a significant growth in the liberal ameliorative approach to prisoners. Advocates of this attitude managed to retain their advantage despite such setbacks as the Dartmoor riot' (a savage outbreak of violence that began over the serving of a cold breakfast to the convicts on 24 January 1932 and had to be quelled with the aid of regular troops; Dartmoor at the time housed 440 prisoners, mostly murderers and violent robbers). Even the great buildings that now seem certain to survive for another century might have disappeared under this benevolent scheme for reform. Impelled by an optimistic approach to crime and its control, in the late 1930s the commissioners were 'preparing an assault on the great architectural monoliths bequeathed to them by the Victorians and intending to move further towards modern, open prisons for men and women'.

The broadly successful prisons of this period were a reflection of the extraordinarily stable and contented society that they served.

They continued to follow the same path, towards gentler conditions and less discipline, well into the post-war period. Quite possibly, conditions could have continued to grow significantly softer without any serious growth in crime. However, the war and the welfare state, not to mention the permissive society and the great consumer boom, were to create a world in which prisons ceased to be the last destination of a small knot of incorrigibles. Instead, they became one of society's few weapons against a wave of unrepentant wrong-doing. As levels of crime grew in the brave new world that was created after 1945, the prisons certainly could no longer claim to be successful.

Just when the prisons needed to make a greater impact on those sent to them and on the new criminal class, a more relaxed outside world undermined old-fashioned discipline. This is well-illustrated by the story of Roger Keith Maxwell. The last disciplinary birching of a prisoner in England was approved (as it had to be before being administered) by R. A. Butler, the Conservative Home Secretary, in 1962. Four years later, Roy Jenkins refused to approve the birching of Maxwell. This was a perfectly reasonable decision. Birching was unacceptable in modern England because it was, simply, too cruel and demeaned those who had to inflict it. But no more civilized punishment was available to replace it.

Maxwell had been sentenced to life imprisonment in March 1966 after murdering Derrick Lambert, a guard at Portland Borstal, with an iron bar during an attempted escape. He was the ringleader of a race riot at Maidstone Prison, attacked several officers there and was sentenced to six strokes of the birch. His parents were constituents of Ted Heath, then Leader of the Opposition, and petitioned him against the punishment. Jenkins ruled on 5 October 1966 that he would not confirm the sentence. Nor did Maxwell get the alternative sentence of solitary confinement. Instead he under-went psychiatric testing and was later diagnosed as a psychopath. Psychopath or not, he was freed in 1982, with many years of life still ahead of him.

The Prison Officers' Association was incensed by his initial offence, saying it had resulted from the abolition of the death penalty. The POA leader, Fred Castell, said, quite correctly, that the Jenkins decision meant birching was effectively at an end in England. 'I will be surprised if Maxwell does not get a medal next. He has killed one prison officer and assaulted four others and I feel very angry.' His anger had no effect on policy.

Hugely increased prison numbers around this time produced overcrowding and squalor not seen since the days of the hulks, especially the insanitary and unsettling cramming of several prisoners into cells meant for one. The disgusting practice of slopping out, never attractive, became unbearable. Prisoners often simply wrapped their stools in paper and flung them from their cell windows in nasty parcels. Sometimes the authorities were forced to house convicted criminals in disused army camps or to keep them in police cells. The pressure on the courts meant a grave increase in the numbers of remand prisoners, in spite of ever-laxer rules on granting bail.

The closure of mental hospitals forced prisons to house the insane as well as the wicked. The growth of the drugs menace outside spread inside, as did greater readiness to use violence. The ending of the death penalty increased the numbers of very long-term prisoners serving so-called life sentences and requiring special treatment to make their lives bearable. A number of embarrassing escapes compelled the spending of millions on greater security, at the expense of treasured rehabilitation projects and badly needed new prisons. Yet the real problem remained the fact that England simply did not have enough prisons to hold its new wave of criminals. Worse, it had no idea what to do with them once they were locked up. This pressure and confusion made nonsense of both rehabilitation and retribution, because it resulted in unending efforts to reduce the prison population through suspended sentences, parole and dishonest sentencing.

The extraordinary Criminal Justice Act 1991 compelled judges to pretend that criminals were going to jail for twice as long as they really were. Next came the introduction of 'tagging', early release accompanied by ineffective electronic monitoring. This led to a serious number of offences committed by men who would otherwise have been in prison. In March 2002 it was disclosed that prisoners freed early under the tagging scheme had committed 1400 crimes when they would otherwise have been in prison. Those crimes, between January 1999 and December 2001, included four rapes, thirty-eight serious woundings and eighty-two serious assaults. About eighty released convicts went missing after cutting off their tags, which were supposed to restrict their movements. The figures, which may themselves be misleading because of the difficulty of obtaining convictions, were released by the Home Office to a Member of Parliament, but not made generally available, probably because of their sensitivity.

From 1986 to 1990 a succession of ugly riots, accompanied by expensive and spectacular destruction of buildings, led to a nervous improvement of conditions, which looked like appeasement, mainly because that is what it was. In 1986 alone twenty-two prisons exploded into riots and in 1990 Manchester's monumental Strangeways Prison was subjected to a lengthy, televised uprising which cost £130 million and left 147 officers injured. The next year's riot at Moorland Prison in Doncaster, a new prison, exploded any idea that Victorian conditions and buildings were to blame.

The relationship between prison conditions, prison population and crime is difficult to work out. Between 1909 and 1938, probation as a substitute for prison, coupled with the introduction of allowing time to pay fines (dating respectively from 1908 and 1914), resulted in a drop in annual prison receptions from 205,216 to 40,430. These Churchillian reforms ended the era of rigorous social discipline described by Jose Harris. This was also a time of generally low or stable crime figures. However, the average daily figures for the prison population underwent such an astonishing increase in the post-war period that full-scale moral panic would be a not unreasonable response. Look back at the table earlier in this chapter and the scale of the change is clear. It is not just a matter of larger numbers, but of a wholly different size and shape of criminal class. At the end of the war the figures were still comparable with the 1930s, at just under thirteen thousand (the highest pre-1939 figure was 20,757 in 1903–4, the highest inter-war figure 12,986 in 1933–4). By 1950–51, the total was at 20,474. By 1960–1, it stood at 27,099. By 1971 it had reached 39,708. By 1991 it was still climbing, at 45,817. By 1999 it had reached 64,770. By the autumn of 2002 the prison population was 72,000, its official limit.

Under present moral and legal conditions, any future fall will not be the result of a decline in the level of crime. It is much more likely to follow yet more measures to make it difficult to get criminals into prison and easy to get them out once they are inside. As the early releases of tagged prisoners have shown, many of those allowed to go free under this policy are violent and dangerous. There is simply no comparison with Winston Churchill's pre-First World War reforms, which benefited only the most minor and harmless of offenders. These likely measures will be taken at a time when criminals are already less worried than ever about being sent to jail. What makes this especially hard to accept is the continued pretence that the existing system serves any positive purpose. These crammed and disorderly holding pens may occasionally achieve miraculous successes of reclamation. There are isolated stories of such heartening events. If so, it is in spite of their nature and ethos. They are unpleasant and frightening, but in the wrong way.

The rule seems to be that the more violent the criminal, the less he has to fear from prison. It is true that child-molesters can seek special protection from their fellow inmates. This is, of course, absolutely necessary, although the best precautions can sometimes fail. However, it says much for the balance of power in the cell-blocks that this has to be so. Many who are not child-molesters also need protection but do not get it. Pressure to get involved with drugs and drug-smuggling, for example, is a serious problem for vulnerable inmates. Many decline special protection because they fear association with the despised 'nonces' on the sex-offenders' wings more than they fear the brutality of the normal wings. Once classified as a 'nonce' or a 'grass', a man is forever in danger inside or outside prison in our depraved and chaotic society. While the establishment and the law have long abandoned the use of physical punishment and fear in dealing with offenders, the criminal classes and successful terrorist groups still clearly believe in both, applying them with vigour when they get the chance. This suggests that criminals and terrorists alike would be deterred by fear and punishment if they were used against them, contrary to current penal and political theories.

What can a modern society do? We cannot re-create the conditions described by Fenner Brockway, even as reformed by Evelyn Ruggles-Brise and Alexander Paterson. That does not mean we should do nothing at all. The combination of comparative austerity, discipline and work, and rewards for consistent good behaviour, could be reintroduced to suit the modern age. The restoration of the death penalty for the worst sort of murder would eventually allow for a revaluation of prison sentences. It would also slowly reduce the number of long-term inmates for whom no hope of release can ever exist. A building programme to ensure one cell per prisoner and a recruiting programme for new officers would greatly reduce the risk of riots. The rebuilding of vanished mental hospitals, in any case an urgent national need, would remove the mentally ill from a system in which they should not be placed. The remoralization of society, the end of the state campaign against marriage and the reintroduction of preventive policing would all have their own impacts. The convicted criminal should suffer for his crime and be known to suffer.

Once in prison, he should long for release. Every day and hour of remission should be earned by positive acts of goodness and self-discipline. Once released, he should wish never to go back and should advise others to stay out. He should do hard physical work. He should wear a recognizable uniform which is distinctly unfashionable and that marks him out for what he is. Under certain circumstances he should be made to work in public places on penal tasks designed to reassure the law-abiding public, such as removing graffiti, picking up litter and repairing the damage done by vandals. He should not have access to television or radio or be allowed to play pool or table-football. He should certainly not have access to the telephone. His visits should be controlled so that there is not the slightest chance of visitors passing drugs to inmates. The use of drugs should be unfailingly and rigidly punished by loss of remission. Almost every normal liberty should be a privilege to be earned by good behaviour, cleanliness, self-discipline and obedience. Remission should be reserved for those who undergo proper education and training, which should be either basic or vocational. It should not be designed to help gangsters to write self-serving sociological epistles to the newspapers. There should be punishments, tangible and telling, which can be imposed by governors, usually involving the deprivation of liberties and privileges. These are illustrations, not an exhaustive list of measures.

Criminals do not offend against their fellow human beings because they have too little self-esteem but because they have too much. The guiding words should be those of Winston Churchill, with his 'hard coinage of punishment', and of the old Prison Commissioners, who talked of the 'due punishment of responsible persons' and stated some important truths when they declared: 'The penalty of crime is in the dishonouring circumstances which must accompany loss of liberty; in the deprivation of what liberty permits in the way of indulgence and self-gratification; in compulsory labour; in the loss of self-respect.'

Our mistake has been to reform our prisons so that they might suit Bertrand Russell and Fenner Brockway quite well. However, the kind of people who actually dwell in them are seldom either philosophers or pacifists.

V

Out of the barrel of a gun

Gun control? It's the best thing you can do for
crooks and gangsters. I want you to have
nothing. If I'm a bad guy, I'm always gonna
have a gun.
*Mafia turncoat Sammy 'The Bull' Gravano,
interview in* Vanity Fair, *September 1999*

More legally owned guns mean less crime. A disarmed people are
more easily oppressed and ignored than an armed people. These
are statements of the obvious. It is a measure of how dim and
limited our national debate is that anyone should think them shocking. It is also evidence of our lack of knowledge of our own history
and our lack of curiosity about it. Those who are convinced that
America's gun law is a crazed relic of frontier chaos do not even
know that this law is based on England's seventeenth-century revolution against autocracy.

Respectable citizens in this country used to own and even carry
guns without a second thought, long after the Victorian police forces
established order in the towns and countryside. In pre-1914 London
there was a famous incident, the 'Tottenham Outrage' of 1909,
where, when police came under fire from an anarchist gang, they
borrowed guns from the citizenry and appealed to members of the
public to help shoot down the gang members. This event was one
of the very few occasions when the police of that time encountered
armed criminals of any kind. These criminals were not English but
foreigners from the repressive Russian empire, entirely unused to
English law and behaviour.

Conan Doyle's great fictional detective, Sherlock Holmes, frequently set out on his private missions with a revolver, as did his colleague, Dr Watson. It is quite clear from the stories that the author expects his readers to think this is entirely normal and legal. Where Holmes and Watson do infringe the law, usually by breaking into the premises of blackmailers, they think about it very carefully indeed. Since this is so – and since that paradise of social peace and order, Switzerland, is among the most heavily armed countries in the world – it is clear that the main belief on which gun control is based is wrong. (Switzerland did suffer a gun massacre during 2001, which was followed by illogical calls for gun control. A far worse massacre in the German city of Erfurt in the spring of 2002 led to no such calls, for the simple reason that Germany already has extremely strict laws on legal gun ownership.) The logically and factually insupportable belief that gun ownership is itself a cause of violent crime is accepted as a self-evident truth among the cultural and media establishment. Those who refuse to believe it or dare to doubt it are reviled as if they are unhinged or possibly malicious. The unstated implication is that they may even be potential mass-murderers themselves. Statistics that undermine this belief are belittled or ignored. Isolated and wholly atypical incidents where guns are used in massacres are treated as if they were common and general. The use of guns in the outrage, rather than the wickedness or perversion of the culprit, is treated as if it were the pivotal feature of such events. Facts and logic are overcome by thoughtless emotion. If the theory that more guns produce more crime were correct, England's own past could not have existed. Switzerland's present orderly peace would also be impossible. Once again, the thing that 'everybody knows' about an important area of the crime and justice debate is false.

Two incidents from the past decade sum up the wild schizophrenia of the public mind on this matter. The first was the Dunblane massacre, when on 13 March 1996 the pervert and outcast Thomas Hamilton murdered a teacher and sixteen little children with legally held weapons (this took place in Scotland but had implications for the whole country). This horror came not long after a similar massacre by the outcast Michael Ryan in Hungerford, and led to a public inquiry and a successful campaign for the banning of all legally-held handguns. This action was specifically not recommended by the inquiry's report, but was taken by the new Labour government in response to an emotional public campaign.

Hamilton killed himself, so saving the taxpayer the unwelcome cost of keeping him in food, clothes, TV sets and shelter for the rest of his life. Regrettably, his suicide also prevented a trial that would have revealed in detail how such an unpleasant and dangerous person was able to exploit his 'human rights' to prevent the authorities from acting against him and depriving him of his legally-held weapons – as they ought to have done. Hamilton was expert in using the many complaints procedures of modern bureaucracy to frighten off or divert those who had realized that he was a serious menace. A more robust society, with fewer rights and more liberty, would almost certainly have found him out in time – but that is another book.

The second significant event was the killing on 20 August 1999 at a remote Norfolk farmhouse of the young thief Fred Barras, shot dead in mid-burglary by the eccentric farmer Tony Martin, using an illegally-held shotgun. Mr Martin, the victim of previous robberies, believed that the police could not be relied on to protect him. Barras and his accomplice Brendan Fearon both had long criminal records, which seemed to prove Mr Martin's complaint that the law did little to deter or even hamper thieves and robbers. Mr Martin was at first found guilty of murder and sentenced to what is called life imprisonment but is in fact a variable sentence of about ten years. In an incident that beautifully illustrates the law's new moral neutrality, the convicted thief Fearon, by then at liberty, was asked his view – as a victim of crime – about the possible early release of Mr Martin.

On appeal, Mr Martin's conviction was reduced to manslaughter, but only after he had claimed that he had been abused as a child and had otherwise sought to excuse his behaviour by his own faults, rather than justifying it by the wicked misdeeds of the men who came to rob him by night. In return for this self-abasement, the Court of Appeal reduced his sentence to five years, which meant that he had to stay in prison but took the edge off public anger.

That anger had always been vague and shapeless, more an outcry against Mr Martin's suffering than an endorsement of what he had done. There was no public inquiry into the inadequacy of policing in rural areas, although this is a serious problem affecting huge numbers of people every day and every night. There was a public outcry at the treatment of Mr Martin, but details of the lonely squalor of his life and his muttering eccentricity made it hard for him to be cast as a hero. What protests there were never became politically important.

The reaction to both these events was the opposite of what it should have been and wholly irrational. The general national desire for gun control is one of the few popular passions that marches in step with the liberal left and the elite state. It is also one of the few subjects on which popular law-and-order newspapers tend to take a left-wing line, although they (in my view mistakenly) view it as a strong law-and-order line. The effect of the Dunblane gun ban was to prevent sportsmen from practising their shooting, to wreck many small businesses and to deprive many decent and peaceful people of weapons. It is unlikely that a single criminal was disarmed or discouraged. Regrettably, it is also unlikely that future Dunblanes will have been prevented, although they will then involve easily obtained illegal guns rather than legal ones.

In its supposed object of making the country less dangerous, the ban was predictably useless. A study by the Centre for Defence Studies at King's College in July 2001 showed that the use of handguns in crime rose by 40 per cent in the two years after such weapons were banned in the UK. This was hardly surprising given that criminals tend to obtain their weapons illegally, both because they have to do so and because they can. If the concern about guns after Dunblane had been genuine rather than an emotional spasm, this survey would have produced a national scandal and calls for urgent action. Nothing of the kind happened. A clear-headed look at Lord Cullen's report into the Dunblane massacre would have shown that the real problem was inadequate and fumbling supervision of existing gun laws, which should never have allowed Thomas Hamilton to buy or keep his arsenal.

Hamilton's fitness to be entrusted with a firearm was rightly challenged by an alert and wise police officer, Detective Sergeant Paul Hughes, in a memorandum of 11 November 1991, nearly five years before the crime. Mr Hughes wrote that Hamilton was 'an unsavoury character and unstable personality', but it was decided at a higher level that no action should be taken. Likewise, after an earlier incident, in 1989, when Hamilton had improperly shown off his weapons to a family in Linlithgow, nothing was done about his firearms certificate. Sergeant McGrane of Lothian and Borders police, who investigated the matter, said he did not think a firearms certificate holder should have acted in that way. Papers were passed up to Deputy Chief Constable McMurdo, yet no memorandum on the incident was placed in Hamilton's firearms file or entered in the criminal intelligence database. Lord Cullen in his report later accepted that 'on balance there was a case for revocation which should have been acted upon'.

Detective Sergeant Hughes had noted about Hamilton:

> He appears to me to be an unsuitable person to possess a firearms certificate in view of the number of occasions he has come to the adverse attention of the police and his apparent instability.
>
> I respectfully request that serious consideration is given to withdrawing this man's firearms certificate as a precautionary measure as it is my opinion that he is a scheming, devious and deceitful individual who is not to be trusted.

Detective Chief Inspector Holden of CID wrote on the same memo: 'A difficult situation – I do agree with DS Hughes' appraisal of Mr Hamilton. Do we have any latitude for progress in respect of the revocation of his certificate?'

Most people might think this would have been enough. However, a Superintendent Millar, now retired, wrote: 'while appreciating DS Hughes' concern, I cannot recommend the action proposed for obvious reasons, i.e. Hamilton has not been convicted of any crime and it seems the PF [procurator fiscal] is likely to No pro [give an instruction of *nolle prosequi*, do not prosecute] the recently reported case.' The memo was passed to Deputy Chief Constable McMurdo who initialled it 'no action'. It should have been placed in Hamilton's firearms file but this did not happen. Nothing was entered in criminal intelligence records. Deputy Chief Constable McMurdo was involved in a great deal of correspondence with and about Hamilton between 1989 and 1992, mainly over complaints about him by the Scout Movement (the Cullen report later noted that Hamilton had 'an extremely unhealthy interest in young boys'). Yet his firearms certificate was renewed on 17 February 1992, with authority to purchase additional firearms, including a .357 revolver. Chief Superintendent Adamson, who renewed it, had never seen DS Hughes's memo and nobody had discussed it with him.

Hamilton had also lied to the police for years that he was a member of a legitimate shooting club – which since the 1920 Firearms Act had been accepted as a good and sufficient reason for owning guns. The police do not seem ever to have checked his claim that he belonged to the Callander Rifle and Pistol Club. An investigation by the Sportsman's Association noted several other failures to enforce existing regulations in regard to Hamilton. They concluded: 'a man suspected of being a danger to children, who had harried police officers, who had been thrown out of the Scottish Scout Movement, and who had acted irresponsibly with firearms was allowed to own four pistols and buy several thousand rounds of ammunition just weeks before he killed 16 children and their teacher.' They complained that 'police failings... have been forgotten while 57,000 law-abiding people have lost their businesses, friends and property'.

Any rational society or government would have said, even without hindsight, that senior police officers had been warned that Hamilton was not a fit person to own firearms. It would have sought above all to ensure that future Thomas Hamiltons would have their certificates revoked before they could do any damage. It might well have accepted that Hamilton would, even then, have been able to obtain illegal guns and that such incidents cannot be prevented even by the most ingenious laws and regulations. However, the British political establishment, on a wave of sentimental and unreasoning populism, responded by banning all legally-held handguns. Why should it have done this?

There is a recent history of unscrupulous and unreasoning attacks on gun ownership in this country and elsewhere. There is a far longer history of the willing acceptance of the right, and even the duty, of free and responsible citizens to bear and keep arms. It is only in the past century that government has sought to restrict and control gun ownership among the law-abiding middle class. The first serious laws restricting gun ownership were devised by people who still accepted that it was reasonable and normal for English householders to keep guns at home to defend themselves. Only since the 1960s' cultural revolution has the state taken restriction to the extremes reached after the Dunblane massacre. This fact suggests that the change may have something to do with the growing gap between the people's idea of the law and that of the elite state. A government at one with those it governs need not fear an armed people. A government wishing to impose a new morality and order on society might well object to arms being held, especially by confident and conservative citizens willing and able to defend their own lives and property. The real issue appears to be not crime or public danger, but the state's desire for a monopoly of armed force.

A retired police officer, Colin Greenwood, has examined and expertly summarized the history of the Englishman's right to bear arms and the state's recent attempts to restrict and destroy that right, in his book *Firearms Control*. It is clear that from the beginning of English society the free subject was expected both to keep and to enforce the law. There was no difference at all between the law-abiding, able-bodied man and the state. They supported each other. Under the 1181 Assize of Arms of Henry II every freeman had not just a right but an absolute duty to keep arms to discharge his obligations under the system of hue and cry. This required all to join in the hunt for a fleeing wrongdoer. The types of arms required were prescribed according to the rank of the freeman.

The 1285 Statute of Winchester, one of the first pieces of 'law-and-order' legislation in English history, commanded that every man have 'harness' in his house 'for to keep the Peace after the ancient assize'. And Greenwood points out that the 1328 Statute of Northampton did not, as is sometimes claimed, ban the bearing of arms, except and only where they were used 'to terrify the people'. The right of citizens to arm themselves under hue and cry was specifically preserved. There was always some doubt about exactly who counted as a trustworthy citizen. Henry VIII passed a law in 1541 forbidding the poor (those with incomes of less than £100 per year) to own pistols. But even this anti-crime measure was eased by many exceptions, including the continuing duty to take part in hue and cry.

James II, whose attempt to establish a Continental type of autocracy was in some ways similar to the policy of the modern British government, sought to restrict gun ownership at the same time as he raised a standing army. His overthrow in 1689 led to the drafting of the Bill of Rights, designed to ensure that this should never happen again (one of the reasons why modern liberals pretend that this document does not exist and frequently ignore its provisions). One of the complaints of the Bill of Rights was that James 'caused several good subjects, being Protestants' to be disarmed at a time when Roman Catholics 'were both armed and employed, contrary to law'. Parliament therefore declared that 'the subjects which are Protestants may have arms for their defence, suitable to their condition and as allowed by law'. This was a restatement of the Assize of Arms, which Parliament thought had been threatened by the Stuart dynasty. It still stands, although if it came before the European Court of Human Rights it would certainly be extended to cover Roman Catholics, Jews, Muslims, Hindus and Sikhs, which would make one of that court's more interesting and entertaining cases. It will not be surprising if the current government seeks directly to amend the Bill of Rights, as too many of its provisions are incompatible with Labour's 'modernizing' intentions.

An eloquent summary of the reasoning behind the right to bear and keep arms was provided in Sir William Blackstone's great statement of the common law of Christian England, the *Commentaries* of 1765. These speak majestically of the English subject's right to have arms for his defence (suitable to his condition and degree): 'a public allowance, under due restrictions, of the natural right of resistance and self preservation when the sanctions of society and laws are found insufficient to restrain the violence of oppression'. So long as personal security, personal liberty and private property remain inviolate, says Blackstone, the subject is perfectly free. However, 'every species of compulsive tyranny and oppression must act in opposition to one or other of these rights... All of us have it in our choice to do everything that a good man would desire to do; and are restrained from nothing, but what would be pernicious either to ourselves or to our fellow citizens.'

In the days before firearms this idea was simpler for governments to accept. It is easy to see why insecure states would want a monopoly of guns, especially of the modern and accurate kind. Yet American opponents of gun control point out that such states are often insecure precisely because they are tyrannies that do not enjoy the consent, let alone the support, of their peoples. England may have dealt with this difficulty partly through the class system, which ensured that supporters of the existing arrangements were generally better armed than malcontents. Since 1181, the higher a man's station the more powerful the weapon he was allowed (or obliged) to keep at home. The sheer cost of firearms probably kept them out of the hands of most malefactors until well into the nineteenth century. Even social revolutionaries in England have usually been concerned with the law and determined to obey it where they possibly could, largely because of the dreadful experiment of the Commonwealth which ended in the lawless repressive power of military dictatorship, worse by far than the lawfully limited rule of Charles I. As for armed crime, it has seldom been a grave problem since the founding of the police force. It has only become a serious menace during these supposedly civilized times of rigid gun control.

It was fear of revolution, rather than alarm about crime, which led to several attempts to limit gun ownership. During the unstable times after the Peterloo Massacre of August 1819, Parliament passed the Seizure of Arms Act 1820 which authorized Justices of the Peace to confiscate 'arms which might be used by revolutionaries'. There was a similar panic at the height of the Chartist movement, although in 1838 the old class system seems to have served its purpose once more in helping to keep order. Police in the capital found that 378 guns and 467 pistols had been sold to gentlemen and other respectable types, while only 122 guns and 162 pistols had been sold to mechanics, labourers and others believed or known to be Chartists. The Vagrancy Act of 1824 punished anyone possessing arms with intent to commit any felony, but the offence was the intent, not the possession.

The next apparent step towards control was the Gun Licences Act of 1870 but Colin Greenwood says this 'cannot be considered in any way as an attempt to control firearms'. It was, he concludes, an excise act mainly aimed at raising revenue and controlling poaching. A gun licence was available for ten shillings, without any questions asked, at any post office, much like a TV licence. Even so, the sum (far more than the literal translation of fifty pence would suggest) was probably enough to prevent many poorer people from licensing any gun they might have. Pistols at this time cost about one shilling and sixpence (again, a considerable sum far more than the eight pence into which this sum literally translates).

A more serious effort to limit weapons was the Regulation of Carrying of Arms Bill 1881, which demanded licences issued by a magistrate, but it never reached the statute book. In 1883, the first Firearms Bill sought to ban the carrying of a loaded firearm in a public place, but it too failed. The Felonious Use of Firearms Bill of 1887 called for a minimum ten-year sentence on anyone who committed burglary while armed with a gun. The House was told that over the previous nine years, London burglars had committed four murders and wounded thirteen policemen and five private citizens. Another eighteen criminals had escaped by using firearms. As Colin Greenwood says, this was hardly a crime wave by modern standards. The bill died when the Home Secretary pointed out that the maximum sentence for burglary was then life imprisonment and that fixed minimum sentences were a nuisance to the courts.

Next came the Pistols Bill of 1893, which sought to license the sale of firearms no longer than fifteen inches. Under-eighteens were to be banned from buying them, as were violent criminals for five years after their release from prison. Chief constables would have had to give permission for anyone to carry a loaded pistol. The bill was killed off after a spirited speech from the Member for Middleton South East, a Mr C. H. Hopwood, who asked: 'Why should Englishmen not arm themselves? It is natural and Parliament should not interfere with such a right.' The Commons agreed with him.

The bill came back in 1895, when the Victorian MPs again threw it out, after Mr Hopwood, sneering at it as 'grandmotherly', remarked that 'to say that because there were some persons who would make violent use of pistols, therefore the right of purchase or possession by every Englishman should be taken away, is monstrous'. The Home Office, in a tactic to be used many years later by Roy Jenkins over other matters, supported the bill even though it was officially 'private', but could not save it from being crushed by 189 to seventy-five. England in 1902, says Greenwood, 'was a country where guns of every type were familiar instruments and where anyone who felt the need or desire to own a gun could obtain one... the right of the Englishman to keep arms for his own defence was still completely accepted and all attempts at placing this under restraint had failed.' Even so, another version of the 1890s' bills, the Pistols Act of 1903, was eventually passed, although it was even weaker than the earlier ones. Its main effect was to encourage the making and selling of long-barrelled pistols in order to evade its ban on weapons shorter than nine inches long. Between then and the Great War, there were several attempts to legislate, encouraged by the Sidney Street incident of 1910, but they came to nothing in that very different England.

The war changed everything, accustoming Englishmen to state control, regulation, rationing, identity checks and conscription, and bringing the government into their lives in a way never before known. Colin Greenwood obtained details of a confidential committee on firearms law which considered the issue in 1918, headed by Sir Ernley Blackwell, a senior Home Office civil servant. Despite a level of crime that was incredibly low by our standards and small by the measures of the time, they feared the aftermath of the First World War, with many ex-servicemen bringing guns home. They also worried about the coming repeal of the strong regulations against carrying weapons included in the Defence of the Realm Act, which had restricted national life in wartime but was now to be scrapped. 'There is good reason for altering the law so as to make it much more difficult to obtain arms than it is at present,' they urged. They wanted to revive a pre-war proposal for chief constables to issue certificates to persons of good character, allowing them to keep weapons if they had grounds for doing so.

In those peaceful and well-policed times, they still thought that a man's wish to protect himself and his household from burglars was a likely and sensible reason for such an application, especially if he lived in the sort of remote farmhouse where Tony Martin was to be burgled nearly eighty years later. As they said: 'The ground could obviously be urged with much more force by an applicant who lived in a rural or out of the way district than by one who lived in a well patrolled street in a town.' They did not, however, say that a citizen living in a town should necessarily be refused a certificate. It is quite clear that, even at this stage, nobody was questioning the Englishman's right to have weapons for his own self-defence. In a way, all that was happening was a rearrangement of the old rule that kept weapons in the hands of the nobility and their allies. Only now weapons would be kept out of the hands of the criminal, the drunkard, the unstable, the young and the mad.

There is a suspicion that the 1920 Firearms Act which followed this committee's work (and which is the grandfather of all that came afterwards) was actually motivated by the fear of a Bolshevik uprising more than by the fear of crime. Those were unstable times and the bloody chaos of Ireland just across the water made the government inclined to panic. There is some evidence for this in the diaries of Thomas Jones, Lloyd George's Cabinet Secretary, who wrote in an entry for February 1920 that in the general atmosphere of panic about possible revolution (which he did not share) he had, among other things, suggested that the coalition government 'make absolutely sure of your arms and munitions'.

Jones records that, during a 'conference on industrial disturbances', Walter Long, a Tory and First Lord of the Admiralty, said: 'The peaceable manpower of the country is without arms. I have not a pistol less than 200 years old. A Bill is needed for licensing persons to bear arms. This has been useful in Ireland because the authorities know who were possessed of arms.' Edward Shortt, the Liberal Home Secretary, replied that 'The Home Office had a Bill ready but in the past there have always been objections.' The Tory leader Andrew Bonar Law believed that 'All weapons ought to be available for distribution to the friends of the government.' At this point Lord Inverforth reminded his colleagues that the United Kingdom then had such a surplus of weapons that it was selling them to the Baltic states. He failed to calm his colleagues. The Home Secretary used the same conference to outline plans for a special temporary force of ten thousand soldiers. And Robert Munro, the Secretary of State for Scotland, said that 'the existing police force was inadequate either for the revolution or for large industrial strikes accompanied possibly by sabotage'.

No mention of this was made when the Firearms Bill came to be debated that summer. The Home Secretary told the Commons that its main purpose was to reduce crime, saying: 'We hope by means of the Bill to prevent criminals and persons of that description being able to have revolvers and to use them.' He said that a number of post offices had recently been raided by thieves carrying guns. While he hinted that crime was the real concern of the bill, he did not produce any detailed evidence of serious problems. For whatever reason, the House of Commons did not raise the sort of objections its Victorian and Edwardian predecessors would have done. Perhaps it was exhausted by the conflict and its aftermath, perhaps, through the experience of war, it had simply grown accustomed to more state regulation. The old spirit of libertarian opposition to gun control had mysteriously died.

During the debate on 10 June, Lieutenant Commander Kenworthy, Member for Hull, alone spoke up for Blackstone's England. He declared: 'It has been a well-known object of the central government in this country to deprive people of their weapons.' He went on to declare: 'I very much object to the power being given to the police to judge whether a person is fit to have a firearm' (the original Pistols Act placed this power with magistrates). He also noticed, as all his parliamentary colleagues failed to do, the significant change in the nature of the police that was buried in the new law: 'In England the police are very respected public servants. On the Continent they are petty officials with tremendous powers, which they use to the full.' The bill was, he said, 'one more attempt to set up a petty police bureaucracy in this country...'. Kenworthy concluded: 'The very foundation of the liberty of the subject in this country is that he can, if driven to do so, resist.' Mr Kiley, MP for Whitechapel, made another trenchant criticism, which remains unanswered to this day. If burglars wanted guns, he said, they would steal them. 'These men are dangerous, but there is nothing in this Bill which will adequately deal with them.'

Actually, the use of firearms by criminals in England was still a minor problem in the 1920s and for many years to come. For example, in the eighteen months between 1 July 1936 and 31 December 1937, only twenty people arrested in the Metropolitan Police area were found to possess firearms. Of these, twelve were airguns and one a toy pistol. These figures are slightly lower than those from before the First World War and similar to those of the early 1950s. There was a brief increase in the totals in the years immediately after the Second World War. All these figures are so small that it is hard to tell whether legal controls had anything to do with the changes from year to year. It seems unlikely. However, during the late 1940s that a significant change in the law was made by the Labour government without any legislation at all. On 17 October 1946 the Home Secretary, Chuter Ede, simply declared: 'I would not regard the plea that a revolver is wanted for the protection of an applicant's person or property as necessarily justifying the issue of a firearm certificate.' This was a complete reversal of the views of the Blackwell Committee just a quarter of a century earlier. It was also an attack on centuries of custom. Blackwell's view had been based on the laws and traditions of the country and on the Bill of Rights. Under the 1920 Firearms Act which followed Blackwell's report the law had obliged the police to grant a certificate if the applicant met the conditions.

The wording of the Act – 'A firearm certificate *shall* be granted by the chief officer if he is satisfied' – emphasized that the police were merely making sure that the right to own weapons was exercised by the proper sort of person. Colin Greenwood argues: 'During the intervening years, chief officers of police, either at the suggestion of or with the support of the Home Office, have withdrawn this right by purely executive decisions until the present position is that any claim to have a firearm for self-defence is certain to fail except in the most unusual circumstances.' He says that there is no certainty that a modern court would uphold the ancient right to keep arms, and he is almost certainly right.

Another significant restriction of liberty came with the tightening of the shotgun laws in 1967. There had always been harsh penalties for the criminal use of such guns, but the law had largely left their owners alone. While banning sawn-off shotguns altogether, the 1965 Firearms Act, rushed through in a panic as a sop to those who feared that the abolition of hanging would produce an epidemic of armed crime, did not try to control ownership of normal shotguns. The then Home Secretary, Sir Frank Soskice, explained, 'there are probably at least 500,000 shotguns in legitimate use throughout the country and the burden which certification would put on the police would not be justified by the benefits which would result.'

Then came a new Home Secretary, Roy Jenkins. Soon after his appointment he was compelled to deal with the Shepherd's Bush police murders, described elsewhere in this book, in which the criminals used pistols, not shotguns. A month later, Mr Jenkins claimed: 'the criminal use of shotguns is increasing rapidly, still more rapidly than that of other weapons.' Colin Greenwood says Mr Jenkins was mistaken, misunderstanding statistics that were in any case unreliable. Only three months previously, presumably using the same information, Mr Jenkins had echoed Sir Frank's unwillingness to restrict shotgun ownership, saying: 'I must pay some regard to the burden of inspection which would be put on the police. The police do not consider that it would be right to make an extension at the present time.' Greenwood shows that between 1961 and 1965, indictable offences involving all firearms had risen from 552 to 1140. Those involving shotguns had risen from 107 to 318 (that is, by 211). This means that the use of other weapons had risen from 445 to 822 (that is, by 377). This does not really justify Mr Jenkins's claim that criminal use of shotguns was rising more quickly than that of other weapons, unless percentages are more important than actual numbers. Nor does it deal with the awkward fact that these 'indictable offences' included poaching by night and thefts in which guns were stolen. They were therefore useless in judging the real growth of armed crime. What is more, the methods of collecting the figures are open to serious question. Greenwood says that they are completely unreliable.

Even so, Mr Jenkins inserted his shotgun laws into the vast and revolutionary Criminal Justice Act of 1967. Given the scope of that Act, it is hardly surprising that the shotgun licensing plan was hardly mentioned at all in the second reading debate. Greenwood says: 'Previous firearms legislation had always provoked lengthy debates and had been the subject of much concern by many members. Could it be that this was what was anticipated when [shotgun licensing] was wrapped up in the midst of vital and controversial legal reforms?'

Greenwood argues that one of the few reliable and consistent measures of armed crime in England during the 1945–65 period is the annual number of robberies in the Metropolitan Police area in which firearms are involved. These figures were continuously kept, and they excluded meaningless cases such as children using airguns. The total stood at twenty-five when first recorded in 1946 and rose to forty-six in 1947 but then fell much lower, to twenty-eight in 1948, nineteen in 1950, a mere four in 1954. It was not until 1959 that the numbers climbed to fifty-one, just above the previous high point in 1947. The next serious rise took place in 1964 when there were ninety-two such robberies. The post-1964 figures are so different that they seem to be from a different series: 114 in 1965, 142 in 1966, 165 in 1967, 225 in 1968 and 272 in 1969. Greenwood also notes that by 1991 the number had risen to 1618 but then fell to 597 by 1994, a drop probably attributable to a concentration on such crimes by the Flying Squad at that time. They were often armed.

In unpublished research under the title 'Do Our Gun Laws Work?', Colin Greenwood analyses the use of certain types of weapons in crime, partly to see if the tighter laws introduced after the Hungerford massacre had any effect on gun crime. First, he notes that the number of legal guns went into steep decline after post-Hungerford legislation. The story was different, however, for shotguns, which were used widely in the then-growing sport of clay-pigeon shooting. Shotgun certificates in force in 1971 stood at 793,092 and climbed steadily so that by 1988 they had reached 971,102. By 1997 they had diminished to 686,294. Firearms certificates in force fell from 228,921 in 1971 to 193,809 in 1988 and 164,960 in 1997.

Then he analyses the use of firearms in homicide and robbery in England and Wales before and during the same period. 'There is no statistical relationship,' he concludes, 'between the numbers of firearms legally held in Britain and the use of firearms in homicide or robbery.' For instance, homicides involving firearms rose and fell without any noticeable pattern: seventy-seven in 1987, thirty-six in 1988, forty-five in 1989, sixty in 1990, forty-nine in 1996, fifty-nine in 1997. Robberies involving firearms were equally random over most of this period, wavering upwards from 2831 in 1987 to 3939 in 1990 and 5827 in 1992, then down again to 3029 in 1997. However, they increased significantly between 1969, when there were only 464, and 1981, when they reached 1893, and only once after that fell below two thousand, often reaching more than three thousand. Something profound had changed, but it was not the result of an increase in the number of legally-held firearms since no such increase took place. What is more, the proportion of homicides committed with guns has not grown significantly. While it occasionally fell sharply, to 4 per cent in 1980, and rose sharply, to 11 per cent in 1993, it generally remained between 6 and 9 per cent throughout the period 1969 to 1997.

Greenwood, whose little-known and out-of-print book and

subsequent unpublished research is indispensable reading for anyone who wishes to debate gun law policy, makes several more powerful points. He cites a three-year Home Office study (Annual Criminal Statistics 1997) into the origin of firearms used in homicides between 1992 and 1994. In homicide involving organized crime and drugs no legally-owned firearms were used at all, but forty-three illegal ones were. In three years only one robbery involved the use of a legally-owned gun, compared with seventeen involving illegal weapons. Even in killings caused by arguments, jealousy or revenge, only four cases involved legally-held guns, compared with seventeen involving illegal ones. In domestic incidents fourteen homicides involved legal weapons, compared with forty-one involving illegal guns. Even given that the legal status of forty-five of the weapons used in such crimes was, bafflingly, unknown, these figures give great force to the view that the criminal's choice of weapon is barely affected by the law.

For armed robbery, the pistol, much more toughly regulated than the shotgun, is very much the criminal's preferred weapon. The illegal sawn-off shotgun is the next most popular. The normal shotgun, probably illegally bought even though it is the most readily available legally, is the least favourite in the thief's arsenal. The law is largely irrelevant since armed robbery is rarely if ever a first offence, so those who use guns to rob would already be banned from holding legal guns.

More alarming is the startling rise in the number of pistols used in homicides after 1992, at the same time as the numbers of shotgun homicides fell. Greenwood suggests:

> The rise in the use of pistols in homicide since 1992
> reflects a most important change in the nature of
> homicide and may well be associated with the rise of
> drug and criminal gang related shootings which are
> being reported...
> A discernible change in the pattern of homicides

involving firearms is taking place which may reflect
a total failure to effectively police a segment of the
community...

Tackling this phenomenon through the medium
of stricter controls of pistols is clearly not an option.
They were extremely strictly controlled throughout
the period and are now effectively banned.

Finally, Greenwood offers an explanation for the increase in gun
crime of recent years that upsets all modern orthodoxy. He found
two extraordinary peaks in the use of weapons (that is, all weapons,
including knives and clubs as well as guns) in robberies, in 1948 and
1956. He notes that 'the period after 1957 marks a general rise in the
level of the use of violence and 1964 marks a further steepening of
virtually every graph' measuring violent or armed crime. These
dates are all highly significant. The death penalty was openly suspended for much of 1948 while its future was passionately debated
in both Houses of Parliament. It was again publicly suspended
during a second such debate, for a period extending from August
1955 to March 1957 (see Chapter 6 for details of these debates). After
1957, a vital change had taken place in the law of murder. Before
1957, if four men went out on a robbery and one of them killed the
victim, all four were liable to hang. After 1957 only the actual killer
would face the noose. As Greenwood points out: 'Previously, each
member of the gang had a vested interest in ensuring that the
others did not kill, but with the passage of the [1957 Homicide] Act,
this interest diminished.' The death penalty was finally abolished
in 1965, but no executions took place after the hanging of Peter
Anthony Allen and Gwynne Owen Evans on 13 August 1964 for the
murder of John Alan West during a theft. Once again, the death
penalty was unofficially suspended, this time never to return.

With these dates in mind, it is interesting to consider
Greenwood's figures, which show a leap in armed and violent
offences in 1948 followed by a return to the previous level. There is

then another leap in 1957 followed by a much smaller fall and a generally higher level of such crimes. There is a third significant jump in 1964 which does not fall again. Nor has it since.

Supporters of gun control often point to the USA as an example of what not to do. During the long slow decline of order in England, this argument seemed to hold. America had a far higher murder rate and its armed crime was out of control. However, this smug comparison cannot now be made. It was based on the afterglow of the old and unique English system of liberty and order created over centuries. Now, as that afterglow fades, the USA has begun to look safer than England – not least because it has turned its back on many of the elite liberal penal theories of the 1960s. In their study 'Crime and Justice in the United States and in England and Wales, 1981–96', Professor David Farrington of Cambridge University and Dr Patrick Langan of the US Department of Justice showed that the two countries have almost swapped positions. Using statistics and victim surveys, they compared the rates of reported assaults, robbery and burglary and found that in this miserable competition England and Wales have now overtaken the USA. By 1996 the robbery rate in England and Wales was 40 per cent higher than in the USA. Rates of assault, burglary and car crime in England and Wales are almost double those in the 'lawless', 'frontier' USA. The USA has better arrest and conviction rates than England, and US courts are far more likely to send offenders to prison.

The homicide rate in the USA remains far higher, as does the use of guns in killings, but this undoubted truth is rooted in the major difference between the two societies – America's unhealed and worsening racial divide, the persistent stain of slavery and the terrible damage it did. Yet again, gun laws are not an adequate explanation. Brazil and Russia, both countries with far tougher gun laws than the USA, have murder rates four times higher than America. Initial research after Australia introduced gun bans, following a particularly grisly massacre in Tasmania in 1996, shows that they may well have had severe unintended consequences. In the first two years of firearms restrictions, armed robberies rose by 73 per cent, unarmed robberies by 28 per cent, assaults by 17 per cent and kidnapping by 38 per cent. Murder did fall by 9 per cent, but manslaughter increased by 32 per cent.

One other statistic is highly relevant to the debate about the effect of widespread legal gun ownership on criminal behaviour. In the USA, so-called 'hot' burglaries, committed while the victim is in the house, comprised 13 per cent of the total. In England and Wales they accounted for about 50 per cent of the total. These facts suggest that the rational thief hesitates to break into a house where he may face armed resistance sanctioned by law. If so, widespread gun ownership by free citizens, combined with a law that generally permits them to defend their property and lives with deadly force, may well restrain crime.

The difference in the law's attitude towards force in England and in the USA is definite but hard to trace. Presumably the two began to diverge in the nineteeenth century as England became an almost wholly urban and suburban society with a universal police presence, while much of the USA remained rural and effectively unpoliced. The view of many American states, that a householder is entitled to defend himself, seems to be based on the English common law but has developed against a background of far more scattered settlements and in the absence of a police force within easy reach, let alone regular preventive patrols. Many states have laws specifically upholding the right to protect one's home. And 'defence of habitation' is a widely recognized principle in American law, allowing the use of deadly force if a citizen has a reasonable belief that someone is trying to enter their home violently. This is different from the English idea of 'reasonable force' where others must judge whether the force was reasonable or not.

John Baker, Professor of Law at Louisiana State University, quoted in the *Daily Telegraph* (27 April 2000), believes: 'It would be very difficult in any state to convict a homeowner even of manslaughter if he shot a burglar who was burgling his home.'

This not confined to conservative southern states where white supremacy and racial barriers could be blamed. In Pennsylvania, for example, the law provides an explicit right to use deadly force either when there has been an unlawful entry, or when the resident believes the intruder is going to commit a felony on the property or is attempting to take property unlawfully. There is no duty to retreat if the resident believes that deadly force is necessary. The defence must assert that the action was taken in self-defence and the prosecution can only challenge this by disproving the claim beyond reasonable doubt.

By contrast, well south of the Mason–Dixon line, in South Carolina, there have recently been complaints that the police are too willing to investigate homeowners for acts of self-defence. This became such an issue that the South Carolina Attorney General, Charlie Condon, felt it necessary to announce in March 2001: 'The State is going to back the homeowner if their home is invaded. I'm putting home invaders on notice that, if an occupant chooses to use deadly force, there will be no prosecution.' Significantly, such cases in South Carolina all seem to have ended with the acquittal of the householder. It was the investigation, charge and trial that angered Mr Condon and the voters.

The contrast with Britain could hardly be sharper. Old ladies have been ordered to remove barbed wire from their fences in case it injures a burglar. Almost any action in defence of property can expose the citizen to grave risk. In May 1997 a former policeman, Edwin Skeates, was convicted of assault by a jury after taking a fourteen-year-old boy by the scruff of his neck and marching him home to complain that he had been trying to damage his garden fence. He was ordered to pay £250 compensation to the youth. Mr Skeates, who spent £7500 on his defence, was acquitted of a second charge of inflicting actual bodily harm by causing the youth 'post-traumatic stress'. The youth's injuries amounted to a bruise, which had disappeared within twenty-four hours, and some scratches. The judge, Assistant Recorder Philip Parker, lectured Mr Skeates thus in the name of the law: 'You must curb your temper, control your emotions and behave more reasonably. You must be more tolerant and less prone to act unreasonably.'

Then there was the strange case of the seventy-six-year-old retired miner, Ted Newbery, who sought to defend his beleaguered allotment against repeated attacks by mounting guard over it. One night in 1988, as he slept in a shed on the allotment, Mr Newbery was woken by the sound of two men trying to break in. They called out 'if you're in there, we're having you'. Mr Newbery took his shotgun, loaded it, poked it through a hole in the door and fired. The shot hit Mark Revill in the arm, armpit and chest. Revill was prosecuted for his offences of that night and pleaded guilty. Mr Newbery was also prosecuted on charges of wounding and acquitted. However, he then found himself being sued for damages and was ordered to pay Revill £4000 because the judges ruled that he had 'used greater violence than was justified'.

The judges believed that the ancient rule '*ex turpi causa non oritur actio*' (no claim can arise out of an evil action) did not apply. Mr Justice Rougier, stung by the public contempt for his ruling, wrote to *The Times* to explain himself. 'Had the defendant tried the less drastic tactic of shouting, turning on the inside light or even firing into the roof, it is virtually certain that the two burglars would have run away at once,' he suggested, with the comforting hindsight of one who was not there and was unlikely ever to be in such a position. He said Mr Newbery had failed to take much care where he was shooting and caused 'severe and lasting injury to the would-be burglar; a few inches either way and he would have killed him'. Many past judges might well have reckoned that he had no special duty to take care where he shot when he was besieged in a lonely hut by two ill-intentioned young men who had threatened to 'have him'. However, this is not the way the elite state thinks.

The recent case of Carlo Vellino reveals the increasing moral neutrality of the judges' bench. Vellino, with a long criminal record, jumped from a window to try to escape arrest for non-payment of fines. As a result, he is now paralysed for life. He sued for £300,000 on the grounds that the police should have stopped him from jumping because they knew he had a habit of trying to escape when arrested. Nobody laughed. On the contrary, one of three Appeal Court judges, the former Communist, Lord Justice Sedley (appointed by a Conservative government), ruled in Vellino's favour. His two colleagues overruled him, but it is probably just a matter of time before judges of the Sedley type form a majority in the higher courts.

Apart from knowing that he may face this sort of judicial neutrality between right and wrong, a citizen who defends himself cannot predict how he will be treated. He will face a legal mechanism that is utterly inconsistent, the rules of which are so capricious and subjective that the wisest course when his home is attacked is to do nothing at all. In May 2000 the Director of Public Prosecutions, David Calvert-Smith, said that the legal system operated in favour of householders in the vast majority of cases where they defended themselves. His reassurance was ambiguous: 'I believe that the test the courts have set over the years has taken full account of the very human situation that people find themselves in, and that we can be trusted only to put cases before a court where a jury is likely to find the force used deliberately on a burglar was disproportionate.' He said that those who reacted spontaneously and did not 'persist' with force once the threat had ceased should not be in danger of prosecution. The problem with such statements is that the judgement of what was reasonable will not be made in a dark hallway at midnight but in the cool orderliness of a courtroom by day, by a youthful jury who may well have no idea of the menace suffered by the victim. Or the judgement may be made in an air-conditioned government office where the gravest danger is a shortage of biscuits. Entirely absent from Mr Calvert-Smith's thinking is the ancient sense of horror, recognized in legal systems as far back as the Old Testament, that anyone should break into a man's home by night.

In 1996 Brian Mackenzie, then chairman of the Police

Superintendents' Association and so in a good position to know the true state of affairs, complained that something was wrong 'when a pensioner who tackles two heroin addicts burgling his home finds himself complained about by the burglar and arrested for assault'. He thought the police and the prosecution service needed clearer guidance on how to behave:

> If you tell the man in the street that someone broke into someone's house and was assaulted by the homeowner they are going to say that it serves them right.
>
> In my view possible attack is the occupational hazard for the burglar. He is liable to be clobbered if he is caught. It is his own misfortune. The same rule applies when someone attacks a police officer. Only in exceptional cases – say where a gun was used but not necessarily when someone dies as the result of a struggle – should there be a prosecution. The fact is that juries are very reluctant to convict in these cases. We shouldn't be arresting victims, rushing them down to the station and charging them. As officers we should be applying the test of what the man in the street would think reasonable.

Mr Mackenzie's views probably were not and are not shared by his superiors in the hierarchy, who have less and less interest in what the man in the street thinks. They care more about the elite state's theories of social control and negotiation, as taught at Bramshill.

It is not only Bramshill and the universities that have undermined the idea of self-defence. The Occupiers' Liability Act of 1984, produced by that elite liberal pressure group, the Law Commission, was enacted by a Tory government, like much of the worst criminal justice legislation of modern times. It was this law that allowed Ted Newbery to be sued in a case that warned the English public that burglars had obtained human rights and were ready to use them. When this law was debated in the Lords in

July 1983, Lord Gisborough warned that it might prevent people protecting their property with barbed wire. Lord Hailsham, then Lord Chancellor, made light of this, saying:

> Supposing you found a burglar putting a ladder up against your house with intent to steal from it or do something even worse? I am not sure whether you need lean out of your window and say 'Look out, the third rung from the bottom is slightly defective'. I suspect you would not be under a liability to such a man. But I doubt whether that is part of the doctrine of *ex turpi causa non oritur actio*. I doubt the application of the doctrine in general to the law of tort. I think that the real application is to raise Lord Atkins' question which he sought to answer in a very different context in Donaghue v. Stevenson – namely who is my neighbour and what duty do I owe him?
>
> I hope this Bill may clarify the law rather than create a revolutionary change in it.

This useless mixture of complacent frivolity and self-righteous piety, typical of a Conservative Party utterly out of touch with real life, left nobody the wiser. It eventually led to the Northampton barbed-wire case, when an elderly lady whose council house was the frequent target of burglars was ordered by the council to take down the wire in case it injured a thief as he climbed in. Mrs Ruby Barber, then ninety-three, resisted the order, as did her son Burt who had spent £450 putting up the wire. After many months of legal negotiation and discussion she was allowed to keep the wire, provided she put up a notice warning intruders of the danger it posed and provided she accepted liability for any injury they might do themselves while climbing into her property.

When the Occupiers' Liability Bill reached its committee stage in October, Hailsham was still more infuriating than he had been in the earlier debate. Lord Stanley of Alderley moved a sensible and prescient amendment to be inserted in the bill to the effect that 'No duty is owed by virtue of this section by an occupier of premises to any person who is on those premises having committed or with the intention of committing there a criminal offence of which that person is capable of being convicted.' Even the most radical ex-Marxist judge could not have got around that. He was supported by Lord Renton, who warned: 'Unless this amendment, or something to the same effect, is introduced into clause 1 we shall have great uncertainty, we shall have confusion and we could have serious injustice.'

It was no use. Lord Hailsham was back waving his Bible and babbling of a lost rural England where children still raided orchards, rather than the real one where drug-addicts raid homes. 'If a man steals apples on your land is it really to be said in a Christian country that you do not owe him any duty? I will not stand for that.' Lord Renton, rightly irritated at the suggestion that he was not as good a Christian as Lord Hailsham, retorted: 'I did not say that.' Lord Stanley pointed out that minor offences such as stealing of apples would be dealt with under the Theft Act. He continued to warn that the bill, as drafted, contained dangers:

> I am not entirely happy, as a layman, about the criminal
> who trespasses and the occupier's legal liability towards
> him, or about the defective ladder or in fact the
> carelessly-left hole and how liable I am, as an occupier, to
> a criminal. However, having listened very carefully to
> speeches made by noble Lords throughout the
> committee, I can only hope that if I come up before a
> court, my noble and learned friend the Lord Chancellor
> will be there and will take a similar view that I do not
> have to tell the chap that the third rung is defective. I
> hope no other court would disagree with that view.

Realizing he was getting nowhere, he reluctantly withdrew his amendment. The ancient truth that the courts will apply the law as it is written, whatever promises anyone gives at the time, turned out to apply. It is hard to imagine this sort of high-minded tripe being accepted by any American state legislature. But in England, where the Conservatives think it is unchristian to put up a barbed-wire fence, while the socialists think burglars should be able to sue the police for failing to stop them jumping out of windows, the robust defence of the free citizen has little chance of being written into the law.

England's gun laws and its confusing rules about self-defence are both quite new things. So is the great expansion of the burglary industry, which recently achieved an astonishing productivity rate of two hundred burglaries per hour. These facts may be connected, although the left prefers not to believe so. But if it cannot be proved that a disarmed and demoralized citizenry encourages crime, there is certainly little evidence that gun ownership by confident citizens will increase crime, as the prejudiced and ignorant anti-Americanism of the liberal elite state would have us believe.

The converse is strongly supported by the revolutionary work of John Lott in his book *More Guns, Less Crime*. Lott, an economist, examined the effect across the USA of changes in gun laws. Laws on firearms vary immensely in the USA, so that, for example, Vermont, a virtually crime-free state, has no gun restrictions at all, while Washington, DC, the eastern districts of which have a fearsome murder rate and where the sound of gunfire can often be heard after dark, has local ordinances threatening dire penalties for owning, keeping or carrying any kind of gun. This variation makes comparisons between different practices possible. Lott was the first to do so. His study followed the widespread passage of 'concealed carry' laws permitting law-abiding citizens to carry a hidden weapon unless police have valid grounds to object to their doing so. By the time he had completed his book, thirty-one of the fifty states had done this, a striking increase over the mere eight that had such laws in 1965.

This development was a response to the severe increase in violent crime that began to affect the USA in the late 1960s, interestingly at about the time that the Supreme Court ruled that the death penalty was unconstitutional. He concluded that violent crime rates were highest in the states with the most restrictive gun laws, next highest in states that allowed local authorities discretion in granting permits, and lowest in states with non-discretionary rules (that is, those that simply say that the police must issue permits unless the applicant is disqualified by his past record). Then comes the real shock. 'Violent crimes are 81 percent higher in states without non-discretionary laws. For murder, states that ban the concealed carrying of guns have murder rates 127 percent higher than states with the most liberal concealed-carry laws.' For property crimes, the difference is much smaller, just 24 per cent. States that allow the concealed carrying of guns have less crime in general, but the main difference is in violent crime.

Lott also goes into immense detail, sometimes county by county, about what happened when the laws changed. He found that rape, robbery, violent crime, aggravated assault and murder fell sharply in areas where the public were permitted to carry hidden weapons. These crimes often then increased in neighbouring areas without such laws, showing once again that career criminals make rational choices based upon calculations of risk. If the next-door areas subsequently introduced their own concealed-carry laws, these crimes fell there too. Property crimes not involving contact with the victim tended to rise as criminals sought the easier option. The largest drops in violent crime following the introduction of legal concealed handguns came in the most urban counties with the highest populations and the greatest crime rates. Very few citizens misused their privileges. In the period 1987 to 1996, Florida issued 380,000 concealed-carry licences and revoked seventy-two because of crimes committed by the permit holder. Most of those crimes did not involve use of the permitted gun. In Virginia, by the year 2000 not one permit holder had been involved in violent crime. In Texas, seventeen out of 114,000 licences had been revoked by 2000.

The facts are also uncomfortable for liberals who claim to be in favour of total sexual equality. Few things equalize men and women more effectively than a gun. Lott says:

> Guns also appear to be the great equalizer among the sexes. Murder rates decline when either more women or more men carry concealed handguns, but the effect is specially pronounced for women. One additional woman carrying a concealed handgun reduces the murder rate for women by about 3–4 times more than one additional man carrying a concealed handgun reduces the murder rate for men. This occurs because allowing a woman to defend herself with a concealed handgun produces a much larger change in her ability to defend herself than the change created by providing a man with a handgun.

Surprising proof that this truth has penetrated the heart of liberal feminist America came in the months following the 11 September outrage, after which many formerly peaceable citizens armed themselves in case they were called on to defeat a terrorist attack. A group called the Second Amendment Sisters united feminists against gun control. A plainly shocked writer from the left-wing *New York Times*, Nicholas Kristof, recounted a visit to Mount Holyoke College in Massachusetts, a liberal campus which staged one of the first bra-burnings of the 1960s' sexual revolution. In 2001, about fifty women students joined the Second Amendment Sisters. The *New York Times* reported: 'It is bizarre to sit on the campus of a liberal all-women's college in Massachusetts talking with students about their yearning for, say, a Smith & Wesson 9-millimetre semiautomatic – but maybe that's because I'm not used to feminists with guns.'

It turns out that, in addition to *Women and Guns* magazine, there is a growing number of such women's groups. These include Mother's

Arms and Armed Females of America, whose website declares: 'Those who push for gun control are of the same mind-set as Palestinian suicide bombers and the Taliban who kidnap women for rape and sex-slave trade. Both don't like the possibility of armed citizens, in these cases, especially an armed woman.' In fact, the idea of an armed citizen, especially an armed woman or member of a racial minority, being better able to resist oppression by an authoritarian state creates difficult contradictions for the left-wing worldview, which the women of Mount Holyoke seem to have resolved.

Lott's work, since it upsets so many prejudices and assumptions, is still the subject of turbulent debate. He has capably defended himself against attacks on all fronts. He was carpet-bombed with abuse and misinformation by America's gun control lobby, which repeatedly and incorrectly accused him of being financed by gun manufacturers, but as yet they have not been able to overturn his conclusions. Their fury at his successful book is typical of intolerant elite liberalism at its worst, unwilling even to consider ideas that contradict its pieties, let alone debate them fairly and rationally. Liberalism will defend to the death everybody's right to agree with it.

Lott also produces a number of facts that blast holes in the assumptions of those who believe that guns in the hands of citizens, rather than a state monopoly, are intrinsically wicked. He takes myths one by one and pulls them to pieces. The claim that individuals are frequently killed by people they know is used to support the idea that most killings take place within families or between friends. In fact, the FBI's category of people who 'know' their victims includes a huge number of rival gang members who know each other. This is not quite what this oft-quoted statistic is taken to mean. Lott says:

> Most people do not envision gang members or drug
> buyers and pushers killing each other when they hear
> that 58 percent of murder victims were either relatives or
> acquaintances of their murderers. If family members are

included, 17 percent of all murders in Chicago for
1990–95 involved family members, friends, neighbors
or roommates. While the total number of murders in
Chicago grew from 395 in 1965 to 814 in 1995, the number
involving family members, friends, neighbors or
roommates remained virtually unchanged. What
has grown is the number of murders by non-friend
acquaintances, strangers, identified gangs, and persons
unknown.

For a professional criminal's view of the issue, which cannot be dismissed as self-serving, Lott quotes the Mafia turncoat Sammy 'The Bull' Gravano on the subject of gun control: 'Gun control? It's the best thing you can do for crooks and gangsters. I want you to have nothing. If I'm a bad guy, I'm always gonna have a gun.' Gravano laughed at planned restrictions, paralleled by those placed on English gun owners after Hungerford: 'Safety locks? You will pull the trigger with a lock on, and I'll pull the trigger. We'll see who wins.'

Lott also deals interestingly with the issue of the massacre, as seen in Hungerford, Dunblane, Tasmania and in such places as Columbine High School in the USA. He makes the point that young men have owned and used guns in the USA for centuries without such events taking place, so some explanation other than the easy availability of guns is needed. This is especially so because guns, even in America, are far harder to obtain than they once were and it is much more difficult to carry them legally than it used to be.

Until 1967, for instance, it was possible for a thirteen-year-old almost anywhere in the USA to walk into a hardware store and buy a rifle. Many schools had shooting clubs and even in New York City it was common for high school students (aged thirteen to eighteen) to take their guns to school with them on the subways. Yet school massacres were unknown. Now students can be expelled for bringing water pistols on to school premises, and primary schoolchildren have been suspended for carrying around pictures of guns. Many schools have guards and metal detectors at their entrances. Yet school massacres continue to occur with dispiriting frequency despite all these supposedly effective restrictions. Given that such horrible events do take place, what are their implications for gun control? First, they are not caused by widespread gun ownership or they would not be a new problem. Secondly, if such events do happen, the presence of legally held guns in society may actually hinder them.

In a school shooting at Pearl, Mississippi, in October 1997, the killer was immobilized by a teacher who fetched a legal gun from his car and stopped the incident before police arrived. Nobody can say how much worse it would have been if the teacher had not acted as he did. Most media did not report that the teacher, Joel Myrick, did this with a legal gun. In a school-related shooting in Edinboro, Pennsylvania, the criminal was again subdued when the owner of a nearby restaurant produced a legal shotgun – again well before police arrived. Lott cites several more such incidents, arguing that liberal elite media coverage has simply edited out these important facts, unable to cope with the possibility that legal gun ownership has helped keep the peace. Coverage of terror attacks in Israel also frequently slides over the fact that the attackers rarely escape and are often killed by armed bystanders before they can do serious damage. Israel's streets are full of heavily-armed people, but armed crime by such citizens seems to be virtually unknown.

The idea that legal restrictions on guns are a useful way of curbing armed and violent crime is simply not borne out by the history of crime in this country or in the United States. The circumstantial evidence that an effective death penalty may deter such crime is strong. Yet the elite state prefers the ineffective method and would rather take away the liberties of lawful citizens than the lives of lawless murderers. All men of power tend to use disorder as a pretext for policies that they favour in any case. In the same way, 'terrorism' has served as an excuse for a grotesque increase in state power, especially since the New York outrage of September 2001. It has also led to the isolation and insulation of the elite from reality, in all the free countries of the world, in a way that threatens the spirit of democracy. It is hard to believe that Englishmen could once walk along Downing Street and pose on the steps of Number Ten to have their pictures taken, or that public footpaths once ran across the grounds of the Prime Minister's country residence at Chequers. These things were true surprisingly recently.

This is really the point of this chapter. I do not seek to argue here that America is a better-ordered country than England used to be. Far from it. It is an entirely different society, with many faults that nobody would wish to import. It pays a high price for its widespread illegal gun ownership, for it is, as usual, the illegal and uncontrolled weapons that are almost exclusively the ones used in crimes. The country is so enormous and often so sparsely populated that the sort of police presence once achieved in England would never have been possible outside a few cities. Thus it requires and accepts a great deal more independence from its citizens.

Nor would the best solution to our problems be mass gun owner-ship by the middle class, although I fear that it will not be long before there is an increasing demand for something of the kind. In our mainly urban and suburban society there should be no need for every home to contain a gun. We are, after all, supposed to have a police force and the rule of law. I believe that a return to preventive policing and to the idea of the punishment of wicked actions, together with a revival of morality and responsibility, would be a far better solution.

These things once produced a unique combination of freedom and order, and could do so again. If they fail to do so, then the former right of the free English citizen to own and use weapons in the pursuit and suppression of crime will need to be reasserted. Those who make our current laws should be aware of that. For most, the arming of the people would be a sad second-best to the revival of proper policing. However, many will soon see it as a good deal better than cowering defenceless in their homes, unable to fend off or deter the lawless predators on the streets, while unprotected by an absent and neutral police force.

There is another point here, too, concerning liberty and the nature of the criminal law. The elite state's attack on gun ownership by the respectable is irrational and actually stupid if its intention is truly to reduce crime. If the pre-1920 law of England still applied and respectable people kept guns at home in large numbers, there would almost certainly be significantly less crime despite the absence of the police from the streets. The intention of the current restrictions, however, seems to be entirely different. The modern elite state instinctively loathes gun ownership and its twin brother, the right to self-defence, for a reason it does not like to state openly. It does not, like Lloyd George, fear some sort of insurrection. But it does fear a challenge to its monopoly by responsible and active citizens who do not accept the new definition of crime, or the radical, egalitarian redrafting of the criminal law that has taken place since the cultural revolution.

If such citizens were freely to enforce the law as it once was, they would be subverting the law as it now is. If burglars were shot in mid-burglary, intruders beaten and delivered to the casualty department by their victims, vandals summarily chastised and forced to repair their damage, and rapists effectively discouraged by their armed victims, the feebleness of the official criminal justice system would be exposed and its moral relativism ridiculed. The elite state would be forced to respond to such competition by improving its own woeful efforts at law enforcement. The current policy seems to be to suppress the competition and warn it off. Citizens must be stripped of any power to defend themselves physically, since they would be defending an absolute right to property which the elite state does not fully accept. It believes that property is held conditionally, not absolutely. It follows from this that some crime is, in effect, a protest against the unfair distribution of wealth.

If the state believes that, then it cannot wholeheartedly seek to prevent such crime or desire to punish it. Nor can it permit others to do so. It must disarm and demoralize them so that they do not dare to do what comes naturally to them. It must intimidate them so that they turn away from actions that they privately believe to be right and necessary. If bold or rash individuals still defy the liberal elite state by protecting what is theirs with force, then they must be taught a severe lesson. The state, in these circumstances, will break all its own principles of moral relativism and abhorrence of punishment. It will abandon its normal methods of coaxing, endless second chances, excuse-making and rehabilitation, which are applied to ordinary transgressors. It will inflict on citizens who actively defend themselves, and on them alone, the exemplary and deterrent punishment that it refuses to employ against thieves and robbers. It will accuse robust and lawful citizens of 'taking the law into their own hands' – a phrase you could only use if you had failed to grasp that the law of England belongs to the people of England.

VI

Cruel and unusual

It requires a superman to survive 20 years of
imprisonment with character and soul intact…
I gravely doubt whether an average man can
serve more than ten continuous years in prison
without deterioration.
Sir Alexander Paterson, Commissioner of Prisons,
1930

In a Home Office museum near Rugby sits the plain, grey-painted
wooden chest that used to be sent unaccompanied by train around
the country to prisons where an execution was due. It contains the
nooses, straps and pinions used to hang murderers, all in remarkably
good condition. Anyone over fifty might have walked past this
object as it sat unguarded and unremarked on the platform of a
country railway junction. It is a strange reminder of another
England, where hardly anything was subject to much in the way of
security but where the state could and did deliberately take the
lives of murderers.

In the Home Office library, in its modern tower high above
St James's Park, they still keep a neatly printed document entitled
'Execution of Sentence of Death, Notes as to Practice', dating
mainly from 1920. To read it is to recall George Orwell's description
of England as 'an everlasting animal, stretching into the future and
the past and like all living things having the power to change out of
all recognition and yet remain the same'. The Home Office is not
only one of the oldest government departments in England. It is the
inheritor of something far older, a state rooted in the Middle Ages.

The instructions remark (in case of any doubts arising) that quartering and beheading for treason were finally abolished by

Parliament in 1870, soon after the state gave up strangling the condemned and took to breaking their necks instead. They specify the fee for hanging a man, set in 1931 at a maximum of ten guineas. Since executioners were not gentlemen, they would be reimbursed for only a third-class rail fare to and from the prison. There are detailed instructions about the stretching and testing of the rope before execution and the exact positioning of the culprit beneath the beam of the gallows.

Reassuringly, it declares that 'no serious mishap' has occurred since changes made in 1891 when there came into force a new set of instructions and a new 'table of drops'. This is a carefully calibrated chart specifying exactly how long the drop should be depending on the weight and build of the condemned man, but only going up to just over fourteen stones. It records the 'mishaps' that had taken place and the measures introduced to avoid them being repeated. They are gruesome and explain why this document was until recently an official secret:

1856   William Bousfield caught his legs against the edge of the pit at Newgate (following this legs were pinioned).

1868   Matthew Atkinson at Durham. Rope broke, drop being too long.

1878   A rope broke, owing to being too worn.

1884   Thomas Harris at Newgate, culprit's neck 'slightly torn'.

1885   John Lee, Exeter. Trap would not fall because part of the apparatus stretched under the weight of the convict. This led to testing of the drop using a bag of the same weight as the convict. In this case the sentence was commuted to life imprisonment after three attempts failed.

1885   Robert Goodall, Norwich, decapitated –

'the man had a slender neck the tissues of which had deteriorated'. A great public outcry led to subsequent executions where the drop was too short.

1888   Robert Upton at Oxford was nearly decapitated, his neck being too thin.

1891   John Conway. Prisoner wished to make a statement and the cap being raised to permit of his doing so, the rope lay against his neck instead of over the cap. This and the long drop 'caused the rope to cut into the tissues and some blood flowed'.

This was the last instance of a serious mishap.

There were several semi-religious rituals, probably introduced to satisfy the need for a ceremonial and visible event after the abolition of public executions in 1868. Until 1902 a black flag was hoisted over the prison after each hanging. Until 1901 the prison bell (or the bell of the neighbouring church) was tolled for fifteen minutes before the execution. After 1901 the bell was not rung until after the condemned man was dead. The prison chaplain did not, as was widely believed, read the full burial service to the prisoner before he was hanged. For those used to the immense delays in executions in modern America, it is the following brisk instruction that will be most surprising: 'Executions should take place in the week following the third Sunday after the day on which the sentence is passed, any weekday but Monday, and at 8 a.m.'

The document records a curious rummage through ancient archives after *The Times* suggested in May 1916, the height of the First World War and soon after the Easter Rising in Dublin, that traitors should be executed in public. The newspaper claimed that the law still allowed it. Civil servants then looked through records of state trials from 1300 to 1600. They discovered just how recently various medieval practices had been abolished. An Act of 1814 did away with drawing (the removal of the condemned man's intestines, generally while he was still alive and before his eyes), the ancient punishment for treason. It substituted quartering, the cutting of the traitor's body into quarters after death and their display in various parts of the country after having been boiled in pitch, a form of state terror last widely used after the bloody assizes of 1685. This, along with the dragging of the condemned man to the scaffold lashed to a hurdle, was not finally abolished by Parliament until 1870. Officials came to the conclusion that the public execution of traitors was not permitted by law even if it had been a good idea, which they thought it was not.

The Home Office document explains how English law managed to prevent public or press witnesses from attending executions, as they are still permitted to do in the USA. The power to grant permission to attend was originally vested in the Justices of the Peace, who were independent of the prison authorities and the government. For some years after the abolition of public hangings, witnesses were allowed to attend closed executions. In 1877, however, the power was transferred to the Home Office's Prison Commissioners who, not surprisingly given the ugly incidents recorded above, simply refused almost all applications.

In the same library is an equally fascinating pamphlet, marked 'Strictly Secret' and evidently prepared by a senior civil servant asked to provide a case for the retention of the gallows. It is an eerie memento of an age when the British official class still had conservative instincts and reflexes, and could defend them with reason and without shame. It is entitled 'Death Sentence: Question of Abolition' and dated 1924. Possibly it was written to answer questions raised by the new Labour government that was about to take office. It reaches deep into the past, pointing out that hanging was far less common in former times than most people believed. In the seven years before 1811, of 1872 persons committed to the Old Bailey for offences other than murder only one suffered death.

It quotes Mr Justice O'Hagan, who favoured abolition in the

hearings before the 1864–6 Royal Commission on Capital Punishment. Even so, he predicted that such a change would disrupt the entire penal system: 'The substitution of a minor penalty would render essential serious modifications to the discipline and machinery of our prisons; and such modifications, while I believe them to be possible, may be difficult, and remain to be devised.' This warning was entirely accurate. The English penal system has still to develop an alternative to execution or to overcome the serious sentence-inflation that followed the abolition of hanging. The character of the prisons has also changed, in many ways for the worse.

The document dismisses the argument that executing killers shows a want of respect for human life, citing the great libertarian reformer John Stuart Mill's pro-hanging speech to Parliament in April 1868. Mill asked: 'Does fining a criminal show want of respect for property, or imprisoning him, for personal freedom?' And it cites Dr Samuel Johnson's similar defence of the penalty as being justified by the special, irreversible horror of murder. 'This terror should therefore be reserved as the last resort of prohibitory sanctions, and placed before the treasure of life to guard from invasion what cannot be restored.' It recalls some of the horrible suggestions for alternatives to execution. The Howard League for Penal Reform would probably not wish to be reminded of John Howard's suggestion: life imprisonment with an annual whipping. The then Earl Russell's liberal version of mercy was a long term of separate confinement 'followed by another term of hard labour and hard fare'.

Returning to 1924, the official raises what has always been the strongest practical objection to abolition, the risk that ordinary criminals would add murder to other crimes: 'They might also operate in gangs. There is already such a tendency, e.g. bank raids, post office raids, motor burglaries etc but murder is usually avoided. There would not be the same inducement to avoid it if capital punishment were abolished.' He made this prophecy, perhaps still to be borne out: 'Not only would the criminals be freer to shoot, but everyone else would be freer to shoot them. The disposition to take extreme measures to protect others or oneself might be aroused in most unlikely quarters.' And he hit on a grave difficulty at the heart of the abolitionist case, assuming that the abolitionist is seeking, as he claims to be, to avoid the needless deaths of innocent people. If the state does not kill, will fewer die, or more? And if more die, is that any better? In the end, the author of the paper, who does not identify himself but whose initials are given as 'A. L.', clearly concluded, against his own personal sentiments, that abolition would be a mistake, writing: 'I could not suggest it though, temperamentally, I am an abolitionist. I could not even consider it seriously again until more cogent facts and arguments are adduced and some feasible and sufficient substitute proposed.'

The debate about abolition was, like prison reform, a nineteenth-century quarrel that persisted into the twentieth century and now seems likely to carry on well into the twenty-first. Before the Second World War the political ruling classes were still divided on this subject. Even the left was not, as it is now, unanimously for abolition. Since the populace was of one mind, in favour of retention, change was long delayed. A Commons committee in the briefly Labour-dominated Parliament of 1930 produced nothing but an explosive row and claims of unfairness. Six of its fifteen members walked out after the abolitionist majority refused them permission to publish a minority report in favour of retention. It was only in the years after the end of the war that the present elite prejudice against hanging took hold of the entire Labour Party.

Old-fashioned England's last stand in favour of capital punishment took place in 1948, when the ancient forces of conservatism still had just enough grip and determination to prevent abolition. The battle led to events close to a constitutional crisis. On 14 April 1948 abolition of hanging was written into the Criminal Justice Bill in a free vote in the House of Commons. At that time of huge Labour majorities there were clear signs that much of the Labour movement was not in favour of the reform. Perhaps Labour ministers and MPs also feared they would be punished at the polls if they got rid of the gallows in a clearly partisan vote. The majority was a mere twenty-three in an ill-attended House with half the Cabinet missing, presumably seeking to abstain.

Not all the Labour front bench were covert abolitionists afraid of unpopularity. Some actively favoured the noose. Present-day left-wing admirers of Clement Attlee and Ernest Bevin should note that they voted to keep the gallows, going into the lobbies alongside Winston Churchill. The Labour Home Secretary, Chuter Ede, spoke powerfully for retention, saying that criminals attempting to escape arrest were using more and more violence, and it was only through luck that there were not more murders. Although the bill was still a long way from royal assent, the government made it clear that, under such circumstances, the death penalty could not be carried out. It was officially suspended.

In June, Lord Goddard, the Lord Chief Justice, took advantage of a debate in the House of Lords to accuse Chuter Ede of acting unconstitutionally by suspending the penalty. Stirred by his intervention, the Lords voted by 181 to twenty-eight to restore hanging. The Bishops of Durham and Winchester and the Archbishop of York supported restoration, actions unthinkable today, although their attitude is explicitly sanctioned by Article Thirty-Seven of the Church's Thirty-Nine Articles. This robust clause authorizes the state to punish 'grievous or heinous crimes' with death. The Commons then voted for a complex compromise which the Lords threw out after several distinguished judges publicly described it as unworkable. As a result, after some parliamentary shuffling, the penalty was restored and the black cap was brought back into use on 17 June 1948.

In the intervening weeks (as noted in Chapter 5 on gun control), Britain had a brief and interesting experience of what abolition would be like. Death sentences were still passed, but everyone knew that the Home Secretary would automatically grant a

reprieve. On 21 April 1948 Mr Justice Hilbery refused to don the traditional black cap and white gloves to pass sentence of death on
Donald George Thomas at the Old Bailey because the Home
Secretary had suspended the death penalty and the ceremony was
therefore a dishonest mockery.

Until this moment English courts had used the same ritual
without a break for hundreds of years. Its solemnity and harshness
are notably absent from modern courts, but it is worth recording the
actual procedure. The sheriff's vicar, an ordained minister, took up
his place behind the judge on the dais. The usher then called out:
'My Lords, the King's Justices do strictly require and command all
persons to keep silence whilst sentence of death is passed on the
prisoner, upon pain of imprisonment. God Save the King.' Once
sentence of death had been pronounced, the vicar intoned 'Amen'
and the judge added: 'and may the Lord have mercy on your soul'.
This form, little changed since the Middle Ages and probably quite
recognizable to a time-traveller from the sixteenth century, was still
practised in an England of jet aircraft, telephones, television, peni-
cillin and the National Health Service. It was also an England of
minimal crime and infrequent murder, where the illegal use of guns
was almost unknown. However, its survival was only temporary.

The first step towards final abolition was taken by Chuter Ede,
who set up a Royal Commission on Capital Punishment in 1949.
(He would himself eventually become an abolitionist, largely out of
regret for having refused to reprieve Timothy Evans, later proved
innocent, although doubts have since been cast on this.) Its report
was inconclusive. It was bound to be. International comparisons are
very difficult to make because of differing definitions of murder.
The effect of abolition elsewhere is also difficult to compute
because it often follows a long period during which the penalty has
been suspended or rarely used. The deterrence argument cannot
be proved either way without lengthy experimental periods – of
execution, its absence and its return – which are politically difficult
to arrange, at least deliberately.

However, the Commission's arguments were the framework for the compromise Homicide Act of 1957. This abolished the rule under which all members of a gang would hang if one of them committed a murder. It also declared that a killing during the commission of a felony was not murder unless it could be proved that the killing was intentional. Those changes removed major theoretical deterrents to armed and violent robbery, and their possible impact on the crime figures is discussed in Chapter 5.

One thing that emerges clearly from the Commission's research is that the English system carried out a surprisingly small number of executions compared with the number of murderers it convicted. This is largely because England had no system of degrees of murder but (except in cases of insanity) required that all convicted murderers should be sentenced to death. Responsibility then passed to the Home Secretary who wielded the royal prerogative of reprieve. The evidence suggests that most occupants of this post were generous with mercy and hated the duty and the burden. It might even be that the fact that the final decision between life and death rested with a political friend or colleague – and might one day fall to themselves – eventually influenced MPs in the direction of abolition. Juries also disliked having to find murderers guilty, although they dutifully did so in many cases, helped by the knowledge that their decision was very likely to be overturned.

Jury recommendations of mercy led to reprieves in 74 per cent of cases (68 per cent of men and 95 per cent of women), while reprieves were granted to 28 per cent of those who were not recommended to mercy (27 per cent of men and 57 per cent of women). Among the reasons for granting mercy were 'pitiable circumstances' (often covering destitute mothers who had killed their babies, or the survivors of suicide pacts), extreme youth, provocation, jealousy, absence of malice or premeditation, and mental abnormality. The Commission accepted that many juries brought in verdicts of manslaughter because they did not think that the death penalty was appropriate, even though they knew that there was an almost even chance of the sentence not being carried out. For the fifty years before 1948 no fewer than 45 per cent of those sentenced to death had been reprieved.

As the Commission said, the penalty 'falls very far short of a threat of instant and certain death to every murderer'. From 1900 to 1949, 7454 murders were known to the police in England and Wales. In 1674 cases the suspect committed suicide; 4173 persons were arrested on suspicion of murder and 3129 sent for trial at assizes. Of those sent for trial, 658 were acquitted or not tried, 428 were found insane and 798 guilty but insane. Of those convicted, thirty-five were sentenced to penal servitude for life or detention at Her Majesty's pleasure, and 1210 sentenced to death. Of those, twenty-three had their convictions quashed on appeal, forty-seven were certified insane and 606 were reprieved. Out of all these thousands, 632 convicted murderers (621 men and eleven women) were actually executed for murder. There was therefore only one execution for every twelve murders known to the police. These totals are not startlingly different from those recorded in the final third of the nineteenth century, when murders known to the police never rose above 190 in any year, death sentences ranged between fifteen and forty, and actual executions between five and twenty-five.

Perhaps because the public was satisfied that the worst killers were being executed, those reprieved often did not have very long to serve. In 1866 the minimum term for a 'life' sentence was set at twenty years. By the end of the nineteenth century twenty years had come to be regarded as the maximum. Fifteen years became normal. Between the wars, the average was quietly reduced further so that by 1939 most life-sentence prisoners were released after between ten and thirteen years. During the war it was reduced to six to ten years, although terms were lengthening in the post-war period. Some, including 'mercy killers' and suicide pact survivors, were released after one, two or three years. Most seem to have been released after serving between seven and eleven years.

At this time, violent offences by released murderers were extremely rare (only one committed a murder during the 1900 to 1949 period). The Commission was reluctant to recommend very long prison sentences as an alternative to hanging. They recalled the words of the Prison Commissioner Sir Alexander Paterson in evidence to a Commons Select Committee in 1930: 'It requires a superman to survive 20 years of imprisonment with character and soul intact... I gravely doubt whether an average man can serve more than ten continuous years in prison without deterioration.'

The 1957 Homicide Act was the inconclusive result of an inconclusive report. It neither abolished nor strengthened the death penalty. It was introduced in November 1956 by the Tory Home Secretary, Major Gwilym Lloyd-George, who noted that there had been no executions for sixteen months. Its main changes were that killings by abnormal people, or under severe verbal provocation or in pursuance of suicide pacts, would be considered to be manslaughter. The murder of police and prison officers, and murder by shooting or by causing an explosion, remained murder. Killing in the course of a felony would not be murder unless it could be proved that it was done intentionally. Most important of all, an accomplice would not be guilty of murder unless he used violence himself. Lloyd-George predicted that the measure would reduce the number of capital sentences passed by three-quarters – that the annual number of murder convictions would fall from twenty-five to six and executions from thirteen to four.

Judging from later debates, many MPs appear to have believed that the Act would effectively end the death penalty while officially retaining it. This would have been a deception of the public, but by the 1960s much of the criminal justice system was already designed to persuade voters into thinking that the law was stronger than it actually was. Major Lloyd-George's hopes were partly disappointed. The Act came into force on 21 March 1957. In the previous year there had been thirty-two murder convictions. In 1957 there were forty, in 1958 thirty, in 1959 forty-two, in 1960 forty-two and in

1961 fifty-one. The killers convicted of 'manslaughter due to diminished responsibility', who would have faced murder charges under the old law, climbed from eleven to forty-one between 1957 and 1964. However, in the final years of hanging, the number of executions per year rarely rose above two. In the whole period between 1946 and 1964, fewer than two hundred murderers were executed, an average of about ten per year, with the highest tally being eighteen executions in 1951.

It was plain in the post-1957 years that the governing class had lost their nerve and will. They doubted their religion and their right to rule. They no longer believed in the rightness or the effectiveness of the death sentence. Those disposed to do evil deeds were quick to scent weakness, as they always are. As Chapter 5 shows, this decline in confidence was accompanied by important changes in criminal behaviour, which may or may not have been caused by changes in the law. Such a link cannot easily be proved, however tempting it might be to assume that the connection was direct. However, it cannot simply be dismissed as meaningless by any reasonable or honest person. The abolitionists had the argument all their own way in the 1960s because most people believed the world was moving into a new era of peace and civilization, and they wanted them to be right. Few conservatives were prepared to challenge them on moral grounds. Now that the abolitionists' victory has been followed by a grave increase in homicides, serious woundings and armed and violent crimes of all kinds, they ought to be asked to restate their case. And if they are honest and fair, they ought to be willing, as the retentionists eventually were, to put their theories to the test of experience.

Abolitionists tend to assert that capital punishment is not a deterrent. They act as if there were nothing further to say. The case is closed on this aspect of the debate because they say so. Many supporters of hanging have asserted, with equal force, that it is a deterrent. They know it is, or think they do. There is no dialogue between these positions, only bombardment. The argument is actually much more complicated and both sides have much to prove. The first point that needs to be resolved is this: if hanging is a deterrent, what exactly does it deter? It is absurd to suggest that it deters murder as such, since many murders, committed in scenes of domestic misery or rage, could not be deterred by anything – never were and never will be.

However, it is reasonable to suggest that hanging alters the behaviour of the career criminal or the calculating conspirator. This sort of deterrence does not affect just murder, but also forms of crime that might accidentally or unintentionally lead to a murder charge. The pre-1957 penalty might have deterred the carrying of weapons by gangs of robbers, because all of them might hang on account of a killing perpetrated by one of them. It might have deterred the carrying of weapons by individuals, because it treated any killing in the course of a crime as being a murder. It was also more credible than the post-1957 law because more executions took place.

Colin Greenwood's figures on armed and violent robbery (see Chapter 5) do coincide quite remarkably with the suspension of the death penalty, with its weakening and with its abolition. It is worth noting that in the very different circumstances of the USA, 90 per cent of murders prior to the abolition of the death penalty in 1966 were 'crimes of passion'. Since then, such crimes have declined to 70 per cent of murders, suggesting that it was 'stranger murders', committed at random or in pursuit of other crimes, that may have been deterred by the death penalty.

The homicide tables themselves are less striking, but should worry anyone who thinks there is no connection between the abolition of hanging and the number of unlawful killings. Once hanging was abolished, the distinctions between different sorts of killing became less important. Anecdotal evidence from the courts suggests that many killers who might once have been charged with murder are charged with manslaughter in order to save time in overcrowded crown courts. It would be invidious to say more, but if this is true it would help to explain important shifts in the statistics over the last thirty years. The dates are chosen because of the significant changes in homicide law in 1957 and 1965.

In 1956 there were ninety-four convictions for homicide in England and Wales. Of these, eleven were for infanticide, fifty-one for manslaughter and thirty-two for murder. The 1957 Act introduced the new fourth category of 'manslaughter due to diminished responsibility', among its other changes. In 1958 there were 113 homicide convictions – ten for infanticide, forty-eight for manslaughter, twenty-five for manslaughter with diminished responsibility and thirty for murder. By 1964 there were 170 homicide convictions, – twelve for infanticide, seventy-three for manslaughter, forty-one for manslaughter with diminished responsibility and forty-four for murder. In 1966, out of 254 homicide convictions, there were twenty-two for infanticide, 109 for manslaughter, fifty-one for diminished responsibility and seventy-two for murder. By 1975, when there were 377 homicide convictions, eight were for infanticide, 196 for manslaughter, sixty-six for diminished responsibility and 107 for murder. In 1985, of a total of 441 homicide convictions, three were for infanticide, 200 for manslaughter, sixty-five for diminished responsibility and 173 for murder. These later figures suggest that diminished responsibility, once an important category, is no longer significant because sentences are in general lower and manslaughter charges more readily preferred. Despite this, the actual number of murders has risen significantly.

Even this turns out to be misleading. The situation is really much worse. If it were not for superb emergency medical services, the national murder rate would be in the thousands and possibly comparable to the American figure. Taking the raw homicide totals – the numbers of homicides actually committed rather than the convictions as shown above – the rise between 1976 and 1996 was significant but not astonishing. It went up from 616 to 745. Attempted murder cases in the same period rose far more sharply, from 155 to 634. And instances of the serious offence of 'wounding to endanger life' doubled from 5885 to 10,445.

These figures suggest that advanced medical techniques are saving many lives that would once have been lost. Human wickedness and murderous behaviour have increased vastly, but human mercy and ingenuity have, so far, outpaced them. Doctors are now capable of saving the lives of men who have been stabbed through the heart. Not long ago, a knife in the arm might well have been fatal because of infection, sepsis or other complications. It is reasonable to think that the knife-wielding assailants do not know how good their victims' chances of receiving such treatment are. It is very possible that they do not care. It is therefore just as reasonable to add these crimes to the tally of those that might have been deterred by a death penalty but are certainly not being deterred now.

An experimental return of the death penalty, during which its opponents agreed not to obstruct it with technicalities or delays, might actually prove or disprove the alleged connection between capital punishment and deterrence. If certain sorts of crime increase in the absence of the penalty and decrease on its return, then a connection between the two seems highly likely. It has been absent now for almost forty years and the world has changed much in this long time. Even so, a ten-year test of a pre-1957 type of law would show conclusively whether the link exists, for we would then have three lengthy periods – before, during and after abolition – for which comparable crime figures would be available.

Here is a unique chance, under agreed and fair conditions, to resolve the question. (Some might argue that such an experiment would be unethical and cynical – but could it possibly be more unethical and cynical than leaving matters as they are today in the knowledge that we might be needlessly abandoning our society to unchained violence?) Whichever side of the argument was disproved would then have to be abandoned. Either capital punishment would be shown to be an essential weapon in the hands of a just state, or the argument for hanging would be demolished forever and could never be revived in a rational society.

The abolitionists will never permit such a test to take place. They have a well-founded fear that it would go against them. And they have no wish to discuss the moral case against execution, for it is laughably inconsistent and goes to the heart of the attempt to replace the English criminal law with an alien code. The way in which the death penalty was finally abolished is described in detail in my *Abolition of Britain*. It is important to remember that at the time the abolitionists had all the best tunes and no record to defend. The world believed in general progress and saw the gallows as a dark relic of a wicked past. It had yet to experience the disappointments and setbacks of social reform. The retentionists, on the other hand, were weakened by several real or alleged miscarriages of justice. And, in the way of English conservatives, they had been in power so long that they had got out of the habit of using reason to defend their instinctive beliefs. They were taken by surprise and overwhelmed because they did not think that they needed to argue for what was obvious to them. If the argument were now staged again on equal terms, the liberal elite would have to be a good deal clearer about the gulf that lies between them and the English people on the whole issue of criminal law.

The socialist left, who have in recent years been the main body of the anti-hanging movement, pose as the righteous opponents of the gallows. Their opposition to the death penalty for murder runs deep, although most of their arguments are easily challenged. The suggestion that the death penalty is 'barbaric' is often made. This claim ignores the sad truth that, when you abolish the gallows, something else arises to take its place, for which you are equally responsible and which may be worse than what was there before. Yet the abolitionists have always refused to think about this problem, believing the goodness of their cause makes such tedious detailed consideration unnecessary.

Murder is a crime of unique horror. No justice system can treat it lightly. The favoured alternative, long years of imprisonment, can hardly be called civilized. In the growing knowledge that prisons are squalid hellholes run by the inmates, the cry that 'hanging is too good for him' is frequently heard from people who actively hope that the convicted man will suffer persecution from his fellow prisoners. One liberal columnist on a left-wing daily newspaper openly made this suggestion. Writing in the *Mirror* on 18 July 2000, referring to the murder of Sarah Payne, a small child, Brian Reade wrote:

> I don't believe and I never will believe in capital
> punishment. It is civilised society stooping to the level
> of the depraved. And cases like Sarah's only confirm
> my belief.
>   If they catch whoever did it, hanging is too good
> for him. A life spent dodging razor blades in his food,
> needing an armed guard whenever he takes a shower,
> fearing every night if he will get his throat slashed
> tomorrow is more fitting punishment for the most
> cowardly of human beings.

What could be more barbaric than consciously and intentionally abandoning a human being to the self-righteous justice of a criminal mob? But is life imprisonment especially civilized anyway? Even if our prisons were models of ordered and purposeful tranquillity, long years of confinement have a terrible effect on the human spirit. Thanks to the abolition of the death penalty, there are many more prisoners now serving very long sentences and their deterioration is a major problem for the authorities.

The police have also begun using weapons far more frequently since (and perhaps because of) the abolition of hanging. In London, many police cars are permanently equipped with guns and a growing number of officers wear holsters. When the Nottinghamshire force experimented with armed officers on a crime-prone housing estate in Nottingham during 2001, the most shocking thing about the event was the public's lack of surprise. Officers are frequently seen carrying sub-machine guns at airports and even outside courthouses, and the English public, which would once have been appalled by the sight, is now accustomed to it. England is now halfway to becoming a society where both criminals and police are armed. While predictions are difficult, we could be slowly approaching the American state of affairs. There, hundreds of suspects are killed each year by armed police officers and hundreds more by armed householders. Why is an armed police force, which must shoot and kill without due process, without jury trial or appeal or the possibility of reprieve, more civilized and less barbaric than hanging after due process?

The weakness of their claim to be more civilized has led abolitionists to advance practical objections to execution. They are feeble and without force or principle, and are certainly not arguments for abolishing an effective and morally potent weapon in the armoury of free nations. One example is the claim that too few rich people tend to be executed given the numbers of wealthy murderers who are convicted. This is quite possible, though arguable. But if it were so, the problem could be solved by executing more rich murderers. It is not a principled objection to execution itself. Again, with the argument that too many of those executed are black – perhaps so, but in that case let us ensure that we execute more white murderers.

Wrongful execution is certainly a problem and certainly happens, but, as we shall see, it is not really an argument against capital punishment. To illustrate its weakness, here is a typical quotation from one notable abolitionist: 'I do feel that the risk of a man being sentenced to death and hanged wrongly is a risk which is sufficiently serious to provide a very strong argument against the continuance of capital punishment.' Parody and caricature often help to simplify a point. The speaker in this case was one Denis Nowell Pritt, KC, giving evidence to the 1930 Select Committee on Capital Punishment. Pritt (1887–1972) was a communist fellow-traveller. He would spend much of the following four decades justifying and explaining Stalin's show-trials and the behaviour of the Soviet Union. There is now evidence that he may well have been a secret agent of the NKVD. There was almost nothing the Kremlin did that he would not defend, even including Moscow's embarrassing attempt to conquer Finland in 1940.

Pritt was prepared to accept wrongful execution and mass murder of political and class opponents condemned in servile and lawless show-trials, by a state of which he approved. Yet he opposed the execution of criminals condemned by lawful trials before independent juries, by a state of which he disapproved. His views were rewarded and valued by those whom he served so well. Had this country ever become a communist state, he would no doubt have been one of its high legal officials, perhaps the prosecutor at show-trials held to dispatch the old regime's supporters to death administered by bullets in the backs of their necks.

Much valued by the communist hierarchy, this crusader against the English gallows was garlanded with Soviet and Warsaw Pact honours for his loyal service in bad times and worse ones. He was awarded the Lenin Peace Prize in 1954, the 'Freedom' of the (East German) city of Leipzig in 1957, and an honorary degree in 'law' from the Charles University of Prague in the same year. All the states involved practised the death penalty on their political opponents, often on the flimsiest of evidence, always without juries or the presumption of innocence, and without clemency or mercy. It is fair to say that Pritt's opposition to the death penalty and to wrongful execution was limited and inconsistent. He is an extreme example, but not a misleading one, of the left's confused view of execution.

In essence, the idealist left has often been ready to excuse or justify judicial killings in pursuit of what it sees as a just cause. Even those who rejected Stalinist Russia generally did so only after long periods when it was quite obvious that it was using execution as a political tool and they could not have been unaware of this. In the post-war world, many socialists who believed themselves more civilized than Stalinists have been willing to defend the Castro regime in Cuba, which has also employed show-trials and political execution. Many have defended the Chinese dictatorship, which certainly executed its opponents and critics, and which even today uses the death penalty against a wide variety of alleged criminals after inadequate trials. Vietnam, another regime that the left is inclined to protect, has in recent years used public executions to dispose of allegedly corrupt businessmen, who have whole lemons stuffed into their mouths to silence them before they are shot in public by firing-squads. Could the selective outrage of the anti-execution lobby be the result of the belief that some forms of execution are more objectionable than others? Could it be that the morality of leftist-liberalism sanctions killings in the name of the socialist elite state but objects to them in the name of a common law based on Christianity?

The USA, for all its faults, does not hold public executions and insists on two jury hearings and a long series of appeals before any murderer can be executed. Liberal leftists like to say that they object to execution in the USA because it is a democracy. However, it is precisely because the USA is a democracy that it has restored the death penalty.

In recent years, the USA's refusal to abandon the death penalty has become a large political issue in the European Union which uses it, quite rightly, to help define the important differences between the EU and the USA. These are well summed up by the distinction between a common law system, where the law serves the people, and a Code Napoléon system, where the law serves the state. This is not just a technical matter. It is a deep and crucial division between the two rival systems, which explains much else that is distinct about them. This is why England's current transition from common law to Continental corpus juris is proving so painful and so difficult.

No doubt most of the leftist-liberal campaigners against execution are genuinely tender about the subject and do not wish to see a soul harmed. However, their inconsistency, and their complete inability to notice that they are inconsistent, are significant. To admit to these faults would be to concede defeat in the main argument. Therefore the safest thing to do is to ignore the contradictions and keep claiming the moral supremacy in the hope that nobody will notice the truth.

Principled opposition to the taking of innocent life is exactly that. It cannot allow exceptions. Yet the great social experiments that such people have always supported take innocent life in great numbers. And their modern equivalent, 'progressive' military interventions in the Balkans or Afghanistan, could not be attempted without accepting the need for a number of innocent deaths. When these deaths take place, some on the left do feel and express an honest outrage at them. Many of the most telling reports of the aerial slaughter of non-combatants in Kosovo and Afghanistan came from the pens of the left and were published in newspapers of the left.

However, no general conclusion about the righteousness of killing innocents in a good cause was reached in the Vaticans and synods of the new elite theology. The thing could not be thought through without exposing its false logic. The new generation of self-christened 'hard liberals' baldly insisted that such things must be accepted as part of the price of the new world order that they are seeking. This is a respectable position, easily understood by conservative supporters of the death penalty. It is another part of the long argument over the limits of just warfare. However, it is simply not compatible with principled opposition to the use of the death penalty against convicted murderers, who are much less likely to be innocent than the accidental victims of inaccurate high-level bombing or wrongly targeted cruise missiles.

Many other public policy decisions cause innocent deaths, with much less justification than the Kosovo intervention. The early release of convicted murderers leads to four deaths each year on average, because some of these people kill again once freed. The 'care in the community' policy, of releasing mentally ill people from asylums and relying on them to take unsupervised regular doses of mind-altering drugs, leads to frequent homicide and bereavement when these poor abandoned creatures go berserk in public places.

It is possible to argue that British government transport policy, which depends on the existence of an astonishingly easy driving test, leads indirectly to thousands of deaths because of the incompetent drivers it allows on to the roads. After all, many of the approximately three and a half thousand deaths each year on UK roads could be avoided if it were not so easy to have legal charge over a lethal machine. If the elite state were truly against the killing of innocents, it would have to make many changes in the way the country is run. In none of these areas is the possibility of innocent death seen as a reason for abandoning a policy generally seen as beneficial – to the world, to the economy, to freedom of movement.

The left's objection to capital punishment is a smokescreen. Nobody who wields power is genuinely and absolutely opposed to the killing of innocents. The real questions are: how many innocents and for what purpose must they die? This calculation is a regrettable necessity of power, although a necessity for which authority can usually avoid direct blame. Pilot error, 'friendly fire', poor intelligence, excessive police zeal and so forth are generally cited as the reasons for this failure of benevolence.

Suicides in prison, which across the EU are at least as common as executions in the USA, are presumably also innocent deaths. Even so, because they are the indirect result of the justice system, they are deemed acceptable. So are shootings of suspects by the police. For the elite particularly dislike the direct responsibility that governments and ministers must take for executions. Most Home Secretaries, even Conservative ones, become abolitionists for selfish reasons. They hate having direct power over life or death and they fear they may misuse it. The Tory Michael Howard, supposed by the liberal left to be the blackest reactionary ever to hold the office of Home Secretary, declared that the danger of wrongful execution had made him an abolitionist.

Other leading pro-hanging Tories have been heroes in safety, calling in public for restoration but never allowing it to become an election issue or a manifesto pledge. That might actually compel them to bring it back. The political class, in all the major parties, has been careful to avoid this, and many must have hoped that the issue was closed for good when Parliament voted, supposedly by accident, to end Britain's exemption from the European Convention on Human Rights, which had until then allowed her to restore the death penalty if she chose to do so.

In totalitarian countries for which the left has sympathy the arguments of necessity are usually sufficient. Omelettes cannot be made without breaking eggs. The truth is that, for vast goals of social improvement and nation-building, modern leftism is perfectly happy to permit the killing of innocents. The older leftism was even happier to do so, as the Pritts and their comrades chorused their mitigations of the Gulag and the Great Terror, the Great Leap Forward, the Thousand Flowers and the forgotten Havana show-trials at the start of the Castro dictatorship. Then why is it so bitterly opposed to the killing of a small number of murderers, most of them unquestionably guilty?

The death penalty is loathed by the liberal elite partly because it is popular but mainly because it is the keystone of a criminal justice system that rests on the idea that each of us is responsible for his own actions. It is not idealist at all. It is anti-Marxist and anti-Freudian at once, and so especially hard for them to bear. The old English system believed that evil deeds should be punished on principle, not to take revenge but to impose justice on men who had committed the worst of all crimes, the uniquely wicked act of murder, the supreme outcome of the arrogant selfishness that comes from immorality. Some murders, especially those of children, are so heinous that society requires such a demonstration.

For execution also pre-empted and prevented blood feuds and the private vengeance known as lynch law. A presage of what might now come about took place in Manchester in March 1998 when a mainly female mob kicked and stabbed Stephen Mills to death because they suspected him of being a burglar. Mr Mills, a schizophrenic, had earlier been forced to flee his house by another mob. An eyewitness of this under-reported incident described how 'It was like a pack of wild animals hunting their prey. He ran behind a house and they went after him. One had a baseball bat and you could hear the sound of it hitting him. He was screaming.' The old law accepted that it had taken away the right of vengeance from individuals precisely because it sought to avoid such scenes. It must therefore offer them strong and convincing justice as a substitute. It also sought to make potential murderers fear that they might themselves die.

Logically, the liberal elite must stand against both retribution and deterrence, because both are founded on the idea that individual moral choice is possible and may be influenced for the better by fear. Modern liberalism believes that the murderer has killed because of his background and circumstances, and that his crime is just one more argument for a better society, to be achieved by higher taxation and greater state authority over everyone. In a way, the repressive notion of gun control is liberalism's answer to conservative calls for the death penalty. But the liberal solution restricts the lives and self-defence of everyone, while the conservative answer menaces only a tiny number.

Retribution and deterrence are also based on the idea that there are absolute standards of right and wrong, which cannot be altered by economic or social conditions. The elite state cannot accept this argument. If it is true, the elite state's own existence is unjustified. It similarly dislikes the religious element of the penalty which assumes that a man's soul might be more important than his life. The state, which believes it can improve a man's life but that he has no soul, sees execution as a failure and a reproach to its own goodness. It would rather the killer were rehabilitated and reconciled than that he died, even if he died repentant. As long as he continues to live, that hope of reconciliation is alive.

One of the most enthralling paradoxes of British judicial history is that of Lord Goddard, a judge reviled by liberals for his support for the death penalty and his willingness to impose it. Goddard was also the judge whose instinctively libertarian ruling forced the government to abolish the oppressive system of identity cards which it had sought to continue in peacetime in defiance of its own promises. Few English judges have struck a greater blow for freedom in the twentieth century. Goddard's support for the hanging of murderers is entirely consistent with his opposition to the surveillance state. And the current government's desire to restrict the liberty of the subject is entirely consistent with its instinctive opposition to the death penalty.

As to the American issue, America now being the only Western democracy that employs the death penalty, it is unwise to deduce too much from what happens there. The USA's crime problems, complicated by racial and cultural divisions, are so different from Britain's that parallels should only be suggested with care. However, opponents of capital punishment constantly repeat the claim that its existence in America makes no difference to homicide rates. They say that there is no noticeable distinction between states that have the penalty and those that do not. This would not actually be very surprising. Most of the states that officially maintain the death penalty use it only very rarely and very slowly. Liberal elitists among judges and lawyers delay executions by every legal means. Even if someone is sentenced to death, he is far more likely to die of old age awaiting execution than he is to be judicially killed.

Only one state, Texas, has achieved a speed and quantity of executions likely to be credible to rational criminals. The Houston urban area is the scene of most murders in Texas, and most of those executed come from there. Between 1982, when Texas resumed executions, and 1996, Houston's homicide rate fell by 63 per cent. In the same period, the US national homicide rate declined by 19 per cent. Across the whole state the figures are equally interesting. In 1991 its murder rate was 15.3 per thousand, the second highest in the country. By 1999, according to research by William Tucker published in the Washington *Weekly Standard* in August 2001, it had fallen to 6.9 per thousand, close to the national average of 5.7 per thousand. Florida, which rivals Texas in willingness to execute, has seen its murder rate fall from 10.7 per thousand in 1990 to 5.7 per thousand in 1999. Contrast New Mexico, which does not execute. The state began the 1990s with a murder rate of 9.2 per thousand and ended it with a rate of 9.8 per thousand.

The civilized case for capital punishment is strong. The liberal case against it is remarkably weak and has been allowed to stand unchallenged for too long. A rational society concerned to reduce its levels of violent and armed crime would give a serious and careful hearing to the pro-death-penalty argument. Britain's elite state is not willing to do so. It treats supporters of the death penalty as political lepers and pariahs whose arguments are morally contemptible. There is no clearer proof that those who wish to be 'tough on the causes of crime' cannot also be tough on crime itself.

There is one other worrying aspect to this argument. The death penalty is only acceptable under certain specific circumstances. These are due process, jury trial, the right of appeal and the existence of an unfettered free press able to expose miscarriage of justice and see that it is punished. Any conservative supporter of capital punishment would withdraw his support if these conditions were absent. The danger is that the elite state, seeking desperate remedies as its egalitarian policies continue to encourage the growth of crime and disorder, will eventually reach for the death penalty – but without these safeguards. The history of idealist and revolutionary regimes suggests that this is more than possible. I venture to predict here that, if the message of this book is not heeded, something of the kind will eventually happen in socialist England and perhaps across the European Union. In that case, the author of this book will certainly be prominent among those campaigning against execution.

VII

Evil drug-dealers

The war on drugs, if it was ever fought, was lost in the late 1960s when the authorities stopped disapproving of them. The struggle against narcotics is a moral crusade or it is nothing. A morally literate people would not want to stupefy themselves. The only thing that the law can do about drug-taking is to encourage and reinforce a generally accepted moral message, that this action is wrong and wicked. It can disapprove and by doing so strengthen the will of the individual tempted to buy. It can punish and so reinforce the message of parent and teacher that this is one of the things the wise person should not do.

The liberal elite, however, has never really felt that it is wicked to seek chemical oblivion. Many of its members have used illegal drugs in the past. Many have children or friends who use them now. Commander Brian Paddick, the extraordinary policeman who stalks through these pages as an exemplar of so much that is wrong, admitted in March 2002 that his homosexual lover had smoked cannabis in his presence. It is tempting to wonder how many other members of the new ruling class have had similar experiences.

That ruling class has tried, not very hard, to discourage an activity that it does not really think of as wrong. In doing so it has helped to spread the idea that narcotics are not wrong in themselves, that those who take them are innocent victims of wicked persons who sell drugs to them. This means that, increasingly, great forces are deployed to attack the suppliers of drugs, while few or none at all are mobilized against the people who buy them. The product is vile and the traffickers in it viler still, but the buyers who obtain these vile substances from these villainous people are to be pitied and exonerated.

However, many citizens do persist in thinking that drug-taking is wrong, making it difficult for the elite to legalize what many of its members see as a normal pleasure. The state is also bound by international treaties to prevent the legal sale of many drugs. To make matters more complicated, some drugs are so unpleasant and devastating in their effects on those who take them that even social liberals disapprove of them. The difference between these drugs and the ones of which they approve is hard to see, except by an ill-defined scale of horror and disgust. Cannabis is supposedly 'soft', although in some genetically-engineered versions it has as potent an effect on the brain as heroin. Heroin is supposedly 'hard', though even this substance has its defenders. Cocaine is halfway between the two but, in the form of 'crack', it becomes 'hard'. Ecstasy pills, widely regarded by teenagers as harmless pleasure tablets, suddenly appear dangerous when, as they occasionally do, they kill those who take them. Their long-term effects are as yet unknown, but they are likely to be significant. Far more public concern is voiced about the possible ill effects of mobile phones.

Much anti-drug propaganda brackets legal alcohol and tobacco with illegal cannabis. This (unintentionally?) makes it hard for a generation who smoke tobacco and drink beer, wine and whisky to tell their children to stay away from marijuana. The comparison is false. While some people drink to get drunk, most do not, whereas nobody smokes cannabis for the taste. All of them smoke it to become intoxicated. And tobacco, although harmful, is hardly a powerful mind-altering substance. Then there is the campaign for the 'medical use' of cannabis, winning the sympathy of millions who would never otherwise listen to campaigns for drug legalization.

Without a clear moral objection to drug-taking as such, or to law-breaking as such, the law and its enforcement do not make sense. As a result, the 'war against drugs' has often been reduced to hysterical slogans, ludicrous advertising campaigns, bizarre self-defeating actions and comically misplaced efforts. In more recent years it has come close to offering the young instructions on how to take drugs 'safely' – an approach for some reason not tried in the official campaigns against cigarette smoking or driving while drunk. And it has utterly failed, to the great cost of the country. As the Royal Navy and the SAS churn the seas or slip through the Colombian jungle in pursuit of drug-smugglers and producers, the Metropolitan Police publicly announce that they will look the other way if they see people openly smoking illegal cannabis. How long before they do the same with the cocaine which the SAS and the Navy try so hard to interdict and suppress?

This feeble approach to the drug issue is yet another result of the elite's rejection of absolute right and wrong. A system based on clear moral choice would condemn all kinds of deliberate intoxication. Interestingly, the same elite state has done much to relax England's alcohol laws over the same period, allowing longer opening hours while claiming, absurdly, that these have had no effect on behaviour. Conventions governing alcohol advertising have buckled so that many drinks are now openly promoted purely because they are strong. The only form of drunkenness that is either officially or unofficially discouraged is drunken driving.

Much of this relaxation is the result of a thoughtless selfishness among the elite themselves. Parental control is now so weak and the fashion for drug-taking so strong that the sons of a Home Secretary and of the heir to the throne have been revealed to be involved with cannabis. No parent, however exalted or morally well equipped, can confidently assume that his teenage children will not do the same. Those who privately believe cannabis to be harmless gravely increase this risk. They themselves have led successful and prosperous lives, and they believe that because such drugs did not harm them they will not harm others. To remove the fear of prosecution from themselves and their offspring, they seek to weaken the law for everyone. In doing so, they forget the many millions who cannot cope so well with such things and the many more millions who must live alongside them and suffer from their behaviour – especially the epidemic theft of portable goods to pay the price of narcotic pleasure.

Enormous amounts of 'petty' crime are linked to drug-taking. The theft of small saleable items, preferably electronic, is the quickest way of raising money to pay a dealer. Aggressive begging, which often comes close to mugging, is another. Mugging itself is, of course, a third. This resort to theft is quite logical. A drug habit, which is a selfish and arrogant form of behaviour in itself, increases the need for money while reducing the inclination to work for it or to care about the consequences of so-called 'petty' crime.

In some poorer parts of the country, boys of eleven and twelve are stealing to pay for cannabis. Measured on the moral scale of the elite, this is unimportant compared with the risk that the child of a media figure might get a criminal record for possessing a few ounces of cannabis. It is considered too much to ask the children of the ruling class to obey the law, but perfectly reasonable to condemn huge swathes of society to lawless dishonesty. Once, this would have been called class justice, but since class is now based on power rather than wealth or moral standing, such expressions are no longer used.

It also does not seem to occur to those who argue this position that a strongly enforced law against cannabis would actually protect their children from pressure to join the drug-culture. If there were a real chance of arrest, conviction and prison for doing so, many would have a good, permanent excuse for refusing to buy or smoke cannabis. Instead, elite commentators complain that enforcement of the existing law would 'criminalize' their young. This view, often advanced by people who consider themselves to be conservatives, reveals an extraordinary attitude to the law. The fact is that users of illegal drugs criminalize themselves by breaking the criminal law. They have the freedom to keep the law or to break it.

Perhaps the most eloquent denunciation of modern England's long, lazy and self-deluding weakness in this matter is to be found in the first volume of Malcolm Muggeridge's autobiography, *Chronicles of Wasted Time*. He recalls his time as a teacher in Egypt in the 1920s and the efforts then being made by the authorities to try to stamp out hashish in an attempt to bring about modernization and national revival, in imitation of Turkey's reforms under Ataturk. After describing the listlessness and sloth of students addicted to hashish smoking, Muggeridge wrote:

> Russell Pasha, the head policeman and the last Englishman to hold the post, was particularly active in trying to prevent hashish getting into the country, and in reducing indulgence in it. At the League of Nations, too, the suppression of the traffic in hashish was one of the few things the member states unanimously agreed about. If anyone then had suggested that all this endeavour was misplaced because hashish did little harm, and was anyway non-addictive, the suggestion would have been received with incredulity and derision. To the best of my knowledge no one at all reputable, or for that matter disreputable, ever did make such a suggestion. I had to wait forty years to hear it made, and then not just by crackpots and wild libertarians; but by respected citizens, clergymen, purported scientific investigators and other ostensibly informed and enlightened persons.
>
> When I hear or read their apologies for hashish, I recall the Zaffaran Palace [seat of Cairo University at the time] and the stupefied faces and inert minds of so many of the students there; the dreadful instances of the destructive effects of this drug on bodies and minds which any resident in the Middle East was bound to encounter.

I know of no better exemplification of the death wish at the heart of our way of life than this determination to bring about the legalisation of hashish so that it may ravage the West as it has the Middle and Far East.

This should be coupled with Allan Bloom's denunciation of rock music and its accomplice, the drug-culture, in *The Closing of the American Mind*:

> Rock music provides premature ecstasy and, in this respect, is like the drugs with which it is allied. It artificially produces the exaltation naturally attached to the completion of the greatest endeavours – victory in a just war, consummated love, artistic creation, religious devotion and discovery of the truth.
>
> Without effort, without talent, without virtue, without exercise of the faculties, anyone and everyone is accorded the equal right to the enjoyment of their fruits. In my experience, students who have had a serious fling with drugs – and gotten over it – find it difficult to have enthusiasms or great expectations. It is as though the colour has been drained out of their lives and they see everything in black and white. The pleasure they experienced in the beginning was so intense that they no longer look for it at the end or as the end. They may function perfectly well, but dryly, routinely. Their energy has been sapped, and they do not expect their life's activity to produce anything but a living, whereas liberal education is supposed to encourage the belief that the good life is the pleasant life and that the best life is the most pleasant life... as long as they have the Walkman on, they cannot hear what the great tradition has to say. And after its prolonged use, when they take it off, they find they are deaf.

Both men have understood what our political leaders have failed to grasp: that drugs are the enemy of the moral society in which effort is rewarded by exaltation and success in this world. Oddly enough, rock musicians and those who surround them immediately understood that the implicit message of narcotics was the same as theirs – a challenge to the hated suburban work ethic. By providing exaltation without effort, while making success an empty matter of cash and possessions, they strip the striving classes of their motivation to be good and to work hard.

The striving classes are not only what is usually called the middle class. They include all those who, in modern economies, have worked hard to better themselves or to maintain a respectable and honest place in the world. Drugs and rock music, in contrast, cause people to stay in the same place or even to sink, and encourage their dependence on the state. Political discontent and criticism of the existing order are rare among the children of the middle class, who have found inner contentment in a culture of easy intoxication, rock music and sex. They are even rarer in what used to be the working class. Heroin is on easy sale in Manchester, Merthyr and Grimethorpe, where it blurs the minds of the losers in the industrial conflicts of the 1970s and 1980s. As for the new generations, uneducated, unemployable, illiterate and yet exposed to all the blandishments and temptations of modern advertising, dope and pills are a double salvation. They make the dull world shine and they offer fast, tax-free income to those prepared to deal and trade in them.

Another argument ignored by the authorities is the one that says that we owe a responsibility to those who nurtured us not to throw the gift of life back in their faces. Given that the effects of narcotics are still only dimly known, no wise or intelligent person should risk such an important part of his body – if not for his own sake, then for the sake of his parents, brothers, sisters and friends.

However, a sternly moral society is needed to reinforce such views with law. Modern England is not such a society. Only the dimmest young person could have failed to notice what happened in 1967 when several members of the Rolling Stones were charged with various drugs offences. At this distance it is pointless to delve into the details of the charges. The truth about the long-ago evening at a farmhouse in the cosy Sussex seaside village of West Wittering will remain elusive and disputed. What is important is that, given an opportunity to make an example of several prominent rock stars, at a time when rock stars were well known to be dabbling in drugs and their actions were influencing the young, Britain's governing classes deliberately missed that opportunity. Mick Jagger was charged with the possession of four amphetamine tablets for which he had no prescription. Nineteen police officers surged into Keith Richards's house where, among other things, they found Marianne Faithfull clad only in a fur rug which kept slipping from her shapely form.

The atmosphere at the time, as viewed by one hormonal fifteen-year-old schoolboy (the author), was of a war between the generations. The dreadful cliché is for once absolutely accurate. The beliefs and morals of those who had been through the war were losing their grip. The giant commercial and emotional power of rock music had harnessed the great flood of self-pity and self-important angst of millions of teenagers. It had turned it into a sort of immoral force. Things that were not important at all, such as the length of a man's hair, were suddenly crucial. Jagger was said to have told the *Daily Mirror:* 'Teenagers are not screaming over pop music any more, they're screaming for much deeper reasons. We are only serving as a means of giving them an outlet. Teenagers the world over are weary of being pushed around by half-witted politicians who attempt to dominate their way of thinking and set a code for their living. They want to be free and have the right of expression, of thinking and living without any petty restrictions.' It sounds remarkably like Anthony Blair's speech in Stevenage thirty years later, in which he spoke of being part of the rock-and-roll generation. Mr Blair's award of a knighthood to Sir Michael Jagger in June 2002 neatly closed a political and cultural circle.

Instinctively, the authorities knew that those four apparently insignificant pills were enormously important. The arrest of Mick Jagger, hero of the teen delinquent and the waking nightmare of the teenage girl's respectable mother, was like the sound of gunfire in the hills outside the city. The rebels were approaching the suburbs. Did what was left of the grown-up establishment have the strength and will to stop them?

When Jagger's trial began on 27 June it seemed as if they did. For a war between generations, it was exceedingly polite. Judge David Block dealt briskly but fairly with such matters as the curious clothes worn by Keith Richards and with the lady in the fur rug, yet the contrast between the judge and the defendants remains astonishing. Block, who was to die in 1980, was a distinguished and decorated former naval officer. He had survived the Japanese sinking of the aircraft carrier HMS *Hermes* in the Indian Ocean in 1942 and was present at the destruction off North Cape of the German raider *Scharnhorst* in 1943. What must he have felt about the people appearing before him, whose liberty to behave in this way he had personally defended at such risk to himself? What did he think when Keith Richards said: 'We are not old men. We are not concerned with petty morals'? Yet he still sought to be fair. 'Put out of your minds any prejudice you may feel about the way Richards dresses, or his observations about petty morals,' he told the jury. 'Disregard the evidence as to the young lady who was alleged by the police to have been in some condition of undress.' Whether they obeyed him or not, the jury found Jagger and Richards guilty and the judge sent Jagger to prison for three months. Despite claims that a mysterious interloper may have brought drugs into the house, Richards was imprisoned for a year. A poll in the *Daily Mail* found that 56 per cent of the population aged between twenty-one and thirty-four thought the sentence on Jagger was not harsh enough. Only 12 per cent thought Judge Block had been too severe. In the end it was the middle-aged establishment which came to their aid.

For the pair were not freed by an enraged mob of teenagers.

The walls of Brixton Prison were not torn down by the bare hands of the young generation. Their salvation came from *The Times* newspaper, supposed to be the voice of the establishment, in words penned by a conservative Roman Catholic, William Rees-Mogg. He managed to compare Jagger to Oscar Wilde in a leading article surmounted by Alexander Pope's words: 'Who breaks a butterfly on the wheel?' Perhaps the comparison was actually unfair to Jagger. Wilde had brought his persecution on himself with a stupid libel action and disdained several chances to save himself. Jagger was also in the throes of a libel action against the *News of the World* (later dropped), but had most certainly not sought his troubles as keenly as Wilde had done. Wilde's offence was loathed by almost everyone, including many of his friends. It would be nearly a century before he would become a hero, except to other outcasts. Jagger's alleged offence was viewed as harmless even by many of his critics. He would be a hero before his appeal was heard.

Rees-Mogg's leader minimized the drugs involved and suggested that the star was suffering from strain and exhaustion. Then he argued against what has always been one of the main purposes of the criminal justice system – to make an example of those who come before it: 'It should be the particular quality of British justice to ensure that Mr Jagger is treated exactly the same as anyone else, no better and no worse. There must remain a suspicion in this case that Mr Jagger received a more severe sentence than would have been thought proper for any purely anonymous young man.' He added: 'There are many people who take a primitive view of the matter. They consider that Mr Jagger has "got what was coming to him". They resent the anarchic quality of the Rolling Stones' performances, dislike their songs, dislike their influence on teenagers and broadly suspect them of decadence.' Indeed they did.

However, decadent or not, the Rolling Stones could afford excellent lawyers. Jagger was rapidly bailed and his appeal was heard with great speed. Davin Seay, in a biography of Jagger, quotes the rock star's counsel, Michael Havers, as saying: 'It was imperative that I get those convictions overturned or Mick and Keith, with drug convictions on their records, would not be able to enter the United States to perform their concerts.' On 31 July, Richards's conviction was overturned on appeal by Lord Parker, the Lord Chief Justice of England, in person. Richards was absent from the courtroom owing to an attack of chickenpox which he said he did not wish to give to anyone else. Jagger, wearing jacket and tie (albeit a mauve, blue and yellow one) for the occasion, stood to attention when the judge spoke to him and actually bowed to the bench at one point. His conviction was turned into a conditional discharge and his prison sentence cancelled. Interestingly, Parker directly contradicted the great Rees-Mogg editorial, saying to Jagger: 'You are, whether you like it or not, an idol of a large number of the young in this country. Being in that position, you have very grave responsibilities and, if you do come to be punished, it is only natural that those responsibilities should carry a higher penalty.' However, he felt that testimony from Jagger's doctor, saying he had verbally approved the sort of pills Jagger was found with, was 'the strongest mitigation there is'. And he said the tenuousness of the evidence against Richards meant that his conviction should be quashed altogether.

Teenage troublemakers everywhere rejoiced. So, presumably, did those who hoped that the Rolling Stones would continue to be profitable, especially in the USA, that largest of all markets for British rock music. The rebels had fought their way out of the hills, taken the outer suburbs and would soon be marching through the streets of the capital. The establishment had suffered a total and unmitigated defeat, although few of its then members could have imagined that thirty-five years later Jagger would become a Knight Bachelor and that neither he nor the public would find this event especially ludicrous.

After his release, Jagger was almost immediately flown by helicopter to an Essex stately home (the property of Sir John Ruggles-Brise, nephew of the great prison reformer) to meet his saviour,

Rees-Mogg. The editor of *The Times* then informed the rock super-star: 'You are often taken as a symbol of rebellion.' The heir of Sir William Haley went on to ask the singer of 'Let's Spend the Night Together': 'Do you feel that society has a great deal in it today that ought to be rebelled against?' The truly rebellious answer to that question would have been: 'No, I am a member of one of the lucki-est, most prosperous, safest, most pampered generations ever to have lived, growing up in one of the freest countries on earth under the benign rule of law. Why should I complain or rebel?' It did not come, for, while it might have been true, it was not what Jagger was expected to say or what he had been encouraged by adulation to think. Nor was it what the producers of Granada TV's *World in Action* – or Rees-Mogg, for that matter – would have wanted to hear. They believed that Britain as it had been was finished. They were only too happy to sit and be chastised for their reactionary fustiness. They liked being congratulated for their open-minded acceptance of the exciting new age. It would be wonderful to know what Jagger actually thought during this absurd exchange. But we probably never shall.

The defeatist attitude of such people as Rees-Mogg was shared in the official world. During the Jagger affair a great band of worthy and fashionable persons had signed an advertisement in *The Times* calling for changes in the cannabis law. Even before they had done this, a Whitehall committee was at work on undermining that law. It was to be the first of many such committees, all determined to establish that the narcotics laws were too fierce, all unmoved by the enormous increase in narcotics use that accompanied their verdicts. On 1 November 1968 the committee, under the leadership of Baroness Wootton of Abinger, reported. They concluded:

> We think that the adverse effects which the consumption
> of cannabis in even small amounts may produce in some
> people should not be dismissed as insignificant. We have
> no doubt that the wider use of cannabis should not be

encouraged. On the other hand we think that the dangers of its use as commonly accepted in the past and the risk of its progression to opiates have been overstated, and that the existing criminal sanctions intended to curb its use are unjustifiably severe.

Witnesses to the committee included R. D. Laing, the ultra-radical and fashionable psychiatrist, William Levy, editor of the counter-culture magazine *IT* (*International Times*), Martin Sharp, a 'representative' of the equally counter-cultural magazine *OZ*, and the radical journalist Peter Laurie. They recommended that there should be no use of imprisonment to punish possession of small quantities of cannabis. They also urged that the use of private premises for drug consumption (which had been an issue in the Keith Richards case) should be excluded from legal penalties. They called for a review of police powers on search and arrest, and said that the law should be recast to give Parliament greater flexibility of control. They urged, too, that the law should separate cannabis and heroin as soon as possible. These recommendations would all eventually take effect in one form or another. Once again, anyone wondering what were the authorities' true feelings towards drugs would have been filled with doubt about their resolve.

In the following years, as the law against cannabis was weakened, its enforcement weakened as well. Quietly, police forces began to ignore the possession of small amounts of the drug. Quietly, the rhetoric of politicians shifted from condemnation of drug-taking to denunciation of drug-dealing. Drug-dealers were constantly described as evil.

By the 1980s it was plain to any thinking person, and to many unthinking ones, that the government did not really know what to do about drugs. A poster campaign warning of the health risks of heroin – 'Heroin Screws You Up' – not only failed to persuade anyone but its artwork, showing tragic, hollow-faced people in dark and desperate circumstances, became a rare collector's item.

A programme was launched to offer heroin addicts the supposedly less harmful methadone instead. Many then sold the methadone to buy heroin. Others found that the substitute was a potent drug in its own right. By early 2002 more than a million prescriptions for methadone were being issued each year. Projects for the treatment of drug-addicts sprang up everywhere. A fashionable doctrine of 'harm reduction' was widely adopted. This assumed that the young would inevitably take illegal drugs and offered them advice on how to do so safely, or at least more safely.

At first this was semi-official, carried on by privately financed organizations. It soon began to be the official view, and was confirmed as such in January 2002 when the government sponsored an advertising campaign urging club-goers to consult the Drugs Helpline for advice on narcotic safety. The helpline, run by a private company but paid for out of taxes, took a 'non-judgemental' view of drugs. Its website described their properties and their effects, often in terms that made them sound quite attractive. At no point did it try to say that drug-taking was wrong in itself. However, it did reveal the legal classification of drugs and state which were illegal. This step had been foreshadowed some years previously when a Tory government bill licensing dance clubs in Scotland had stipulated that they should provide 'chill-out' rooms where users of the illegal drug ecstasy could drink water and rest after taking it. In March 2001 similar advice was offered by the government to clubs in England, and a Home Office minister, Robert Ainsworth, said that society had to recognize that illegal drug use had become an integral part of a clubber's night out.

Meanwhile the assault on respectability and the ethic of sobriety continued. An independent charity grandly calling itself the Police Foundation (which actually had no direct connection with the police) produced a report calling for the effective decriminalization of cannabis and ecstasy. The report was taken seriously in some highly conservative quarters. Few noticed that the group of people who had prepared the report contained not a single person who believed that drug-taking was morally wrong.

The Dutch government's experiment with relaxing cannabis laws in Amsterdam has been widely and one-sidedly praised by the British media. In fact, the project has had many problems and is widely disliked by many people in the Netherlands, who object to the easy availability of drugs and the large number of cannabis cafés that have opened near their homes. The reform was followed by a 250 per cent rise in the use of cannabis by Dutch adolescents and a 22 per cent increase in the number of registered hard-drug-addicts.

Interestingly, almost nothing has been heard of another experiment with legalization, in the American state of Alaska. The experiment, significantly, was imposed by the State Supreme Court and overturned by democracy. From 1975 to 1990 Alaskans could legally possess four ounces of cannabis for private use at home. Crime, welfare dependency and health problems all increased during this period. The argument that making a drug legal reduces its glamour for the young also proved false. Use among Alaskan teenagers rose to triple the USA's national average. In 1990 the state's citizens organized a 40,000-signature petition to hold a referendum on the law. Despite being outspent ten to one by the pro-cannabis lobby during the campaign, they restored the anti-cannabis law by a vote of 55 to 45 per cent. If decriminalization is such a good idea, so free of problems, this result is hard to explain. Rather than seek to explain, however, cannabis legalizers generally either do not know about it or prefer not to discuss it, referring instead to Amsterdam which they misleadingly represent as a pure triumph of enlightenment.

The sobriety ethic has also come under attack from those who claim that cannabis is a useful medicine. They have been given a kindly hearing by academics and the media as well as a government research project to test their claims. This is absurd. The University of Mississippi has literally thousands of research papers on the medical effects of cannabis, all of them critical. The evidence for the miracle properties of cannabis is scanty, to say the least. For instance, a glaucoma sufferer would have to smoke cannabis every two hours to obtain relief (that is, four thousand times per year), and would be too intoxicated to make sense of any improved vision that might result. Many promising drugs, which do not need to be smoked and are available in easily measured quantities, never make it to the market because of much smaller problems than this. It is also interesting that the powerful and wealthy pharmaceutical industry, which could make a vast fortune out of a pill that provided euphoria without harmful side effects, has yet to produce any such product. Perhaps euphoria always exacts a price.

Because of the way it is smoked, cannabis causes disfiguring mouth, tongue and lip cancers. It is also more dangerous to the lungs than tobacco. Modern versions of the drug, intensively cultivated, are vastly stronger and more dangerous than Beatles-era marijauna. Cannabis can trigger latent schizophrenia and wipes out the effect of anti-schizophrenia drugs. It remains active in the body for days, and is found ever more frequently in the corpses of dead drivers after accidents. Any prescription drug that had one-tenth of these effects would be withdrawn from sale amid a national panic.

One rare opponent of cannabis among the liberal elite has been the Oxford Professor, Susan Greenfield, who, as she launched her TV series about the brain, told liberal pro-drug campaigners they were fools. 'You've got this beautiful, lovely thing that's evolved, and it's all yours, and then along comes this drug and it goes... splat!', she said graphically. Knowing how the brain works, she could not understand drug-takers: 'They wouldn't go about slashing up their muscles. Why on earth would they want to damage their brains?' Professor Greenfield's opposition is rare among her generation. So is detailed knowledge of the working of the human brain, her speciality.

The main ingredient of cannabis, tetrahydrocannabinol (THC), has been available for years on hospital prescription in the UK as the anti-nausea drug nabilone, which can be given in proper measured doses and is sometimes supplied to patients undergoing chemotherapy. However, it cannot provide a euphoric 'high', which is perhaps why campaigners for medical cannabis prefer to forget its existence. In fact, the whole 'medical use' argument is consciously false, as was unwisely admitted by the leader of America's pro-legalization campaign, Keith Stroup. He told an audience at Emory University in 1979 that the pro-cannabis campaign would use the medical marijuana argument as a red-herring to give pot a good name. This was recorded in the campus newspaper, the Emory *Wheel*, of 6 February 1979: 'We are trying to get marijuana reclassified medically. If we do that... [we will] be using the issue as a red herring to give marijuana a good name.' In which case it must be one of the most effective red-herrings in history.

The alternative approach to the British one has been partly tried in America: strong moral and cultural resistance supported by decisive prosecutions and police hostility. For years the US federal government campaigned resolutely against drug abuse and backed its moral arguments with legal punishments. The number of illicit drug users dropped from 24.3 million in 1979 to 11.4 million in 1992. In the following years, crime of all kinds also began to fall. Researchers are still arguing about the reasons for this decline. It is at least possible that reductions in crime were the result of reduced drug abuse.

Strangely, many conservatives in Britain (and America) would not be interested in that fact if it were the case. To the delight of the liberal elite, who would not relish a proper debate on this subject, these conservatives have adopted what they believe to be a 'libertarian' position on drug abuse. This allows them to support the dismantling of the laws against cannabis. Presumably, in the future it will permit them to attack the laws against other drugs as well. (An article to this effect by the noted conservative pundit, Bruce Anderson, was published in the *Spectator* in March 2002.) They contend that drug-taking is a private decision in which the law has no business. They also say that the law, by persecuting suppliers, does nothing but encourage the growth of crime. They suggest that keeping the existing laws against drugs is the equivalent of American alcohol prohibition in the 1920s and 1930s, doomed to fail and a boon to gangsters.

The parallel is false, since alcohol was already well established in the USA, and especially among Italian, German and Irish immigrant groups, before prohibition was attempted. Drugs, even cannabis, are not yet accepted as part of British culture and remain a minority pursuit. They could become part of the culture, but only once all legal and moral sanctions against them have been removed. The problem of gangsters benefiting from the illegal nature of their goods is more difficult. Such people have always profited from evading the law, under many different circumstances. No doubt the rewards of drug-smuggling are increased by its legal prohibition. That would not in itself be an argument for relaxing controls. If the substance involved is dangerous and unwelcome, this kind of thing will happen during the effort to banish it. If the effort is successful, the problem will be temporary. The real difficulty is that controlling the supply while effectively encouraging demand is bound to fail. If the suppliers faced severe penalties for smuggling and a diminishing market as well, then they would eventually abandon their efforts.

But the main foundation of the 'libertarian' argument is in some ways more insidious. It is a folly that paralyses conservative democracies faced with an assault on the culture of effort and reward. It has captured influential journals, including the *Economist* magazine, where Frances Cairncross recently cited an argument of the great libertarian John Stuart Mill – that the individual is sovereign over his own mind and body – in support of the legalization of cannabis, and explained that the *Economist* would in future support that cause. Her arguments, however, were elegantly answered by Norman Dennis, Director of Community Studies at the Institute for the Study of Civil Society. Dennis, in an article published in the *Salisbury Review*, points out that Cairncross bases her case on only one of Mill's positions and retorts: 'That does not mean, for Mill, either that other people must accept that the sovereign individual is right, or that his free choice must be costless to him. Other people can properly display their dislike and disapprobation of the sovereign individual's choice. They can properly offer him advice and employ persuasion. They can legitimately shun him.' Dennis continues:

> The sovereignty of the individual is not Mill's only principle. He says just as firmly that 'whenever there is a definite damage, or a definite risk of damage, either to [another] individual or to the public, the case is taken out of the province of liberty and placed in that of morality or law.'
>
> It is true that he comes down against the legal prohibition of the only drug he deals with, alcohol, while fully admitting that the mischief a person does by intemperance can seriously affect those nearly connected to him. In reaching all his concrete policy conclusions, Mill makes it clear that the application of his two principles depends on the circumstances of the time.
>
> He says there are some times and some places where there is no advantage at all in people breaking the rules. At other times there is an advantage in them doing so, namely when they act 'not only differently but better'. He was specifically concerned with an increasingly powerful Victorian public opinion, demanding and securing more and more elevated and rigid moral controls from the community and the state.

For this reason, Dennis says, it is an anachronism to use Mill's arguments against oppressive Victorian morality to support the case for drug legalization in twenty-first-century Britain:

> Oppressive morality scarcely exists and British teenagers are now the heaviest drinkers, smokers and drug-takers

in Europe. The most effective argument today for freedom to take drugs is that it is impossible for either public opinion or the police to do anything to diminish drug taking, and that therefore the moral and legal towel should be thrown in, in defeat and despair. That is the complete opposite to Mill's argument for liberty in 1859.

Dennis quotes Mill's warning that civilization can become 'so degenerate that neither its appointed priests or teachers, nor anybody else, has the capacity or the will to take the trouble to stand up for it'.

Failure upon failure – the failure of a free country to recognize a peril, the failure of an elite class to understand the moral basis of its own influence and power, the failure of the criminal justice and police systems to support their own laws, and now the failure of conservatives to distinguish between liberty and licence – have together combined to make narcotic drugs effectively legal in England. The consequences of this have only just begun to be felt. As the resulting selfishness, indolence and theft spread through the country many may come to regret it. As the resulting separation of effort and reward destroys sobriety and the work ethic, all these problems will be doubled and redoubled so that what used to be an efficient and functioning civilization stumbles down the staircase into a condition of Third World confusion and squalor from which only the rich will be able to escape.

During 2001 and 2002, many senior police officers openly supported the relaxation of laws against cannabis and, with government approval, publicly abandoned any effort to enforce the law against this drug in Brixton, one of the most crime-stricken areas of the capital. This 'experiment' was swiftly classified as a success and extended to the rest of the country. The excuse was advanced that this would free officers to fight other sorts of crime – an excuse that appeared particularly feeble when crime, and especially robbery, immediately increased sharply in the same district. In July 2001 the number of street robberies in Lambeth reached 760, a 56 per cent increase over the previous year. Later, it would be claimed that street crime had diminished following the introduction of the softer approach to cannabis and that this was a beneficial result of the switching of resources. In fact, there were widespread complaints from residents that dealing in all drugs had become more intense. As for the reduction in street crime, it was not what it appeared. In February 2002 the number of street crimes was 556, slightly below the 562 of February 2001. However, at this time Lambeth was one of nine London boroughs specially targeted by the Metropolitan Police in an attempt to combat street crime, by diverting officers from their 'normal' duties to patrolling the streets. Reductions in street crime were recorded everywhere that this strategy was introduced, not only in Lambeth. The idea that the drop in street crime was the consequence of the softer approach to cannibis was, to put it mildly, questionable. Yet it was claimed by the policy's supporters that it was so. The abandonment of proper law enforcement was alleged be a rational use of resources. On closer examination, it looks much more like the degeneration of civilization.

VIII

Twelve angry persons

The jury is more noble in theory than in reality. There is nothing especially elevating in the sight of twelve people crammed into a room trying to decide whether to ruin a fellow human being's life. Yet for once, the idea *is* more important than the practice. As long as these strange committees continue to exist, governments are less powerful and citizens are more free.

Two things happen to trials when a jury is present. First, there is an element of doubt about the outcome that is quite beyond the control of the state. This turns the presumption of innocence from a mere slogan into a real possibility. Some on the jury may actually be prepared to believe that the police have the wrong man. Secondly, the prosecution's huge advantage over the defence is greatly reduced. The defence is not an interloper among officials but one of two contestants before a panel that owes nothing to either side.

Regrettably, this arrangement can help some criminals escape justice, although it is certainly not bound to do so. This is the price we pay for its benefits to freedom of thought and speech. It is why it is better, not just in general but for human liberty, that a hundred guilty men should go free than that one innocent man should be imprisoned. The question 'better for whom?' is often asked. The answer must be 'better for everyone'. These freedoms have until recently been considered so valuable that wise people accepted the painful cost. Now, however, that wisdom is repeatedly overruled on the grounds of expense or convenience. Governments constantly make it easier for wrongdoers to mock the law or escape justice by changing the rules of evidence, by weakening the police, by seeking to empty the prisons and reducing penalties to the point where they are meaningless. The same governments become piously self-righteous about plans to remove or reduce jury trial, claiming that restricting this right is a 'crime-fighting' measure designed to strengthen the law. They even claim that jury trial is not a right at all. The blazing hypocrisy of this attitude is matched only by its sheer nerve, its oppressive brutality and its small-mindedness.

Without a jury, the legal process is like any other government action. Strip the process of arrest, trial, conviction, sentence and appeal down to its basic parts and it is quite simple. A series of state employees, few of them especially brave or intelligent or perceptive, are asked to approve the original decision of another state employee. The chances are strong that they will do so at every stage, and will feel that this is what they are paid to do.

Police, prosecutor and judge are all representatives of power, reluctant to admit that they might be mistaken. There is a danger that the defence lawyer will become the state's advocate to the defendant, rather than the defendant's advocate to the state. In fully totalitarian countries, lawyers are either too afraid to act for the defence, or accept their client's guilt and do no more than plead for a lower sentence. In those without juries but with a measure of freedom, the defence starts at a disadvantage and the defendant is required to co-operate in the investigation of his own alleged offence long before he comes to trial. And when guilt is assumed, habeas corpus and other protections against long pre-trial detention seem idle.

In short, jury trial is a grave nuisance to the authorities, especially to governments which believe they have a moral purpose, as the

Blair administration does. It is constantly under attack because of the benevolent state's instinctive impulse to take absolute power so as to be more effectively benevolent. Even where juries exist, they can face severe intimidation from judges and governments. Their right to exist at all, let alone to act freely, is not always guaranteed. When, as in the USA, they are part of the holy writ of the constitution, they can still be avoided by such methods as the use of military tribunals under the excuse of a 'war against terror'.

When, as in England, they are supported by nothing but ancient custom, they can be attacked on the grounds of incompetence, delay and cost, and gradually removed from the courtroom. All too many democrats and libertarians will not come instinctively to the defence of juries. Totalitarians, quicker to see their true purpose, unfailingly recognize them as an enemy and attack them on sight. French juries were abolished in 1940 by the German National Socialist occupation authorities. Dictators fear not only what juries do now but what they might do in a tight corner. However, it is not only naked tyrants who mistrust them. All governments do so, and when France was liberated and the republic reborn juries did not return.

The assault on juries in England has been far more subtle than on the Continent where, after a brief vogue following the French Revolution, jury systems were established and later suppressed or abandoned in several countries, including Prussia, Hungary and the Netherlands. In England, and in a different form in Scotland, they simply continued uninterrupted. However, thanks to a series of changes and reforms, the institution is now significantly weaker in England than it was at the start of the 1960s. It is soon likely to become weaker still.

In the 1950s, an innocent person might well have been convicted of a crime, but only through the incompetence of the police or the courts, or very occasionally through the malice and dishonesty of individual officers. A guilty person might well have walked free, but only through the incompetence of the prosecution. The danger came from imperfections in the justice system itself, not from a state machine with a desire to increase its power at the expense of its citizens. By the start of the twenty-first century, England was slowly approaching the point, unknown for centuries, where an innocent person could in theory be convicted *at the wish of the state*. At the same time, and for connected reasons, acquittals on the grounds of class prejudice and hostility to the prevailing ideology were also slowly becoming possible.

The first whisper of approaching danger came with the report of the Departmental Committee on Jury Service, chaired by Lord Morris of Borth-y-Gest, set up by the Tory Home Secretary, Henry Brooke, in May 1963. It reported to a Labour government almost two years later, and although it took some time for its recommendations to gain government support, they came to pass in the end. The England of the time simply could not cope with the idea that middle-class, property-owning people were the best source of juries.

As it turned out, the committee could not come up with a better scheme. However, in the fashion of the time, change was deemed to be good in itself. It did not have to be for the better, as long as it acknowledged the growing fashion for egalitarianism. The inquiry began respectfully at the beginning. It took the view, preferred by traditionalists, that English juries dated from Magna Carta and replaced trial by ordeal, rather than that Henry II had brought them into being. It also accepted that juries had often been overridden by naked power and needed to be strong to be effective. The courage of jurors and judges alike had won juries a measure of true freedom by the end of the seventeenth century. The great confrontation of 1670 known as 'Bushell's case' involved the acquittal of two prominent Quakers, Penn and Mead, accused of taking part in an unlawful assembly. The crown was furious at the verdict. The jury were kept without food or drink for three days until they almost starved. Then, when they still refused to alter their verdicts, they were marched into prison. In a revolutionary judgement, however,

Lord Chief Justice Vaughan released them on a writ of habeas corpus, ruling simply that the law of England forbade the punishment of jurors.

This, combined with the astonishing English reverence for the law which had been so greatly reinforced by the dictatorial behaviour of the Cromwell regime, changed the history of the world. By liberating jurors from the fear of oppressive judges, it made possible the defiant acquittal of the 'Seven Bishops' which destroyed the autocracy of James II. It was the free jury, as much as any other power, that made possible the Glorious Revolution of 1688 and the limited constitutional monarchy that followed. Otherwise, the course of the seventeenth century, so decisive in the history of England, France and America, would have been utterly different. The freer England of the late eighteenth century gave still more independence to the jury. The 'Fox Libel Act' of 1792 provided juries with an invaluable weapon in the defence of freedom. This law took away the power of judges to order juries to convict in cases of criminal libel, a charge then often used to persecute political dissenters.

It is clear from this history that the main effect of independent juries was to prevent the prosecution of *political* cases, although the Morris committee, deliberating at a time when political freedom was taken utterly for granted, did not dwell on this. The benefits to those accused of ordinary crimes were incidental, though important. The existence of independent juries so completely prevented the use of the courts to pursue political matters that the idea of a political offence became absurd in the eyes of most Englishmen. Directly political trials likewise became almost unthinkable. The suffragettes were prosecuted for public order offences, and the First World War conscientious objectors for defying the conscription laws. Opinions differ about compulsory military service in a free society, but these people were imprisoned for their actions rather than their opinions.

The privilege of jury trial has benefits for the criminal justice system, especially in promoting the belief that most of those in prison have been rightly convicted rather than arbitrarily locked up. It also has a much greater importance in the national constitution. Jury trial for those accused of common crimes is the price society pays for freedom of thought and speech. The same could be said of the rule preventing anyone from being tried twice for the same offence. There will always be criminal cases where it will be tempting to break this rule. However, if it is broken for criminals, it is broken for everyone that the state may come to view as a criminal, and so it leaves dissenters open to the danger of state harassment by repeated prosecution. It also weakens juries by giving the state another method of overturning verdicts it dislikes.

The Morris inquiry did not seem to be challenging any of these fundamentals. At that time a largely peaceful society could reasonably feel confident that its institutions were safe and permanent. Now, many of the props of English liberty are threatened from all directions because of the grave rise in crime that has since occurred. Then, the government was simply seeking a way to get rid of what was seen as an archaic and unequal method of selecting juries.

The main purpose of the inquiry was to look into qualifications for jury service, which since 1825 had been based on property. It was careful to set out the reasons for the existence of juries, and treated the history of the jury with interest and respect. It quoted the potent words of Blackstone: 'The trial by jury, or the country, *per patriam*, is also that trial by the peers of every Englishman which, as the grand bulwark of his liberties, is secured to him by the Great Charter', which promised that no free man should be deprived of life or liberty or property save by the judgement of his equals and by the law of the land. The original Latin sealed at Runnymede thundered across the centuries: '*nullus liber homo capiatur, vel imprisonetur, aut exulet, aut aliquo alio modo destruatur, nisi per legale judicium parium suorum, vel per legem terrae*' (No free man shall be arrested, imprisoned, exiled or otherwise punished, unless by the judgement of his peers or by the law of the land).

The inquiry report approvingly cited Blackstone's description of the jury as the 'strong and two-fold barrier between the liberties of the people and the prerogative of the Crown', thanks to 'the unanimous suffrage of twelve of his equals and neighbours, indifferently chosen and superior to all suspicion. So that the liberties of England cannot but subsist so long as this palladium remains sacred and inviolate.' Its development here as a defence of liberty seems to have been a fortunate accident which only became truly important many years after the jury system was first instituted. In fact, it is hard to believe that any state would intentionally have invented or encouraged such a restraint on its own power. No wonder so many governments of all complexions have since sought to rescind the concession they had so unwisely made.

Juries were first used as a form of inquiry or inquest on the Continent under the Carolingians. They were brought to England by the Normans, who used them not to try cases but to compile the Domesday Book. Henry II brought them into civil and criminal law. After the prohibition of trial by ordeal in 1215, judges turned to juries as the best available alternative oracle. At first the distinction between the Grand Jury of Presentment, which decided if there was a case to answer, and the Petty Jury of Inquest, which decided the outcome, was not clear-cut, but in 1352 it was enacted that no accuser should be put on the petty (or trial) jury. Since then the role of jurors has been transformed from that of witnesses chosen for their expert local (and therefore far from impartial) knowledge and qualifications, into their present role as independent arbiters who come to a case without any previous knowledge of the facts.

The all-powerful Court of Star Chamber, not abolished until the reign of Charles I, often punished jurors who had in its view corruptly returned a verdict of acquittal. Star Chamber, not surprisingly, tended to treat as 'corrupt' any verdict that *it* considered to be against the weight of the evidence. The original function of jurors, as experts knowledgeable about the case and the accused, had faded away when it became difficult to find juries who were personally well informed about the case. This was dealt with at first by introducing additional jurors brought in for their knowledge, but in the end juries became judges of fact and fact alone, with the law being decided by the judge. There seem to be no historical reasons for keeping jurors in ignorance of the previous convictions of the accused, or for the extraordinary measures taken nowadays to keep them from knowledge of the background to the case before them. The original juries would certainly have known a great deal more.

The Morris committee did not openly seek any major changes to the powers of juries, to their secrecy or to the right of defendants to appear before them. In fact, they flatly stated that their purpose was based on the 'need to maintain the system of trial by jury as one that both merits and commands public respect'. Rather movingly, they explained the ancient words used in the old form of pleading at assizes: 'Q: "How wilt thou be tried?" A: "By God and my country."' They said: 'When in a criminal case an accused pleads not guilty, he "puts himself upon the country". The jury are "the country".' This feeling that a man convicted by a jury has been sent to prison not by the state but by the people is one of the reasons for the general popularity, until recently, of the English criminal justice system.

The committee assumed that all this would continue. Lord Morris himself was an experienced judge who had at one time been a Liberal parliamentary candidate. They were, however, unhappy about the way in which jurors were picked solely on the basis that they were householders. In practice this meant that juries were chosen from the lists of those who paid the rates, the council tax of the time, generally levied on the head of the household. In most families this was the husband, ensuring that the majority of jurors were male, although sometimes a husband and wife were jointly registered. In some parts of the country it excluded those living in blocks of flats and council accommodation, because they did not pay rates directly. The age limits were then from twenty-one to sixty.

The committee complained that the property restrictions belonged to 'a period in which only those who possessed property were considered to have a sufficient stake in the country to justify their being allowed to take part in public life'. They did not suggest any other measure of responsibility and solidity that might be better. If anything, there was evidence that the pool from which juries were drawn was becoming wider, rather than narrower. They estimated that there were 7.15 million names marked as eligible for jury service, 22.5 per cent of the 31.77 million names on the registers. A series of property revaluations had recently produced steep increases in the number of people qualified to serve. In February 1955 there had been just 1.51 million, a year later 3.71 million and by February 1964 there were 7.15 million. Yet even this modest expansion of the jury-serving classes was affecting verdicts.

The Metropolitan Police Commissioner, Sir Joseph Simpson, complained that there had been 'a marked deterioration in the quality of jurors'. The Association of Chief Police Officers said that the quality of rural jurors had stayed high while that of urban juries had declined, perhaps because of middle-class movement to the countryside. This presumably meant that rural juries were readier to convict than urban ones. An unidentified (but non-police) witness was quoted as saying that price inflation in the property market had widened the basis for selection and so led to 'an ever-increasing number of men and women of poor education who are ill-equipped for such service... the position must be expected to deteriorate still further'.

The committee dithered over whether there was any serious problem, saying: 'We do not feel able to express an authoritative view of our own... the majority of witnesses have expressed their confidence in the ability and determination of juries.' One thing on which all agreed, already seen as an issue even in 1964, was that far too few women served on English juries. One way of dealing with this would have been to adopt the Scottish system of the time, which allowed 'women with heritable property' to qualify. In practice, this resulted in a near-equality between men and women on Scottish juries, and it could easily have been adapted to English law.

The inquiry admitted: 'there is perhaps some force in the argument that to be a householder, or the spouse of a householder, is to some extent at least an indication of maturity and responsibility.' However, they shied away from the conclusion to which this might have led them, adding hastily: 'We have received no convincing evidence to the effect that householders would necessarily make better jurors than non-householders.' And they sought to use hard cases to make bad law by citing a problem that they had not actually shown to exist on any scale: 'It would be difficult to defend a system under which a householder and his spouse were eligible, whatever their standards of intelligence, education or integrity, while a lodger in their house, who might be a person of outstanding qualities, was nevertheless ineligible.' It would, in fact, have been quite easy to defend it so long as such a case was rare and the system as a whole served the interests of justice. It would also have been possible to devise a system of educational and other qualifications to overcome the problem. The committee, however, did not think in this fashion.

Instead, they seem to have been anxious to dispense with the property qualification altogether, rejecting any plans to change its levels or extend it to women. 'We do not see how property values, laid down in 1825, can be related, 140 years later, to any rational principle whatever,' they insisted. The fact that the existing system was working reasonably well – and that an extended franchise was already worrying the police – did not deflect them from their chosen reform, the abolition of almost any selection at all. They sought to replace the old method with another far less rational system, one that excluded nobody from the jury box save criminals and lunatics. This was their logic, as they dressed up their surrender to unthinking egalitarianism. They resorted, as people tend to do when they are unsure that they are right, to lofty gibberish: 'Our view is that jury service should be regarded as a duty which is a counterpart of the privilege of being a citizen. From this view it follows that

citizenship should be the basis from which the duty to serve arises.'
Unless you believe that everyone is equally qualified to serve on a
jury, which the members of the Morris committee plainly did not,
this sentence does not make sense.

The committee raised perfectly sound arguments against their
own ideas, saying: 'The householder qualification, whatever its
other defects, does have the advantage of being to some extent at
least a guarantee of the maturity and sense of responsibility of
young jurors.' Surely, if maturity and responsibility were desirable,
some sort of selection was required that would exclude the imma-
ture and irresponsible?

They could not have foreseen just how young future juries would
be, once their recommendations came into effect. They admitted
that juries would be younger but argued that this would not be a
bad thing in itself: 'We recognise that unless the present lower age
limit is raised, the effect of our other recommendations will be to
increase the number of young jurors, but we recommend nevertheless that the qualifying age should continue to be 21.' The
committee took the view 'that there is a greater measure of maturity
in people between the ages of 21 and 25 than some of our witnesses
were prepared to concede', and that 'while such people may have
less experience than their elders they may nevertheless possess
experience which is relevant to the duties of a juror'. By the time
their ideas were put into practice, a government in love with youth
culture would have lowered the age of majority, and so of jury
service, to eighteen. Few of the Morris committee's witnesses in
1964 or 1965 would have argued that there was much maturity to be
found in citizens aged between eighteen and twenty-one.

The Morris committee also conceded one of the most valued
benefits of the householder qualification: 'Although we can find no
compelling justification, in principle or practice, for the retention of
the householder qualification, it is only right to say that it probably
does at present serve the purpose of excluding a significant proportion of the criminal classes.' They even quoted from Lord Devlin's

Trial by Jury, with its prescient warning that a wider selection system might lead to pressure for majority verdicts: 'If unanimity is insisted upon and the narrow franchise is preferred, it is no doubt right that juries should be taken from out of the middle of the community where safe judgement is most likely to repose.'

There might have been another way of achieving this. The committee studied American methods of jury selection, which at that time involved searching literacy tests and other inquiries to ensure that jurors were fitted for the task. 'We would expect such a procedure to produce jurors of high calibre,' they concluded, but then they made it plain that they wanted nothing to do with such a scheme: 'Although it would be possible to devise ingenious tests for prospective jurors, we do not think that they would be appropriate or acceptable here. We have already rejected any proposal that there should be an organised basis for making up a jury on the recommendations of some selecting body.' Such an exhaustive process would take some time. If the test were rigorous, the selecting officer would have the task of telling large numbers of people that they had failed it. If it were simple, it would be useless. So in the committee's view there could be no test.

Nor could the property qualification be modified in some way to suit the times.

> The proposal to retain even a limited form of property qualification would be resented, and justifiably so, by those who consider that jury service is a right as well as a duty and that they should not be deprived of this right by the accident of not being a householder, any more than they are for that reason denied the other rights of citizenship...
>
> If our view is accepted that a jury should be a cross-section of the community as a whole, it would seem somewhat curious to draw jurors exclusively from those who are householders or the spouses of householders.

How strange this sounds now, when home ownership is so much more common. If they had simply left things alone, most of the unfairness and the anomalies of the old method would have disappeared. The property qualification looks far less snobbish and rigid than it did in 1965. With the sensible Scottish rules on spouses extended south of the border, it would also have meant women had an equal chance of jury service. The Morris committee seem to have been quite determined to choose the system of random selection from the entire electoral roll, not because it was best, or even better, but because it was the most egalitarian and so politically the least troublesome. The committee's proposals eventually became law in the Criminal Justice Act of 1972 and were confirmed by the Juries Act of 1974, which opened jury service to anyone registered as an elector and aged between eighteen and seventy. This did not come into full force until April 1974, and its effects took some time to be felt.

In the years in between, however, an equally important change had been imposed on juries, in one of those all-too-frequent episodes that make Parliament look like the easily-wielded tool of the executive. On the pretext of 'jury-nobbling' by criminal gangs, for which the evidence was vague and elusive, Roy Jenkins greatly altered the courtroom balance of power in favour of the state by introducing majority verdicts. It was a heavy blow, but like many such blows, not much felt at the time. Yet its significance was known and understood by experts. Lord Chief Justice Hewart had ruled in 1922 that the value of a jury's verdict lay precisely in its unanimity, not in the process by which it was reached.

No research has been permitted into juries, for fear that it might call their verdicts into doubt, but it is quite plain that a tough-minded individual can sway a jury in either direction by force of argument and personality. He can take courage from the knowledge that he has a complete veto. If he holds out to the end he can at least force a new trial – no mean threat. Even so, the bravest and most determined individual is likely to fail in such a lone stand if he does not have right on his side. This is the plot of the famous American film about a deadlocked jury *Twelve Angry Men*. Such a drama could still take place in most of the USA, but not in Britain where ten angry persons can now overrule two equally angry persons who refuse to join the majority. Here, a juror who swims against the stream can be dismissed as a tiresome nuisance, quite possibly at the exact stage where he might once have been on the verge of winning converts. And not just one individual but two can now be overridden.

Without the protection of their all-or-nothing unanimity, juries – like any other group of fallible humans – are far more easily divided and conquered. The change is colossal. A unanimous verdict and a majority verdict are not two different degrees of the same thing, but two quite different things. Yet the change passed through Parliament with very little protest or controversy. And, in an age of demonstrations and protests, there do not seem to have been any marches through the streets urging that England should Save the Jury. Vietnam was more important then, as veal calves and genetically-modified tomatoes would be later. The modern English have an extraordinarily unselfish inability to protest against anything that actually menaces their own liberty and well-being.

There *were* sharp protests from acute and knowledgeable people. Lord Denning told the House of Lords on 6 June 1967 that majority verdicts undermined the whole idea of guilt being proved beyond reasonable doubt. As usual, he struck at the heart of the thing. If one juror has doubts, let alone two, then how can guilt have been proved to the high standard demanded? In an earlier debate, on 10 May, Lord Morris of Borth-y-Gest, who, thanks to his inquiry, had become one of the greatest experts on the subject, had told the Lords that the majority verdicts proposal was 'retrograde'. Lord Denning said on that occasion that it was a fundamental part of the constitution that the jury should be unanimous. Among those who thought the principle of unanimity should be maintained, he said, were some of the wisest and most experienced judges. Lord Brooke, a former Tory Home Secretary, favoured majority verdicts but doubted if Roy Jenkins had enough evidence to prove his case for the change. Lord Stow Hill, formerly the Labour Home Secretary Frank Soskice, urged the government to reconsider its plan. Interestingly, the Lord Chancellor, Lord Gardiner, said that the main reason for majority verdicts was 'cranks on juries', only later adding the official line that there was also a risk of jurymen being bribed or intimidated. To the prosecution-minded, or the tidy-minded government servant, any nonconformist is a crank.

When Roy Jenkins introduced his enormous and far-reaching Criminal Justice Bill on 12 December 1966, with all its changes to court procedure, sentences, parole and gun control, he said of his plan for majority verdicts that 'in the present state of the crime wave we can feel less equanimity about the acquittal of the guilty'. Yet he made modest claims for the immediate practical effect of the change, saying the new procedures 'are not likely to result in different verdicts in many cases, but these few cases may well be crucial from the point of view of law-enforcement and the breaking-up of big criminal conspiracies'. At that time, he said, about 35 to 40 per cent of cases that went to juries resulted in acquittal. In about 3.5 per cent of cases there was jury disagreement that could not be resolved by the ordinary process of argument and persuasion. At the Old Bailey this had affected forty-nine out of 1180 cases in the previous year, hardly an enormous crisis requiring a radical change in the standard of proof. He spoke of an unidentified bank-robbery trial in the previous January where there had been repeated peremptory challenges and attempts to bribe jurors. In the end, four out of the five accused in the case were acquitted.

It seems likely that there were such problems at the time, but that they were confined to small areas and could have been dealt with by prosecutions for perverting the course of justice. The question again arises as to why Roy Jenkins and the Home Office were so insistent on a change the main effect of which would be to weaken jury independence and, while leaving the jury in being, gravely reduce its ancient power to stand in the way of the state.

Here it should also be mentioned that at about this time the old institution of the lay magistracy, another independent part of the system, also began to be weakened. By dispensing with the requirement for evidence to be heard before the lower courts, the Criminal Justice Act 1968 greatly reduced the power of magistrates to throw out a charge at the committal stage. In 1973, to protests from Lord Denning, Lord Hailsham, then Lord Chancellor, first introduced full-time, paid, 'stipendiary' magistrates into rural areas. He promised that the numbers involved would be very small, but in later years this promise has been broken. Many local courts have also closed, usually on the grounds of economy or lack of disabled access. Between 1996 and 2001, 108 magistrates' courts, mainly in rural areas and suburbs, were shut, thus weakening the link between Justices of the Peace and their localities, and making justice more remote in general. In 1973 the Home Office also began to talk about limiting jury trial to certain types of case.

It is hard to chart the effects of these changes. Official figures conceal as much as they reveal. But if they were intended to strengthen the prosecution they have not so far succeeded. In recent years prosecutions have been failing at about twice the rate of thirty-five years ago. By 1999 the number of unsuccessful prosecutions approached the politically important level of 25 per cent. Many other prosecutions fail at an earlier stage thanks to the Crown Prosecution Service's unwillingness to risk cases that do not have a good chance of success. In the most recent year for which figures are available, almost one in eight (12.3 per cent) of cases intended for the crown courts were dropped before trial by the CPS.

However, changes may run far deeper than this, and further detailed research is needed to establish the full truth about the past. Figures produced in early 2002 by the Lord Chancellor's Department suggest that the difficulty of persuading a jury to return a guilty verdict is increasing at an alarming rate. Figures on the outcomes of *contested* jury trials are available only back as far as 1990. They exclude cases where the jury acquitted on the judge's direction, where the trial collapsed or the defendant died. They therefore deal with a significantly smaller number of trials. They are, however, a better guide to the actual mood of juries when faced with a choice.

These figures show that in 1999 38.7 per cent of contested jury trials in England and Wales resulted in acquittals, while in 2000 the figure was 36 per cent. This percentage had changed remarkably little since 1990, the earliest figure obtainable from the Lord Chancellor's Department, when it stood at 37.7 per cent. Regrettably, no statistics of this kind are currently available for the 1960s, 1970s or 1980s, when the effects of majority verdicts and the abolition of the property qualification would have first been felt. Almost as striking is the variation between different parts of the country. The acquittal rate in 1999 in Salisbury, for instance, was 21.1 per cent. In Liverpool it was 61.9 per cent (the 1990 figure was 45.7 per cent), in Caernarvon 66.7 per cent (30.9 per cent in 1990), and at the Old Bailey 34.5 per cent (39.0 per cent in 1990). The results in 2000 were much the same, and in some cases the number of not guilty verdicts was higher. When judge-directed acquittals are added in, 79 per cent of defendants in contested trials in Liverpool were acquitted despite the best efforts of the prosecution in the year 2000.

The immensely complicated guidelines and codes of practice that now beset the police obviously have something to do with this. Any procedural slip-up or delay can kill a prosecution even before it gets to the point where the evidence would be weighed. Meanwhile, the willingness of juries to disbelieve the police and to treat prosecution evidence with suspicion has obviously greatly increased.

The author visited Liverpool Crown Court in March 2002 and found a near-breakdown of respect for justice. There were reports of general truculence and contempt, such as judges being sworn at and mobile phones ringing during cases. Judges were supposed to remove robes and wigs when dealing with defendants under eighteen, in case they intimidated them. Such defendants, often hulking six-footers facing charges of serious violence, were frequently allowed to sit outside the dock next to parents and social workers, supposedly because of their tender years. The old joke, 'Q: "What do you call a Liverpudlian in a suit?" A: "The defendant"', is now obsolete. Most defendants wear street clothes, as do juries. Tattoos, nose-rings and pony-tails were common among jurors, but jackets and ties were unheard-of. Jurors often lounged in relaxed attitudes. The old tongue-twisting jury oath, referring to the 'several issues joined before our Sovereign Lady the Queen', has been simplified so the illiterate or incoherent are no longer found out by it. The huge courthouse containing twenty-two criminal courtrooms is equipped with pictorial direction signs to help the growing number of illiterates find their way about.

Experienced court-watchers, speaking on condition of anonymity, believe that there is widespread but unacknowledged intimidation of juries and witnesses. Witnesses are followed into the lavatories or when they leave the building. Some estimate that as many as 20 per cent of contested cases collapse because witnesses either fail to appear or 'forget' critical evidence when in the witness box. Judges sometimes order the public to move their seats out of line of sight of the jury because of complaints that jury members are being subjected to intimidating stares. There are no police officers on duty in the building apart from those waiting to give evidence. Security, such as it is, is provided by shirtsleeved private guards, many of them women and few of them physically impressive. If there is serious trouble, as there sometimes is, the police must be called from their nearby headquarters.

There is no one obvious reason for the failure rate and demoralization of this place. Some believe that the split between the police and the Crown Prosecution Service leads inevitably to bureaucratic slip-ups and the postponement of cases. Some suspect the CPS is too worried about failing and drops charges too easily. Some blame the youth, inexperience and anti-authority attitudes of modern juries.

Others blame unscrupulous defence lawyers for exploiting the pet-tifogging provisions of the Police and Criminal Evidence Act 1984 and the current disclosure rules. All of these charges are partly justi-fied. However, they add up to more than the sum of their parts. The system has no force or self-confidence and criminals know it.

The abolition of the property qualification, in the still-settled and restrained society of 1974, may have had little effect. However, it could equally have been a slow-burning fuse within the jury system which has finally detonated its bomb. At the present time, in which respectability and middle-class values are widely questioned, espe-cially among the young, it may be starting to have a significant effect on attitudes towards the police and prosecution. It would certainly seem to be so on Merseyside.

Since research into individual jury decisions is sensibly and rightly forbidden by law we can only guess at the truth, although the figures for Liverpool, one of the least middle-class cities in the kingdom by any measure, seem to suggest that something of the kind may be involved. Another influence is almost certainly the age of jurors. The unintended result of the Morris committee's inquiry was that eighteen-year-olds, far younger in years and experience than the twenty-one-year-olds Morris envisaged, now serve on juries. Harold Wilson's decision to lower the age of majority to eighteen was not then in the manifesto of any organization except the Monster Raving Loony Party. Anecdotal evidence suggests that juries have been growing significantly younger in recent years, perhaps because of the over-sixty-fives' right to be excused, perhaps because older, employed people have taken advantage of the ease with which they, too, can avoid jury service.

It may even be that the new system is unintentionally discrimi-nating in favour of juries containing high proportions of younger, unemployed men and women. With its long, time-wasting trials and seedy courtrooms, it repels the respectable, steadily employed and better-off, who have other things to do with their time and have the skill to avoid having to serve on juries. Research on this would be possible without invading the secrecy of the jury room and needs urgently to be undertaken if a serious campaign for jury reform – as opposed to jury restriction or abolition – is to get under way. Acquittals at the current rate will only increase political demands for the end of jury trial, when it is quite likely that it is the political reforms of the 1960s and 1970s that have brought juries to their present state. The acceptance of majority verdicts may also be having its effect – the exact opposite of the effect it was intended to have. In an anti-establishment culture it is those who want to convict who are likely to be in the besieged minority.

The bravely won independence established in the seventeenth and eighteenth centuries is now in doubt. In October 2001 the new establishment revealed its true feelings about the jury system in Lord Justice Auld's *Review of the Criminal Courts*. The Auld report followed three failed attempts by governments of both parties to abolish the right to jury trial. It was sidelined by the government in early 2002 when it became clear that a powerful coalition against it was still in being and that its proposals would be alarmingly expensive. Even so, its naked hostility towards defendants having any right to jury trial, and its desire to create a new tier of jury-free courts, provided a warning of what the elite state wants to do and will certainly do later if it can gain full control of the House of Lords. It was lack of parliamentary time, not a sudden rebirth of libertarian principle, that led to the temporary shelving of Auld. In July 2002 the government proposed judge-only trials in complex fraud cases and violated two ancient principles by suggesting the retrospective abolition of the rule against double jeopardy.

In the late autumn of 2002 a highly significant development signalled the determination of the Blair government to use crime as a pretext to limit liberty. This was made much easier by a major but little-noted constitutional reform in October, under which the Commons abandoned its main remaining power to obstruct the executive. Until that date, a bill which ran out of parliamentary time was completely lost at the end of the session. This gave opponents in the Commons and the Lords a powerful weapon with which they could force compromise on Downing Street. But under reforms sponsored by Robin Cook, leader of the Commons, this power was abolished.

Within two weeks the Prime Minister and the Home Secretary made it plain that jury trial should be even more restricted than the July 2002 White Paper suggested, and that the rule against double jeopardy would be dropped. They argued that this was part of a 'modernizing' and 'rebalancing' of the criminal justice system. In fact it was a recognition of the failure of all their anti-crime initiatives of the previous five years. It was also a clear sign that they had chosen the authoritarian route, rather than libertarianism, and that crime was to be the excuse for it. The basis of their proposals was plainly the Auld report.

Auld urged radical changes to the right to jury trial, effectively abolishing it as a right (a right that he did not believe has ever existed). He also suggested a law making it clear that 'juries have no right to acquit defendants in defiance of the law or in disregard of the evidence'. He argued:

> I regard the ability of jurors to acquit, and it also follows, convict, in defiance of the law and in disregard of their oaths, as more than illogicality. It is a blatant affront to the legal process and the main purpose of the criminal justice system – the control of crime – of which they are so important a part...
>
> They are not there to substitute their view of the propriety of the law for that of Parliament or its enforcement for that of its appointed Executive [Auld's capitalization], still less on what may be irrational, secret and unchallengeable grounds.

Auld urged that the law should be amended to allow the trial judge or the Court of Appeal to inquire into 'alleged impropriety by a jury, whether in the course of its deliberations or otherwise'. This power would have to be tested in use, but it is hard to see how it could exist without putting greater pressure on jurors to convict. Auld also noticed, as others eventually will, that Article Six of the European Convention on Human Rights, requiring reasoned judgements and verdicts, could be interpreted to mean that jury trial was contrary to the Human Rights Act. This unsettling discovery illustrates very clearly just how violently the Convention conflicts with English traditions of liberty and how the two cannot indefinitely coexist.

While he urged the creation of a law to rob juries of the right of defiance, Auld also mentioned an alternative which he seems to have found unthinkable but that actually exists in two American states, Maryland and Indiana. Their constitutions, he said, 'come close to conferring upon the jury the right to determine the law and the facts'. If adopted in England, stated Auld, a law of this kind would require judges to tell juries that they need not convict if they disagreed with the law or with the decision to prosecute. In truth, English juries believe that they have this right anyway and do not need to be informed of it by a judge. Only a judge would think that he needed to tell them about it. Auld, however, described such a clarification of the law as an 'enormity'.

Others might use the same word to describe his plan to extinguish jury independence. Such a statute, in the wrong hands and interpreted by the wrong judges, could cancel the liberties achieved in Bushell's case and the Fox Act, and might take England back to the days when Star Chamber tore up verdicts that did not suit the state. Perhaps because resistance in the House of Lords had recently defeated three government attacks on the right to jury trial, Auld's oppressive scheme did not attract very much attention on its publication in October 2001. Its burial, according to an unattributable government leak to the newspapers in January 2002, was not irrevocable and it has swiftly heaved itself out of the grave. With both Commons and Lords now severely weakened, the jury is in more danger than it has been for two hundred years.

Auld's view of juries contrasted with Lord Morris's attitude thirty-six years earlier. Gone was the reverence and awe for lamps of liberty and twofold protections. Gone was the awkward independence of the judiciary. In its place was a brusque, hard, official practicality and a seeming desire to serve the executive which, if typical of the modern judge, is quite alarming. Like much modern illiberal thinking, it was camouflaged with the cloak of the vaunted fight against crime. Yet there are many other ways in which the courts could be changed to shift the balance in favour of the prosecution of criminals. What Sir Robin Auld and a succession of Home Secretaries of both parties have not explained is why they are so determined to reduce the rights and powers of the jury rather than to take any other possible route. Yet that determination is blatant and unashamed.

Auld swept aside the idea that a right to jury trial existed in England at all. 'In England and Wales,' he declared, 'there is no constitutional or indeed any form of general right to trial by judge and jury, only a general obligation to submit to it in indictable cases.' He rejected Lord Morris's version of history: 'It is often claimed that Magna Carta, traditionally regarded as the foundation of our liberties, established such a right. The claim is incorrect.' This would-be reformer proclaimed:

> Quite independently of Magna Carta there is no legal basis for regarding the claimed 'right' to jury trial as a constitutional entitlement, that is as an entrenched right overriding all other legal instruments, as in the United States for offences carrying more than six months' imprisonment or under the Canadian Charter of Rights and Freedoms for offences punishable by five years' imprisonment or more, or as a right at all.

He was technically correct, but only because no such entrenched rights exist in English law. They are entrenched only in the minds of the people, but plainly not in his. It was interesting that Auld's brief history of the jury system did not mention Star Chamber, Bushell or Fox.

Irrelevantly, however, he said that juries had failed to prevent miscarriages of justice in the late 1980s and early 1990s. This is hardly surprising, as Auld himself pointed out that these miscarriages resulted mainly from falsification or concealment of evidence. Juries could have known nothing and done nothing about them. They could only decide on the basis of what was put before them by police and prosecution and what the judge allowed them to hear. Auld's interest was in showing that since 1855 the law has let accused citizens choose between jury and summary trial for a growing number of offences. This choice, actually granted so that defendants could avoid the length, exense and unpredictability of a jury trial, did not seem to Auld to be an argument for keeping a right to insist on a jury trial. He had a point, but not a very good one. His interest was in the workings of the jury system after it had already secured liberty of thought and speech. He failed to see that removal of the defendant's right to choose would give the state a dangerous power that it would be better off without.

As it happens (and as Auld noted), subtle methods of encouraging defendants to plead guilty, by rewarding them with lighter sentences, have already hugely reduced the numbers of jury trials. This has been achieved without forcing defendants to forgo jury trial, and was introduced in the recognition that many had simply been trying to spend more time in the better conditions given to remand prisoners. Auld, however, was not put off, even though his own evidence showed that criminals playing the system could be outmanoeuvred without the need to dilute the jury system. He revealed why in these telling words: 'I regard it as a matter of principle that the decision [about] where a defendant should be tried is one for a court, not for the defendant.' Why was that?

'This is a decision in which the public as well as the accused have an interest, and the decision should be an objective one, bearing both in mind, not a subjective choice of the defendant based solely on his own self-interest.' In this statement we hear again the cold voice of the elite state, so convinced of its own rightness and goodness that it requires no restraint.

Auld recommended that magistrates, not defendants, should decide whether the accused in so-called 'either-way' cases would go before a jury or a summary court. This would presently affect only a minority of trials. However, combined with his plan for a new bottom tier of courts without juries, his proposals were startlingly radical. If implemented, they would have removed a de facto right to jury trial for many offences and opened the way for its removal for many more. They would almost certainly have been the first stage in a restriction of jury trial that would eventually lead to its effective abolition.

Some hint of the reasoning behind this hostility to jury trial is to be found in Lord Hardie's words during a House of Lords debate in January 2000 on one of the present Labour government's anti-jury bills. Lord Hardie, approvingly quoted by Auld, said: 'What is essential in any system is that the various interests are balanced; that society's interests, as represented by victims and witnesses, are balanced against the interests of the accused. What must be ensured is that the accused is protected from the effect of arbitrary decisions. Who better to perform such a task than an independent judiciary?' These are curious words. Society's interests are not 'represented by victims and witnesses'. Society has an interest in justice and liberty, which is owed to itself as a whole. Sometimes that interest may lead to witnesses being disbelieved and victims seeing the defendant go free. In extreme circumstances (for example, burglars injured in the course of a burglary), it may even lead to truthful witnesses being discounted. The victim, which may be the state itself, may even have to see the defendant go free because the jury thinks he has committed no crime.

The idea that the courts act on behalf of victims is false. They act to enforce the Queen's peace, the property of us all, and the law of the land, also the property of us all. They also act to enforce the constitution and the liberties it guards, and, as long as they contain juries and are presided over by freedom-minded judges, they can even help to make the constitution. Without them, it is hard to see how judges can long remain independent, since all the forces acting on them will be the state's. The pity is that, when juries need as many friends as they can get, they have been so badly weakened by majority verdicts and the abolition of any kind of qualification based upon maturity, education or responsibility. The lower age limit of eighteen is also absurd. Who, remembering his own teens, would wish his future liberty to be in the hands of a teenager? If the politicians were serious about jury reform, they would re-examine these hasty and ill-thought-out changes rather than threatening the principle of jury trial. However, the elite state fears and mistrusts the independence of juries on principle, and sees an opportunity to get rid of them while appearing to pursue the objective of justice and order.

The worse crime becomes, the noisier and cruder the courts will become. When the Metropolitan Police Commissioner, Sir John Stevens, attacked the inadequacies of the criminal justice system in a ferocious speech in March 2001, he called for the implementation of the Auld report, while making little of the other factors that have paralysed the courts. His speech was instantly welcomed by the government and by its semi-official newspaper, the *Sun*. Had he attacked the Police and Criminal Evidence Act 1984, which has subjected the police to absurd codes of practice and rendered convictions far more difficult to achieve, he might not have received such kind treatment from the politicians or their press supporters. Had he urged the re-establishment of some sort of qualification for jury service, he would have been denounced as a snobbish elitist. It was an alarming moment for supporters of jury trial who also believe that crime should be punished and deterred. One notable supporter of juries, the conservative commentator and author, Simon Heffer, declared on the BBC's *Any Questions* programme that he might in future support the Continental inquisitorial system. Much of the attack on the present mess was directed at lawyers, who undoubtedly profit greatly from the adversarial jury system. The fact that lawyers profit from it does not, however, blot out the vital advantages of the jury for a free society, or the need for independent defence lawyers.

The increasing use of trials as crude propaganda is, however, a forewarning of the likely direction of the debate unless the defenders of freedom and the enemies of crime can combine. A combination of noisy 'tough on crime' populism and repression seems likely to be the elite state's response to increasing disorder. From the statements of the Home Secretary, David Blunkett, it is evident that he is politically unable to understand why crime is out of control. Mr Blunkett said in March 2002 that he knew the streets were not safe. He plainly did not understand why this was so, and could offer only the usual New Labour remedies of initiatives, targets and street crime summits at Downing Street. There was also talk of putting more police on the streets, without any understanding of why they are not there already, or why they can do so little when they are there.

With such people in charge of criminal justice, it is likely that the government will shortly resort to more populist measures designed to give the impression of resolution and action. The limiting of liberty can always be made to seem attractive in such times. Such crude crowd-pleasing will undoubtedly be used to undermine the principle of jury trial. This process, of using the courts as government anti-crime propaganda, has already begun. A worrying development of recent years has been this confusion of justice with propaganda, with policemen giving celebratory press conferences after convictions and prosecutors wasting the court's time with emotional descriptions of the victim's plight and wounds, often to disguise the fact that they have no proper evidence against the accused.

The idea that victim and court are in some way on the same side is a worrying and totalitarian one, reminiscent of the sort of state where the public prosecutor demands a heavy sentence. Such states do not have independent judiciaries. They have government servants who cannot be trusted to look after defendants' rights because it is not what they are paid to do or what will please their political masters. However bad the victim's injuries and loss, the court still has the same duty to find out the truth, and to acquit those against whom there is not enough evidence to secure a conviction. In this way, the interests of a truly just court have always been different from those of the victim, and always ought to be. So the answer to the question, 'who better to protect the defendant against arbitrary decisions than an independent judiciary?', is 'an independent jury'.

The attempt to remove the right to jury trial is a serious menace to liberty. Attacking juries will do nothing to aid the fight for the re-establishment of justice. However, it will greatly strengthen the elite state. In the end, if a time comes when it is in the interests of authority to suppress its opponents, restrictions on jury trial will threaten liberty of speech and thought. There is no clearer illustration of the way in which the failure to punish wrongdoing will lead in the end to the punishment of us all.

IX

Institutional defeatism

'A racist incident is any incident which is
perceived to be racist by the victim or any
other person'
Macpherson report

The British establishment is now in favour of racial discrimination
by the police. Officers of the law are supposed to assume that
people of a different colour should be treated as if they were automatically people of a different culture. It is there, in bold print, on
page 316 of the much-praised and almost universally accepted
Macpherson report into the murder of Stephen Lawrence.
Paragraph 45.24 states: '"Colour-blind" policing must be outlawed.
The police must deliver a service which recognises the different
experiences, perceptions and needs of a diverse society.' These
words ended forty years of efforts to abolish racial discrimination in
this country. Until they were published, opponents of racialism (this
book's preferred term, as explained below) could still believe that
they should act as if colour did not matter, in the hope that eventually it would not matter.

From Macpherson onwards, rather than seeking to absorb new
citizens into British society through a policy of tolerance, this
country embarked on an official programme of adapting itself to the
supposed cultures of those new citizens. It assumed that a different-
coloured skin was the outward sign of a different cast of mind and a
reason to apply different rules of citizenship. For the previous forty
years enlightened people had been striving against any such belief,

insisting that colour was a meaningless distinction and that all could and should be absolutely equal in the eyes of the law. Any adaptation was expected to be by the new citizen to his adopted home.

Now the adopted home must adjust itself to its new citizens, treating them differently and with special consideration along more or less racial lines. The idea of a 'White Police Association' would have been repellent in the old era and also in the new. However, the idea of a Black Police Association is so acceptable to the new order that such a body actually exists, with official approval, and gave evidence to the Macpherson inquiry. Yet the new process of adaptation has been a highly selective one. Only some parts of some cultures are to be accorded this treatment. Open, official discrimination of this kind has not existed since the 1960s, when London police stations still displayed unashamedly racialist official notices advising different and special treatment for what were then called 'men of colour'.* To those who came to maturity in the years when racial discrimination was considered to be absolutely wrong and wicked in itself, the change has been disturbing.

The Macpherson report (*The Stephen Lawrence Inquiry: Report of an Inquiry by Sir William Macpherson of Cluny*, CM 4262-1, published by the Stationery Office in 1999) is one of the most extraordinary documents ever to be published by any British government. Its language, tone and style are quite unlike anything else ever printed by the austere presses of the state. Its accusation of 'institutional racism' against the police is by definition impossible to prove and therefore impossible to refute. Yet it has highly disreputable origins. The inventor of this idea and expression was the American black radical Stokely Carmichael, an anti-Semite who was at one time banned from this country and who proclaimed that Hitler was a

---

* The author clearly recalls seeing and being shocked by such notices when under arrest in two London police stations, West End Central and Cannon Row, in August 1969.

genius. Carmichael, originally a Black Panther, changed his name before he died to Kwame Touré in honour of two of black Africa's most disastrous despots, Kwame Nkrumah and Sékou Touré. He once suggested that the people of Brixton should be armed with hand grenades. Despite this tainted source, it has been difficult for anyone to combat the new ideology presumably for fear of being damned as institutionally racist themselves.

A full and devastating examination of this peculiar report's assumptions and attitudes was made in *Racist Murder and Pressure Group Politics* by Norman Dennis, George Erdos and Ahmed Al-Shahi, published by the Institute for the Study of Civil Society. This chapter cannot range so widely. It seeks only to examine the effects that the Lawrence affair, and the official interpretation of it, have had on the police. It also examines the similar but different impact of the 1981 Brixton and other riots and the Scarman report on them.

The strange nature of Sir William Macpherson's report suggests that it was aimed not only at the organization and discipline of the police but at their whole reason for existing. The report argued for a revolutionary change in the official attitude towards solving the country's racial problems, which has now affected every corner of the public sector. The words calling for an end to 'colour-blind policing' quoted above are wrapped in an apparently reassuring blanket of tolerant worthiness. The paragraph in full reads:

> The message is uncompromising. A new atmosphere
> of mutual confidence and trust must be created. The
> onus to begin the process which will create that new
> atmosphere lies firmly and clearly with the police.
> The Police Services must examine every aspect of their
> policies and practices to assess whether the outcome
> of their actions creates or sustains patterns of
> discrimination. The provision of policing services to
> a diverse public must be appropriate and professional

in every case. Every individual must be treated with respect. 'Colour-blind' policing must be outlawed. The police must deliver a service which recognises the different experiences, perceptions and needs of a diverse society.

This declaration has to be read together with one of the report's other revolutionary statements, namely the one appearing almost immediately before it on page 314 (paragraph 45.17). This declares: 'A racist incident is any incident which is perceived to be racist by the victim *or any other person*' (author's italics).

Before returning to these words, it is worth recording the main objections to the Macpherson report voiced by Dennis, Erdos and Al-Shahi. These criticisms, although published by a conservative organization, did not come from the classical right. Dennis is a distinguished scholar of the left and active Labour Party member, Erdos is a Hungarian-born ethical socialist. Al-Shahi, a British citizen of Kurdish origin, is an anthropologist who is an expert on tolerance and integration. After examining the Lawrence inquiry and its report in great detail, they came to the unexpected conclusion that 'no evidence of racism on the part of the police was ever produced.' They went on:

> There was no attempt to show that the Metropolitan Police Service was racist in the sense of being formally structured to put members of ethnic minorities at a disadvantage. Nor was any evidence produced that individual officers dealing with the murder of Stephen Lawrence had displayed racism, unless one includes the use of words like 'coloured', which are currently out of favour with professional race relations lobbyists. No evidence was produced to indicate that the police would have handled the investigation differently had the victim been white.

They added that: 'To question whether the murder of Stephen Lawrence was a purely racist crime was, in itself, adduced as evidence of racism. This was despite the fact that the suspects had been accused of violent offences against white people and were heard, in tape recordings made of their private conversations, to express violent hatred against white people.'

There is much to regret about the Lawrence case, most of all the murder itself, which, like all such crimes, is an immense and irreplaceable loss, made worse by the failure to bring the culprits to justice, and a woeful illustration of the lawlessness now infecting England. However, it is open to question whether it was so special as to justify the enormous controversy and campaign that grew up around it. Doubts have been cast on the competence of the police inquiries, which cannot be judged a success. But such police failure is all too common. The real issue is whether their behaviour in this case was in any way untypical of police work in modern Britain and whether, if so, it was untypical because of racial prejudice within the police.

The Lawrence family is one of many, black and white, who have yet to see justice done to the killers of close relatives. There is as yet no strong evidence that it was untypical, let alone that its failings were the result of racial prejudice. The Lawrence case is by no means the only unsolved murder on the books of the police forces of England. More to the point, it is not the only racial killing to have taken place in that part of London. As Macpherson says (paragraph 7.18 and others, pages 38–9):

> It should be recorded that racist crime and violence were
> not new to the district. Both Eltham and Thamesmead
> had bitter experience of such crime by 1993 [Stephen
> Lawrence was killed on 22 April 1993]. In May 1991 a
> black youth called Orville Blair was killed by a white
> man called Snell. Eventually Snell was convicted of
> manslaughter on the grounds of provocation. There is

some doubt whether this was in fact a racist crime, but it was so regarded by the community.

In February 1991 a white man named Thornburrow murdered a young 15 year old black youth named Rolan Adams, in a gross racist attack made at a bus stop after some altercation between rival gangs of white and black youths... Thornburrow was sentenced to life imprisonment...

On 11 July 1992 an Asian boy called Rohit Duggal was stabbed to death by a white youth named Peter Thompson outside the kebab shop in Tudor Parade. Thompson was found guilty of the murder in February 1993...

Macpherson mentions these cases to show possible connections to the suspects in the Lawrence killing and to complain about the 'lack of co-ordinated information about them', but also to 'highlight the regularity of such offences'.

They also show that, whatever their faults, the police were capable of catching such killers and of providing evidence on the basis of which they could be convicted. If there was a racial bias among the police in the area, then it was not so powerful that the families of Orville Blair, Rolan Adams and Rohit Duggal were deprived of justice. If all these cases had ended without convictions, then a serious case might have been made that there was something *institutionally* wrong with the area's police. Given that these other killings were all cleared up, Macpherson's evidence for a racial or general explanation for the Lawrence failure is remarkably weak.

But perhaps it had no need to be any stronger. It is worth remembering that the Macpherson report (1997–9) was not a response to the murder itself (1993), nor to the initial failure to bring suspects to trial or to the failure of the private prosecution against three men (1996). It was not until July 1997 that Macpherson was asked to set up his inquiry, after Kent Police had already investigated the matter. The Macpherson inquiry was a response to the campaign that followed Stephen Lawrence's death. That campaign had a wider purpose than justice for Stephen Lawrence's family and punishment for his murderers. It had political objectives. The decision to set up the Macpherson investigation was also one of the earliest acts of a Labour government determined to extend Britain's cultural revolution into those institutions that had until then been only partly affected by it.

So in that light, let us return to those extraordinary words in the closing pages of the Macpherson report, that '"Colour-blind" policing must be outlawed', and that 'A racist incident is any incident which is perceived to be racist by the victim or any other person.' There is a third extract, too, which is also quite astonishing. It forms part of a lengthy quotation from a speech given in 1992 by Sir John Woodcock to the International Conference on Policing. At the time, Sir John was Her Majesty's Chief Inspector of Constabulary, a man with immense influence over the conduct of the police throughout England and Wales. His words give a startling clue to the real thinking of many senior police officers today.

Macpherson quotes him (paragraph 6.61, pages 34 and 35), alongside witnesses who called for a radical cultural transformation of the police. If the report had been solely about the Lawrence affair, the Woodcock speech really had no place in it at all. Its presence in the report is a clear sign that Macpherson was inquiring into the socially and culturally conservative culture of police officers and not just into one failed murder investigation. Admitting that the context was different, he specifically said that, even so, he believed Woodcock's words were apt. Since they have absolutely no direct bearing on the case, one has to wonder why. The central passage from Woodcock runs as follows:

> The workplace values of the modern police service have
> not yet fully cut free of the past and the police service

faces a massive task if it is to hold, as the community now demands, integrity and respect for human rights, above all other considerations...

What is happening to the police is that a 19th-century institution is being dragged into the 21st century. *Despite all the later mythology of Dixon, the police never really were the police of the whole people but a mechanism set up to protect the affluent from what the Victorians described as the dangerous classes* [italics added]. I believe that the events of the last few years have not only presented British policing with a challenge so formidable that it has come close to disaster: they have also now given the opportunity to the British Police to reinvent themselves. It is now possible to see that, through a fundamental shift of culture, the British police service will remain at the worldwide forefront of policing, with a style which draws its legitimacy from an understanding of current public needs and of the nature of the contract between police and a new generation of the public.

Where did her Majesty's Chief Inspector of Police get such ideas? Dennis, Erdos and Al-Shahi comment: 'To ordinary non-affluent people – the "labouring nation" who suffer from the crimes and insecurity imposed on them by their neighbours, the idea pronounced by HM Inspector of Police, that the police service is needed by nobody but the affluent, is incredible. Yet this is included in the Macpherson report as particularly "apt in the context of this Inquiry".'

Macpherson stated (paragraphs 6.62 and 6.63): 'Our conclusions and recommendations are designed to guide all police officers towards a transformation of their culture in partnership with others, in the context of policing this present multi-cultural and multi-ethnic Britain... We are confident that the Home Secretary and the Government will perceive the pressures for change which this inquiry has uncovered, so that the necessary transformation will start to take place. The Inquiry itself cannot mould the future, but Government and society can together go forward.'

These three passages are the moral core of Macpherson. The first states clearly that it is the police who must change, rather than the society whose laws they seek to enforce. How must they change? No real suggestions are made about ways in which they might become more efficient and effective in their struggle against crime and disorder. Yet the need to increase their effectiveness is surely the main lesson of Stephen Lawrence's revolting murder and the failure of criminal justice that followed. However, almost all of Macpherson's recommendations concern elaborate and often bureaucratic steps to be taken against 'racism'.

Two of these – a new power to prosecute people for using 'racist' language in private and the suggestion, now adopted, that an accused person might be tried twice for the same offence – are frontal assaults on liberty which would be hard to justify in the midst of a war for national survival. Such ideas are typical of the 'liberal' response to disorder – an increase in the power, even over thought and speech, of the benevolent elite state. As such, they are a warning of what lies ahead for England under its new ruling class.

The police, meanwhile, are to be judged mainly on whether the 'outcome of their actions creates or sustains patterns of discrimination'. Taken to its limit, and put together with the statement that something is racist if anybody thinks it is, this leads to an astonishing conclusion. It means that any action the outcome of which is condemned as racist, even (perhaps especially) by a person of extreme and revolutionary views, is unquestionably wrong. In practice, the operational effect on the police will be unlimited. No officer, however junior, can take any action without fear for how it might one day be presented before some politically-correct inquisition in which his presumed attitude of mind, rather than his actions, will be on trial.

Add to this mix Sir John Woodcock's belief that the English police have until today been a shield guarding the rich from the poor and must now reinvent themselves, and you have a prescription for a cultural revolution in the police force. On another occasion, in his annual report quoted in *The Times* in June 1992, Sir John spoke of the need for cultural change which had to involve viewing the public as customers and meeting their demands. He went on: 'The abusing husband, the foul drunk, the lager lout and the belligerent squatter are customers, different but equally as much customers as the victims of crime, the frightened child, the tourist asking the time.' He said that the police had to be much more answerable and open because society had changed and was no longer acquiescent: 'Police can no longer say "These are the rules, this is what you must do." They must persuade, and answer, the public.' He said that changing the culture would take time but that younger officers had little difficulty in dealing with a discerning public.

In fact, changing the culture of the police has not been easy. Police officers, with a few interesting exceptions, have generally been conservative people. They are bound to be. The nature of the job does not attract individuals who reject the existing social order. Nor, until recently, were they educated much beyond grammar-school level. This did not mean that they were ignorant or stupid. On the contrary, a pre-1960s' grammar-school education probably provided more knowledge and understanding than most modern university degrees. It did, however, mean that they were not sympathetic to idealist or theoretical views of life. Their own store of experience as constables would in any case have contradicted most such views. But, as I have shown elsewhere, this type of officer is rapidly disappearing. There are now many thousands of university graduates in the police and a far greater number of women, who could not apply the old-fashioned rough rules of policing even if they wanted to. These university-educated officers have been removed from conservative parental influences at an impressionable age and exposed to the egalitarian and socialistic theories that pervade most British university courses and are accepted as normal and obligatory among college students.

By the end of the twentieth century, the police force was balanced between the new graduate wing and the old common-sense and hard-knocks wing. Among senior officers, the academic, theoretical, business-school style had become dominant with the mergers of the late 1960s and the increasing influence of Bramshill and the Association of Chief Police Officers. However, the lower and middle ranks still contained many socially conservative people, imbued with older beliefs about what the law was and how it should be enforced. The distinction is best summed up in the difference between the old expression 'police force' and the new one, 'police service'. The older style of officer was often highly effective, although rarely promoted to high levels. Anyone seeking to transform the police as Sir John Woodcock wished to do would meet opposition from this large conservative body of men. And their continued existence and culture would affect and embrace many young recruits.

A forgotten aspect of the Labour Party's lurch into open extremism in the early 1980s is the widespread demand for political control over the police – 'police committees' in the language of the time. The left regarded the police much as Sir John Woodcock did, as the rich's army against the poor. They also viewed them as racialist and hostile to the sexual liberation and relaxed attitudes towards drugs that are common in leftist politics. However, that was in the days when Labour still clung to the old methods of openly seeking to change the nature of society by attacking or taking over established institutions. The left's great discovery in the later 1980s and early 1990s was that there was another method, less direct but equally effective: to leave the institution standing and apparently the same, but revolutionize its culture by more subtle means. Such an approach allows the left to win elections while appearing to be conservative, and to pursue radical policies once safely in office. It is at least possible that the left's desire to change the police has found a new and irresistible weapon in the form of political correctness.

That weapon can be wielded in the unending hunt for traces of 'institutional racism', the presence of which needs no objective evidence and can therefore be alleged whenever necessary.

There is no doubt at all that many individual policemen of the old sort are racially prejudiced in their private minds. It would be difficult for them not to be, given the backgrounds from which they come and the sort of people they are. There is also no doubt that the vast majority of them rightly keep these feelings to themselves and in many cases are actually ashamed of them. Yet it is also true that most of the operational successes of the police are still achieved by these old-fashioned, conservative, male officers. As a result, they still have the upper hand in the 'canteen culture' which determines how the mass of officers act, what they think and which idea of the law they cling to.

The cultural attack on them has been long and sustained. They were the main target of allegations of corruption and evidence-planting pursued by radical lawyers and activists from the 1960s onwards. The famous *Prime Suspect* series of television dramas about a female, culturally liberal officer challenging the sclerotic male dinosaurs of the force had an important impact on police and public attitudes. It has been much imitated. The effect of such programmes is enormous. Now, hardly a month goes by without a tribunal case or a complaint that exposes older male officers as boorish and out of step with the 'modern' world. Such officers and their 'canteen culture' were also the main target of the Police and Criminal Evidence Act 1984 and of the Police Complaints Authority, which acts on the assumption that the police cannot be trusted and that every action they take must therefore be recorded, regulated and subject to disciplinary inquiry.

The effect of Macpherson has been greater even than the impact of these exercises in cultural propaganda. For the first time, it has linked police blunders with racial prejudice in the public mind. Since racial prejudice affects only the old type of officer, it has dealt a wounding blow to their morale and prestige. It has also greatly strengthened the new wave of social-worker policemen and women. As a result, it is likely to lead to the final triumph of the new view of the law as mediator between offender and victim in an egalitarian and multicultural society – that is to say, in a society in which traditional deference, religion and morality have been dethroned. If the police force at all levels is dominated by those who believe in the new type of law beloved of Sir John Woodcock, then that will be the law that is universally enforced. The old type of policing, meanwhile, can be dismissed as wrong and false – as it was by Sir John, who believes that the police never really were the police of the whole people.

This result was not inevitable. It is particularly wretched that Britain's black people and their undoubted problems have been used for this purpose. Many black Britons were and are supporters of the traditional order. In fact, they suffer more than most from the crime and disorder of our society. Much of it is inflicted on them by other black people with whom they have nothing in common but their colour. In a strange inversion of racial prejudice, their plight and their decency alike have both been forgotten. They are black, therefore they must desire the changes recommended by Macpherson.

This liberal, racialist desire to confuse colour with culture is very difficult to oppose. If colour and culture are the same, then those who try to criticize a culture linked with a particular racial group can be attacked as 'racist' and be driven from the stage as personally odious. Yet such an attitude is profoundly racialist in itself because it classifies people by their race rather than by their actions. This book continues to use the term 'racialist' which the author remembers as being in common use in the days when he used to go on demonstrations against Enoch Powell in the 1960s. This is because it preserves the original straightforward meaning of the time: a racialist is one who judges a man by the colour of his skin rather than the content of his character, as Martin Luther King himself put it in his great speech at the Lincoln Memorial, Washington, DC on 28 August 1963.

The word 'racist' did not enter the language of England till much later and it seems to the author that it has an entirely different purpose. It is a slogan word which sucks meaning from a sentence, rather than an honourable word that aids understanding. It is easier to shout or paint on walls than 'racialist'. It sounds and looks like that other great vague abuse-word 'fascist' (so that it is sometimes written 'rascist'). Most significantly, it is often used against people who have no racial prejudice but who honourably object to cultural and moral change. Thanks to this verbal trickery, changes in culture and morals, and the growth of multiculturalism, have frequently been successful because opposition to them is deemed to be 'racist'.

A caricature of this problem is to be found in the attempted prosecution of the elderly retired seaman George Staunton in Liverpool in 1999 for 'racially aggravated criminal damage'. His offence was to paint on the wall of a derelict building the slogans 'Free Speech for England' and 'Remember the 1939 War', neither of which contains any racial sentiment whatever. The charges were eventually dropped, but only after newspaper criticism. The interesting thing is that he was charged at all. Mr Staunton's experience was an extreme example of what is happening to many other well-intentioned people. At some point, principled opposition to racial hatred ceased to be enough to guarantee political respectability. Active support for radical changes in English society became necessary to avoid the thought police and their irrational condemnations.

A significant moment in this process was the Scarman report into the Brixton riots of April 1981 (*The Brixton Disorders 10–12 April 1981, Report of an Inquiry by the Rt Hon the Lord Scarman OBE November 1981*, Cmnd 8427). What took place in Brixton was mass disorder by black and white youths, quite possibly organized, accompanied by a great deal of looting. During its two fiery and bloody days and nights 320 people were arrested and 587 injured, more than four hundred of them police officers. The country was deeply unsettled by such sights, unknown for many decades in mainland Britain.

Policing and criminal justice, although few were aware of it at the time, had already been greatly undermined by the reforms of the 1960s and 1970s, dealt with earlier in this book. Contact between the police and the people they served had diminished because of the abolition of beat patrols. Self-discipline, school discipline and family authority had also been weakened by liberal reforms of the schools and by the general demoralizing effect of the permissive society. An ambiguous official attitude towards narcotics had encouraged the widespread misuse of illegal drugs, only occasionally and unpredictably attacked by the law.

Mass immigration from the New Commonwealth had been badly mishandled, with pathetically little done to ensure that the new arrivals settled well and quickly. The housing policies of urban local authorities had led to the creation of disastrous pockets of social and moral deprivation and misery. Criminal gangs were seeking to take advantage of racial tension and social disorder to create areas where they could work undisturbed. All of these facts contributed to what happened on those two spring days in south London.

Much was wrong with that England. In 1981 much of it would have been a good deal easier to put right than it is now. However, the Scarman report made the disorders an occasion for an attack on police methods and attitudes. And, in anticipation of Macpherson, it sought to make England adapt itself to what it thought was the culture of Afro-Caribbean citizens. The strange and rather insulting implication of this was that the rioters were in some way representative of all such citizens, which, of course, they were not. For the report managed to admit quietly that the Brixton 'community' was divided on the issue of crime and law enforcement and that the majority was on the side of the law.

Scarman opened his report by offering only two significant reasons for the riots: one, that they were an anti-police protest caused by oppressive policing and the harassment of young blacks; and two, that they were a protest against society by 'deeply frustrated and deprived' people who saw 'in a violent attack upon the forces of law and order their one opportunity of compelling public attention to their grievances'. Scarman dismissed neither explanation out of hand, although he rightly said that both were oversimplifications and that neither, even if true, was the whole truth.

A third explanation – that lawless people, angered by a brief return of proper policing to what had become almost an outlaw zone, seized an opportunity to drive the police from the streets and to loot the local shops, and that political opportunists later sought to use the riots as a pretext for restraints on the police in future – seems not to have occurred to him. Why not?

His own report can be read in an entirely different way from the official interpretation. Take, for instance, the early hours of the rioting. Scarman wrote (paragraph 3.25): 'The crowd of black youths felt, with some reason, that they were being pursued. They turned and fought. Their action was criminal and is not to be condoned. It was not, however, planned. It was a spontaneous act of defiant aggression by young men who felt themselves hunted by a hostile police force.' This scene followed what many would think was entirely justifiable behaviour by the police in intercepting a suspicious vehicle, finding a wounded man in it and trying to get him to hospital because they feared he was seriously injured. It is quite extraordinary that one of Her Majesty's most distinguished judges should say that the fighting by black youths was criminal and not to be condoned and then go on to describe it as a 'spontaneous act of defiant aggression' by people who 'felt themselves hunted by a hostile police force'. If that is not exactly condoning the fighting, it goes a long way towards excusing it.

Dealing with Operation Swamp, the police attempt to contain and control street crime which preceded the riot, the guardian of the law is once again ambiguous about enforcing the law: 'I understand why it was decided to continue with the operation: street crime was a grave matter in Brixton, upon which the *silent law-abiding majority of residents* [my emphasis] felt very strongly. But I am bound to say that the wise course would have been to have discontinued the operation.' So protecting the interests of the law-abiding was understandable, but failing to protect them was wise. Which was *right*? The learned judge did not say.

And anyone searching for an actual cause for the outbreak of the riot will be disappointed. There was none. What is interesting about the account is that there is no major incident – only the searching of a minicab driver for drugs and the subsequent arrest of an allegedly abusive youth, not major incidents by the standards of the area at the time. Quite suddenly, there was a fully-formed riot, as if out of nowhere. Chief Superintendent Boyling 'noticed that the crowd in Atlantic Road was covering the full width of the road. Suddenly there was a cry of "Look out!" Looking through the air the Chief Superintendent saw bricks and stones coming through the air towards him.' Earlier, a Mr Tony Morgan (a young black man) had warned Mr Boyling (paragraph 3.37) that 'if he did not get his officers out of the area there would be a riot'. People with cameras had been seen at 4.40 p.m. on a nearby roof taking photographs. How did they know that there would be anything worth photographing at that place and time?

Mr Boyling had responded by toning down the police presence, walking round the crowd talking to as many people as possible. Scarman says: 'The general criticism was of the number of police officers present' (paragraph 3.38). He states that there were then about fifty or sixty in the area – hardly an army of occupation. By 5.45 p.m. the first petrol bombs were thrown. At 5.55 a number 2 bus was 'commandeered' (Scarman's curious term for a criminal hijack) by people in the crowd. The conductor was 'assaulted and *robbed of his takings* [my emphasis]', suggesting that this was not a wholly political act if indeed it was political at all. Meanwhile, the existence of demolition sites in Railton Road provided almost unlimited supplies of ammunition for stone-throwers. At 7.00 p.m. (paragraph 3.57) 'community leaders', including an Anglican vicar and two councillors, explained to the police commander 'that in their view the only way for the police to reduce tension was for the police to withdraw from the area and allow the crowd to disperse'.

The commander, Brian Fairbairn, said he would not withdraw and refused to go with the quartet to speak to the crowd, but lent them a loudhailer so that they could do so. The mediators were 'seized by some of the crowd' (paragraph 3.58) 'who told them their terms for dispersing. They wanted the police to withdraw, they wanted an end to police harassment and they wanted those arrested to be released.' Soon afterwards, there was an outbreak of wide-spread looting by *both whites and blacks* (paragraph 3.61, author's emphasis), again suggesting that the incidents were not exclusively racial or political. Scarman (paragraph 3.76), however, concluded:

> The inference is irresistible that many young people, and especially many young black people, were spoiling for a row as a result of their frustrations, fancied or real, and of their beliefs as to what happened on Friday. The young people who crowded the streets believed Friday's events to be yet another typical instance of police harassment of young blacks. And many of them were deceived by rumour into thinking that police callousness on the Friday had actually led to the death of the wounded man. The tinder for a major conflagration was there: the arrest outside the S & M car hire office was the spark which set it ablaze.

Another way of putting this is that false rumour, presumably spread by malicious people, led to a wholly unjustified confrontation between the police and a small, inflamed section of the Brixton public. The false rumour about the dead man was actually based on the decision by officers to call for an ambulance when they found a wounded man in a car they had stopped. He was not in fact seri-ously wounded and certainly did not die. Their action was humane and justified. Scarman has no thoughts about how the police are supposed to prevent the spreading of false rumours about humane actions.

He then (paragraph 3.77), astonishingly, adds:

> There is no need to probe deeper for the immediate cause of the Saturday riot. I have heard no evidence to suggest that there was any prior organisation or conspiracy. There was no 'D-Day' or 'H-Hour'. But many young people were itching to have a go. The spirit of defiance and aggression was in them. Many observers noted their elation as events developed to the disadvantage of the police. *They were enjoying themselves* [my emphasis]. Deeper causes undoubtedly existed and must be probed: but the immediate cause of Saturday's events was a spontaneous combustion set off by the spark of one single incident.

Yet, despite this insistence that there was no prior organization or conspiracy, Scarman earlier records (paragraph 3.53): 'A white man and a black youth appeared to one officer present to be directing operations' at the time of a concerted attack on the police line in Railton Road. He also notes that the fact that terms were offered by rioters to the police 'indicates plainly enough not only that there was a degree of direction but also that, after the disorders had begun, some strangers participated in the attacks upon the police, some leaders emerged and some used the disorders for the deliberate commission of criminal offences'.

Both these statements cannot simultaneously be correct. Spontaneous riots, if such things exist, do not need leaders either before they begin or after they have started. Scarman also refers (paragraph 3.104) to other events that suggest that the outbreak was not entirely spontaneous:

The evidence does suggest that a sinister contribution
was made by strangers in making and distributing petrol
bombs. Indeed, it is possible, though the evidence is not
sufficient to warrant a finding, that without the guidance
and help of certain white people, the young blacks, who
were the great majority of the rioting crowds, would not
have used the bomb. Be that as it may – and I have to
leave it as an open question – clear and credible evidence
was given to me in private session by two witnesses who
reside in streets adjacent to Railton Road, that they saw
white men making, stacking and distributing petrol
bombs in the Railton Road/Leeson Road area on Saturday.

What a question to leave open.

Yet it is easy to see why it was left open. The whole theory of
spontaneous popular revolt by an oppressed and harassed racial and
cultural minority is deeply undermined by a series of observations:

a) the possibility that petrol bombs were being made in an organized fashion;

b) the riot had enough of a directing intelligence to offer negotiating terms to the police;

c) the rioters lost no chance to loot and steal;

d) poisonous and lying rumours were spread in the hours before the riot;

e) there was not even a definable incident that can be said to have triggered the first violence;

f) white people were involved in both rioting and looting.

There is also the point, clearly made by Scarman himself, that the
rioters were enjoying themselves. This is hard to square with the
idea that the smashing, looting and violence were the expression of a
rooted resentment.

Scarman argues (paragraph 3.105) that it is unlikely that the use of petrol bombs was premeditated. He says forward planning would not have been necessary because of the existence of materials readily to hand. These materials were looted bottles and petrol stolen from what the judge once again calls 'commandeered' vehicles – a strange use of a military term to describe an illegal act, especially from a judge. This is odd logic, since the making of petrol bombs requires not only materials but the wish to make and use them and the knowledge of how to do so, which has then to be shared among several people. They, in turn, must gather the bottles and petrol, find material for fuses, pick a site for bomb-making and organize the distribution of bombs to the crowd. Perhaps recognizing that he is contradicting himself, he adds: 'The bombs indicate the existence of a degree of organisation among the rioters *once the disorders began* [my italics]. There is convincing evidence of the existence of at least one makeshift "factory" in which petrol bombs were made for use by the rioters in Brixton on the Saturday.'

But if there was organization once the disorders began, does it not suggest that there might have been organization beforehand? At a distance of more than twenty years it would be quite impossible to establish this. At the time of Lord Scarman's report, when memories were still fresh, an investigation might have yielded some interesting results. And even if an organization only developed once the troubles were under way, what was its purpose and whom did it serve?

Repeatedly, Scarman reassures his readers (and himself) that (paragraph 3.109) 'The violence erupted from the spontaneous reaction of the crowds to what they believed to be police harassment', and (paragraph 3.110) that 'The riots were essentially an outburst of anger and resentment by young black people against the police'. Perhaps this is the right explanation. What is important is that Scarman's own report gives plenty of reasons to think that there might be another explanation altogether. Yet, as in the case of

Macpherson, one senses that Scarman's conclusions were designed to deal with the political aftermath of the riots rather than with the riots themselves.

There are many fascinating facts in the report that support the idea that the real issue was crime rather than discontent. One is the information (paragraph 4.40) that during the period of Operation Swamp (the allegedly tactless name of which was not publicly known at the time of the disorders) the number of robberies and burglaries in the area halved. Another is that a 'home beat' officer, expert on the neighbourhood, thought that the youths outside the car hire office where the disorders began were not local and were seeking a confrontation.

A vital section (paragraph 4.45) illustrates the police's dilemma and the existence of opposing views within a community that is usually portrayed as being united behind the rioters. The police had to do something about rising levels of street crime, but if they did so they would be criticized: 'There was an underlying feeling that no matter how hard they tried to meet the apparently conflicting expectations of the community and no matter what measures were adopted, their efforts would continue to be the target for unreasonable criticism.' Many police officers must have thought that much of the Scarman report, with its extensive use of hindsight about their behaviour, was yet more of that unreasonable criticism. We also learn (paragraph 4.44) that local 'community leaders' had withdrawn from a liaison committee with the police in February 1979, but nowhere does the report either question the right of these leaders to speak for the entire community, or subject them to the sort of criticism heaped on the police.

At the time, many police officers were baffled as to what they were now supposed to do about crime in Brixton or any other area where race might become an issue. Not yet worn down by two decades of political correctness, some officers were prepared to express doubts. James Jardine, the chairman of the Police Federation at the time, said: 'In my view Lord Scarman has not been able to provide a satisfactory answer to the most important question that he asked "How do the police in the inner city deal with a very high level of street crime, while at the same time retaining the support of all".' He spoke of an 'upside down world' in which Scarman was persuaded to believe that action against mugging was a probable cause of the riots. Commander Brian Fairbairn, head of Lambeth district police and involved at the very centre of events, responded thus to the criticism of Operation Swamp as a serious mistake:

> I think perhaps in hindsight I should have got round the problem we had in a different manner... one wants to work with the community. It clearly pays the police to relate to and to have the full support of the community. At the same time if you are going to try to curb what in this instance is a very high crime rate, you may sometimes have, paradoxically, to do things which seem to work against this. It is difficult to please everyone all the time. In fact, it is impossible.

But others were already beginning to recognize that they were going to have to adapt to the new order. The division between old and new emerged during the hearings. Stephen Sedley, a former communist and future high court judge, was counsel for the Commission for Racial Equality at the inquiry. He contrasted the evidence given by Assistant Commissioner Wilfred Gibson with that of Geoffrey Dear, Deputy Assistant Commissioner in charge of training. He said: 'Through them the Metropolitan Police has spoken with two voices. Mr Gibson was basically defensive, un-self-critical and unseeing, while Mr Dear looked forward and was farseeing.' It is not difficult to work out what Stephen Sedley's idea of a far seeing policeman would have been. Probably it was not that different from Sir John Woodcock's.

The issue here is not one of whether police are able to stop and search black people more often or less often, or even of whether most muggers are black. So what if they are? The real point for most people is that mugging should be prevented, whoever does it. Most burglars are white. The answer is the same. The police record on race is not faultless. It would be absurd to pretend that it was. Stupidity and inexperience, and the chasm that car-borne patrolling has opened up between police and public, play their part in fraying relations between the police and *all* the public, not just black citizens. What is more, the methods of modern policing, with its inconsistency, unpredictability and temporary 'targeting' of certain areas, almost seem designed to cause trouble between police and young men. Years of laxity on drug possession have made the re-establishment of order in some districts a near-impossible task. Part of the magic of the old police uniform was based on its familiarity and its instant recognizability as a symbol of order and safety. Many younger people have never had a chance to develop the instinctive respect for the police that their elders feel. Stop and search, and actions such as Operation Swamp, are a poor replacement for the proper beat patrolling that might well have brought about a real relationship between the police and the law-abiding public in Brixton and many other areas. It might also have prevented the murder of Stephen Lawrence. He was casually knifed to death on a busy suburban road by people who obviously, and correctly, reckoned that they had a good chance of getting away with murder.

The question is whether the issue of race should be used to impose a new code of law on the police and thus on the people of this country. Should black Englishmen be insultingly stereotyped as prone to riot when subjected to the law? Should black Englishmen be assumed to be incapable of co-operating with the justice system, even in their own interests, unless treated with special consideration? Surely such ideas, in their naked simplicity, are grossly prejudiced and likely to create and fix racial divisions within our society? And who benefits from them? Certainly the black people of England do not, since these theories are used as excuses to withdraw what police protection there is from the areas where black people are concentrated.

There have been many racial riots since Brixton, some of them involving Muslim Asians who would once have been thought the least likely citizens in the country to take to the streets. There will, inevitably, be future murders similar to that of Stephen Lawrence. The Scarman and Macpherson inquiries, for all the talk of 'this must never be allowed to happen again', have failed in their supposed main purpose. However, they have succeeded in their less obvious purpose, which was to impose on the police of England a new kind of law, the law of the elite state rather than of the common people. That new kind of law originated with the wealthy liberal stratum whose religion is a guilty egalitarianism. It spread into the legal profession and the world of politics. However, it could not be finally effective until the old spirit of English policing, so despised by Sir John Woodcock, could be eliminated. The grievances and difficulties of black Englishmen have been used as the pretext for a reform that will leave them just as unprotected from crime as the rest of us, and which will in the end threaten the freedom of all Englishmen of every colour, race and creed.

X

Justice denied

And judgment is turned away backward, and
justice standeth afar off: for truth is fallen in the
street and equity cannot enter.
Isaiah 59:14

There is usually a short interval between the crisis and the catastrophe. The barbarian raiders did not descend on the defenceless coasts of England the minute the Roman legions departed. It took some time for them to realize that the lush, comfortable land was defenceless. There is a long, slowly fading afterglow in the sky for some time after the sun has gone down below the horizon, during which the light survives though its source has gone.

We are now living in such an interval, gradually becoming aware of the grave change that has overtaken this country, but still living for the most part as if the legions had not departed and the sun had not yet set. Habits of mind, among those who are inclined to crime and those who are not, have still not adjusted to the real nature of things. For most of us, the moment when we become aware that we are no longer safe will be a personal shock, the grab at the handbag, the robbery on a corner we have passed in safety for years, the sound of broken glass and footsteps where there ought not to be footsteps in our homes at night.

Those who scoff at the law are also discovering their new freedom inch by inch. The young men and women who today beg aggressively for 'change' on the streets of many cities would once have been milder and more cautious. Not many years hence they will be more aggressive still, and probably violent. The burglars who hesitate to enter a house when its owner is at home have yet to digest the news from the courts – that they can most likely break in without fear that they will face a serious defence from the occupants. The thief faced by an inconvenient witness is not yet armed with a lethal weapon and is only slowly learning that it is a rational calculation to close that witness's mouth for ever.

They have not yet understood, and neither have their victims, that the police have permanently withdrawn from the streets and are unable to detect or prosecute most crimes. They are only just beginning to grasp that there is no reliable right of self-defence and that their victims are restrained by a fear of the law that does not trouble them. Only among sub-teenage children in the abandoned, marriage-free zones of the great housing estates is there already perfect knowledge of the feebleness of the police, the array of 'human rights' that prevent them from being prosecuted and the unwillingness of the authorities to punish them if by any chance they should ever be convicted. These people already behave with complete lawlessness, as those who live within range of them know painfully well. When they grow to manhood, we will all have much to fear.

The catastrophe will be gradual. If it were to happen overnight there would be a national revolt. Citizens have slowly grown used to the likelihood that they will return to car or home and find that thieves have broken in and stolen. Neighbourhood by neighbourhood, the puddles of broken glass left by the car thieves begin to appear, at first alarming, then commonplace. Word spreads quietly that it is not wise to use such and such a cash machine late at night. The yellow 'murder-boards' appear, at first a novelty, then a tedious and dispiriting nuisance. It is now generally thought unwise to intervene in violent or angry incidents in public places, and many who would once have gone to the rescue think twice before doing so, mainly for fear of knives.

It is foolish to expect help of any kind to come in incidents on the street or on public transport. Shopkeepers in many areas accept that their goods will be pilfered by violent youths who will return and attack them and their shops if they are challenged. They know that it is futile to call the police, and probably worse than futile since it will only bring about some sort of vengeance. It is a new and crude form of protection racket, instinctive rather than organized. In large parts of the big cities residents are accustoming themselves to the sound of gunfire by night, to the blood-encrusted needles of the drug-takers and the whispered commerce of the drug-dealers. Dangerous and demoralizing narcotics which ought to be discouraged are effectively legal and ignored by the police even when they see them being sold in the open. Once-normal roads and highways are consciously or semi-consciously avoided, especially by women and at certain times, because they are considered to be unsafe. Homes and vehicles must be protected with all the resources of technology, although the main effect of this has been to displace rather than to suppress crime. CCTV cameras in town centres send thieves to the unwatched suburbs. A burglar alarm system says 'rob the house next door, not mine'. Car alarms and immobilizers persuade thieves to hijack cars with their owners, and keys, still in them. The lock and bolt industry has never flourished as it is flourishing now, along with the alarm manufacturers. The only sort of alarm that the public cannot obtain is the sort that would alert the political classes to the true state of affairs.

If all these things had happened at once there would have been outrage and political anger. Because they are gradual and happen to each of us as individuals, we adapt to them and, while we complain, we are not angry enough to act or to try to make sense of what is happening to us. The realization that, if we are in serious trouble or danger, there is nobody out there to help has come to many thousands of people in recent times. However, it has happened to each one of them in isolation. The fear and even shame at their humiliation and defeat that now infect their lives are experienced alone or inside the family. Many probably blame themselves. They ought to be blaming the rulers of the country who have utterly betrayed them while pretending to guard them.

As for those rulers, whose failure in their most basic duty is one of the true scandals of modern England, they have so far escaped most of the consequences of their own folly. Since most crime is about geography and convenience, the political classes have not yet experienced it very much. They drive rather than walk, they live in areas of the capital where there is still some sort of police presence and where trouble is still some distance away. If they are politicians, they are surrounded by uniformed policemen. In fact, the Houses of Parliament are probably the last remaining place in the country where a uniformed constable is a frequent and regular sight. If the police guards of MPs and ministers were to be withdrawn, as ours have been, they would quickly realize how serious matters have become. This will not happen. The deployment of the police as bodyguards for the governing class is part of their new function. Because the new type of policeman serves power rather than the law, the seclusion of the elite from normal life has become one of his main activities.

Our rulers throw us sops and concessions. Schemes for community policing come and, more usually, go. Neighbourhood Watch, supposedly an advance in crime-fighting, is in fact an insulting invitation by the police to the public – to do for themselves the job that the hired constabulary ought to be doing. Packages of noisy 'tough' legislation are rammed through Parliament, frequently damaging civil liberties. They make no difference because the problem does not arise from there being too few laws, or laws that are too weak, but from the fact that laws must be enforced to be effective, and the police refuse to enforce them or are prevented by other legislation from doing so.

That is why so much of the current public argument about crime and punishment is futile. Why quibble about the length of a prison term when professional criminals do not fear prison and are most unlikely to end up there? When the main objective of the Home Office is to keep the prisons from overflowing, or from exploding into riot, and when it openly and specifically states that it does not want to punish convicts, it is hardly surprising that prison has no deterrent effect. Indeed, most criminals have to be exceptionally unlucky and incompetent to get sent to prison at all, or to be made to stay there for more than a few months before being tagged, paroled or otherwise returned to the 'community'. It may well be true that some of the people in our prisons ought not to be there. It is certainly true that thousands who ought to be in them are not, either out on bail, tagged, or left at liberty by the anti-establishment juries created by government folly.

The refusal of the English system to take human life more seriously than property means that levels of violence and the use of weapons increase unchecked. Carrying a gun or a knife is now most definitely worth the risk for the professional criminal, making victims more likely to give up their goods and aiding escape. The slow and unco-ordinated arming of the police, and the rapid and draconian disarming of the lawful population, do nothing to check this trend and make mistaken state killing more likely than ever.

The police themselves are the victims of the mistrust of the liberal elite. No doubt many of the methods used by the police in former times were not ideal. It was an open secret that the police might use violence and other types of rough justice against what they regarded as the criminal classes. The use of informers, still the most effective way of detecting crime, was always bound to be close to corruption and sometimes was corrupt. No system devised by humans can be perfect. But generally fair and just courts usually ensured that the police could not go too far in this direction. The public, it has to be said, were also satisfied with the way in which the old system worked. While it operated criminals feared the law, and both property and lives were far safer than they are now. It was prejudiced in favour of the public, and especially in favour of those who 'worked hard and played by the rules' – to use an expression so much liked by the present government that they stole it from President Clinton.

The growing influence of socially liberal thought on the legal and political elite in the 1960s and 1970s destroyed the informal independence of action against the criminal classes that the police once enjoyed. When cases of police wrongdoing were exposed, punishment of the individuals involved was not enough. Each event became the pretext for a general cause – that of restraining the police with rules and forcing them to do all their business on the record. The various commissions and campaigns whose work led to the Police and Criminal Evidence Act of 1984 and the establishment of the Police Complaints Authority were not set up because of public discontent with the performance of the police. There was little or no such discontent at the time, outside left-wing circles.

Nor were they intended to have the effects they did have. Legal liberals do not like crime any more than the rest of the population and usually try to live as far away from it as possible. They were set up because this country was passing through a revolution – a revolution that needed to change the nature of the law, the police and the courts. The Police and Criminal Evidence Act, with its pages of codes of practice governing every minute action by an arresting officer, is often blamed for the current state of affairs. However, it merely finished the work already done by the abolition of the beat system. The constable was already a radio-controlled automaton sent to crime scenes after the event, robbed of his initiative and of his main function, the enforcement of the public will. Now, bound by the Act and threatened with the career-ruining procedures of the Police Complaints Authority, the police officer is almost powerless to act even when an arrest could be made. Officially, he is not trusted to do the job for which he is paid. The removal of the police prosecution function and its transfer to the Crown Prosecution Service, a body governed by central bureaucracy and fearful of risking defeat in court, completed the transformation of effective police force into ineffectual police service. There are now proposals to remove even the right of the police to charge suspects and hand that over to the CPS as well.

At the same time, the state has obtained powers for itself and for the police force that make it theoretically possible to use immense pressure against those of whom the state does, from time to time, disapprove. On the excuse of fighting against terrorism suspects can be held for lengthy periods without charge, yet actual terrorists are released early from prison and their political spokesmen serve as ministers. Under the pretext of the fight against crime a suspect's exercise of his right to silence can now be taken by the courts as a sign of guilt, yet actual criminals are rarely brought to court, and the sacrifice of this ancient principle (in the Criminal Justice and Public Order Act of 1994) has brought few obvious benefits. Strong public order powers to restrain demonstrations are also a new feature of English law. A police force reluctant to take to the streets singly in pursuit of crime is curiously ready to appear in hundreds to confront demonstrators or protestors. Any excuse serves to denigrate the ancient principle of jury trial. The courts, the police and the prisons now serve the new benevolent elite state rather than the law of the land.

In February 2002, an extraordinary event revealed just how far this process has gone. One of the most senior officers in the Metropolitan Police, Commander Brian Paddick, revealed his innermost thoughts to a website, rashly believing that they would stay private. Commander Paddick, a highly intelligent Oxford graduate plainly marked for rapid promotion, was already known for his open and frequently declared homosexuality. Something that would once have endangered his entire career had become, in effect, an asset and an advantage, and there were those who whispered that Mr Paddick was promoted by the Metropolitan Police because they wished to show that they had fully adopted the new moral and social agenda. Such claims cannot be proved or disproved. He was also well known for his decision to abandon the prosecution of those possessing supposedly 'soft' drugs such as cannabis in the Lambeth district of London where he was in operational charge. This policy had been keenly endorsed by the Home Office and was extended to other parts of the country.

In his Internet conversation, Mr Paddick revealed a worldview that owed a good deal more to Rousseau and other revolutionaries than it did to the stolid reassurance of George Dixon. 'The concept of anarchism has always appealed to me,' he wrote, 'the idea of the innate goodness of the individual corrupted by society or the system. I believe many people are forced into causing harm to others by the way society operates. They would not behave in this way if the current system did not exist or was radically different.' Other samples of his thought included: 'What to do about crack and smack, especially in Brixton? Bottom line – screw the dealers, help the addicts', and 'Do not treat all police officers as lapdogs of a corrupt capitalist system. Dogs sometimes turn on their owners.'

Mr Paddick is plainly a taker of risks. Perhaps comparable to the London mayor Ken Livingstone, he is open about matters that others do not yet have the nerve to discuss. His rash pioneering will make it easier for his successors to say such things as if they were normal, even if he becomes a marginal figure as a result. But there is not all that much of a gap between him and the thoughts of Her Majesty's Chief Inspector, Sir John Woodcock, quoted approvingly in the Macpherson report.

In fact, in many ways Mr Paddick is the ideal post-Macpherson senior officer, a committed member of the liberal elite, equipped with correct ideas on sexuality, gender and 'racism', seeing drug-takers as victims, viewing the police as the defenders of wealth rather than of law. And in the same week that his words were published, the Metropolitan Police took another step away from their traditional duties. It was revealed, in the *Daily Mail* in February 2002, that they are considering 'downgrading' some supposedly minor crimes by no longer automatically sending officers to investigate them. These include burglary, shoplifting and the epidemic crime of driving away from petrol stations without paying. This, if implemented, would not make much difference in practice since arriving after the event is in any case fairly futile. However, it does demonstrate the complete defeat of Sir Robert Peel's original, conservative concept of a police force ranged on the side of the public, sharing its morals and culture.

In the same week a group of traders who sought to sell their goods in the ancient and picturesque imperial measures, known to generations of Englishmen and women, lost an appeal against convictions for breaking the law. But what law had they broken? An Act devised to protect the public from short measure and cheating was used instead to attack entirely honest men for defying an aspect of the cultural revolution. This was an entirely novel use of the criminal law in this country, a fact lost in the justified and equally important legal arguments about its constitutional implications. The 'metric martyrs' were convicted and fined for something that is not an offence against any form of natural law. They were not dishonest, violent or destructive. They were, however, not modern men like Commander Brian Paddick. Both cases are extreme. But, since one was carried to the Court of Appeal and the other involved one of the highest-ranking police officers in the capital, they cannot be dismissed as marginal.

I have sought to explain in this book what appears to be the driving force of the new law. It is based, like the other changes that have overturned English life since 1960, on the new secular religion of the educated elite. Socialist and collectivist in origin, it worships the welfare state. It believes neither in absolute truth nor in absolute right and wrong. It demands special protection for cultures and lifestyles that consciously and deliberately undermine the morality and beliefs of the older generation. It uses the grievances of activists within racial and sexual minorities as the pretext for general change. It rejects the whole idea of punishment and affects to believe in rehabilitation while failing to pursue this objective with any real consistency. It is careless of the ancient liberties of the English constitution, which it often has not heard of, preferring arbitrary group rights granted to favoured lobbies over binding restraints on the power of the state. Having taken possession of the state, it believes that government is essentially benevolent and does not need to be restrained. It is hostile to individual self-improvement by the masses, although members of the elite are permitted to improve their own lives and even to become extremely rich. It is suspicious of individual wealth and most types of property. It sympathizes with the drug-abuser and can see the burglar's point of view. It sees respectability and restraint as repression. It regards what remains of the police force as the army of the rich against the poor, of the morally conservative against the liberated.

However, the elite state hardly ever declares its purpose openly. Often it is too inarticulate or incoherent to do so and merely gropes towards its objectives, seizing opportunities as they come. Since the repeated electoral defeats of radical leftism from 1979 to 1992, it has been justifiably cautious about disclosing its aims in public. Because of this its purpose can only be divined from the results of its actions, which have now had thirty years to reveal their true effects: demoralization; lawlessness; licence; unchecked public debauchery and violence; disrespect for the old; contempt for private or public property; indulgence of hedonism at almost any cost; scorn for the lawful and neglect for the robbed, the injured, the bereaved; furious prosecution of those who defend themselves and feeble pursuit of those who attacked them in the first place; courts that are not respected and prisons that are not feared; an utter complacency about the great misery that all this has caused to the gentle and the good. These are the consequences of the elite state's great project to 'modernize' England into something and somewhere else. In that, at least, it has had great success.

If that were the end of it, things would be bad enough. It is not. Having overthrown a successful and functioning system of law enforcement and justice in the pursuit of an unattainable ideal, the elite state finds that the resulting disorder is unpopular with its own supporters, who are the first to feel the pain of lawlessness. Year by year, the fear and hatred of crime and chaos grows among all classes, as do the demands that something must be done.

There are simple and obvious measures that would begin to deal with this: the return of preventive patrolling; the disciplining of the prisons; the removal of the ludicrous codes of practice which hamper prosecution; the scrapping of the Crown Prosecution Service and the Police Complaints Authority; the breaking up of the merged police forces into smaller units linked to the places they serve; the restoration of the death penalty for premeditated murder; the introduction of educational and other qualifications for jury service. These would hold the line while a remoralization of society was begun in homes and schools, and broadcasters were held to account for their encouragement of violence and licence.

None of these ideas, however, is even contemplated. Instead, the elite state reaches increasingly for instruments of repression long abolished in this country. Some of them it thinks of itself, like the Auld report's assault on juries, the centralization of the police sought in the Police Reform Bill, Mr Blunkett's 'anti-terror' measures, identity cards, the abolition of the rule against being tried twice and the end of the right to silence. Others it welcomes from the European Union, like the abolition of habeas corpus implicit in the European arrest warrant, and the construction of an unaccountable and all-powerful European prosecution service and police force, based upon a European constitution, court and 'charter of rights', which simply ignore the practical success of centuries of English experience and ask us to rely instead on purely theoretical protections.

Arrayed as a 'fight against crime', or against drugs, or against terror, or whatever happens to be the suitable bogeyman of the moment, these measures are in fact the gravest threat to English liberty since the seventeenth century – not least because they are highly popular with a badly-educated public which increasingly believes what it is told and would tolerate much in return for a real attack on crime. In truth, such measures are unlikely to have much effect on crime unless they are taken to the point where the country actually becomes a police state.

There may be people on the left, and on the right for that matter, who genuinely and sincerely believe that this country would be happier if it were less free. There must surely be many more, from both traditions, who believe that freedom is our most precious possession and that no arguments of necessity should be allowed to weaken or destroy it.

Postscript

Shortly after I finished writing this book, a series of disturbing events took place which suggest that there is now a direct, as well as an indirect threat to liberty. This danger comes mainly from attitudes within the reformed police forces and the increasingly politicised Crown Prosecution Service. I believe it originates from the same source as the wider attack on liberty, namely the elite state's certainty that its benevolence and goodness are beyond dispute. This means, by implication, that opposition to its ideas and beliefs are actively offensive, dangerous and subject to legal sanction. We may be witnessing the early stages of the gradual transformation of a free country into a closed society in which some ideas can no longer be publicly expressed. If this is so then the message of this book is even more urgent than it otherwise would be.

The most important of these events was the prosecution of the late Mr Harry Hammond, an elderly eccentric living in Bournemouth. I visited Mr Hammond shortly before his death, and – with colleagues from the *Mail on Sunday* – investigated the background to his arrest and prosecution in great detail. The case is extraordinary in almost every way, and reveals the depth of the conflict between the two traditions of policing now striving for mastery.

Mr Hammond, a passionate evangelical Christian in his late

sixties, liked to preach the Gospel in the open air of Bournemouth, whether anyone was listening to him or not. In April 2002 he was prosecuted under the Public Order Act of 1986, which makes it an offence to display any writing, sign or other visible representation that is threatening, abusive or insulting, within the hearing or sight of a person likely to be caused harassment, alarm and distress thereby. Mr Hammond's crime was to display a placard – now destroyed by order of the bench – on which was written: 'Stop immorality. Stop homosexuality. Stop lesbianism.'

As Mr Hammond hoisted his six-word manifesto in the centre of town on a busy Saturday in October 2001, a small crowd gathered round him, partly hecklers but mostly curious onlookers. The hecklers were rough with him. A young woman tried to tug the placard from his hands. During this tussle, Mr Hammond fell flat on his back and had to be helped to his feet by security guards from a nearby shop. Soon afterwards, Mr Hammond's enlightened liberal critics flung clods of earth at him, one striking him on the chest and one on the head. Another of these campaigners for tolerance crept up behind Mr Hammond and emptied a bottle of water over his bald cranium.

Yet when the police were called, it was Mr Hammond who was arrested. Mr Hammond's case may well be the most bizarre arrest in the history of English policing, since the two officers involved disagreed over what to do and did not resolve their disagreement. A more experienced male constable, Wayne Elliott, thought that Mr Hammond should be protected. His younger female colleague, Nicola Gandy, thought that he should be taken in. They argued for 20 minutes before her view prevailed. At the trial the two officers gave evidence on opposite sides, PC Elliott appearing for the defence, while PC Gandy spoke for the prosecution. The Crown Prosecutor laid into Mr Hammond as if he were a serious malefactor. He said the offending placard was 'insulting to people and people's intelligence. It was insulting to gay people and gay people's friends and he knew that'. A magistrate ruled that the sign 'clearly insulted members of the crowd who had gathered round him'. She pronounced him guilty and fined him £300 plus £300 in costs. She also ordered that his placard be destroyed. Afterwards, PC Elliott said: 'I did not want to arrest him. He was entitled to his viewpoint.' But she felt very strongly about it: 'My attitude was to protect him from members of the crowd rather than protect other people from what he had to say.'

But PC Gandy stood by her decision to arrest Mr Hammond. She said: 'He was provoking and inciting violence with highly inappropriate behaviour.' Asked about her motives for taking a strong stance, she explained: 'My agenda was to try to maintain the peace. I was not very impressed with Mr Hammond's conduct, I don't think he is a very good representative of the Christian faith.' It is interesting that police officers now feel able to comment in public on the religious opinions of citizens.

Mr Hammond planned to appeal, but died in the summer of 2002, before the case could be heard. It is still possible that he might be cleared posthumously, if the Courts agree that the matter is important enough to justify a further hearing. It is worth noting that there is a 1999 precedent in his favour, and that it was set by none other than Lord Justice Sedley, who features more than once elsewhere in this book as a champion of the new liberalism. However, in this case, he stood up nobly for an older principle, which is encouraging news for those, like me, who hope that the civilized left may yet rally to the support of liberty. He allowed an appeal by a fundamentalist preacher, Alison Redmond-Bate, convicted of obstructing the police on the steps of Wakefield Cathedral, saying that freedom of speech covered the 'the irritating, the contentious, the eccentric, the heretical, the unwelcome and the provocative.' It remains to be seen whether the times have changed so much even since 1999 that Lord Justice Sedley's view no longer prevails. It certainly had no influence over the policewoman who arrested Mr Hammond, the prosecutors who took him to court or the bench that convicted him, and many in his position might have been in no position to mount an appeal.

Such prosecutions are based on an assumption which is dangerous to proper free speech. They suggest that condemnation of an action is deemed to be insulting to anyone who does that action. If this is so, then the public declaration of almost all absolute morality is outlawed, since in law it is both disturbing and offensive to those whose actions are condemned by it.

A different sort of unease arises from the prosecution of Alistair Scott, of Exeter, sentenced in October 2002 to 200 hours of community service, and ordered to pay £100 compensation, for having rude and emotional arguments with his Muslim neighbours. It is very difficult to find out exactly what Mr Scott said to these neighbours, since his account differs from theirs – one of many objections to prosecuting people for what they say. Mr Scott denied saying several of the things he is accused to have uttered, but admitted to having been rude, which is why he pleaded guilty. It is not clear whether he really said he hated Muslims, as was alleged against him. 'I deny being a racist although I would say I'm a faithist,' Mr Scott said after his trial. 'I accept that the way I went about it was wrong and unacceptable.' Mr Scott certainly did not behave well. But his opponent Mohammed Hudaib, who was not prosecuted, was also far from saintly. In an argument about the destruction of the Twin Towers Mr Hudaib said that September 11 2001 was a 'glorious day' and that Osama Bin Laden was a great man. He also called Mr Scott a Zionist pigf*****.

The police charged Mr Scott with harassment, though in a free society they would not have charged either man with anything, as nobody was hurt and both had used pungent language. Since the Macpherson report, all British police forces are nervous that they will be accused of institutional racism and so would probably charge a brick wall with harassment if a member of a racial or religious minority drove into it. But the Crown Prosecution Service then altered the charge to 'religiously aggravated threatening behaviour'. This offence – to which Mr Scott pleaded guilty – was invented in the unbalanced few weeks immediately after the Twin Towers outrage, which Mr Hudaib believed was a glorious day. During this period most politicians simply took leave of their senses, which is presumably why the enemies of free speech in the Home Office chose this opportunity to slip such legislation past them. But they succeeded and in the way of such, things, it is now the law and the authorities were presumably anxious to apply it at the first available opportunity. Having done so once – and Mr Scott's guilty plea rules out any chance of an appeal – there is every reason to think that they will do it again.

The third unsettling event was the arrest in November 2002 of Robin Page, a former presenter of the TV show *One Man and his Dog*. Mr Page was arrested and locked in a filthy police cell, more than two months after he had spoken to a countryside rally in Gloucestershire. He began by saying: 'In case any of you are of a fragile disposition and easily offended, please go for a walk round the lake and come back when I have finished. If there is a black, vegetarian, Muslim, asylum-seeking, one-legged, lesbian lorry driver present then you may be offended at what I am going to say, as I want the same rights that you have got already.'

Some time later, he was approached by Gloucestershire Police, who said they had received complaints about his speech. Then he learned that the following advertisement had been placed in at least one Gloucestershire local newspaper, the *Stroud News and Journal*: 'Propaganda Claims Investigated: Claims that Frampton Country Fair was hijacked by the pro-hunting lobby are being investigated by Stonehouse police. Countryside campaigner Robin Page was accused of bombarding visitors with pro-hunting propaganda during his commentary at the fair in September. Sgt Geoff Clark would like to hear from anyone who was upset by the commentary.'

Mr Page says that, when Sergeant Clark arrived at his home, he told him he was there to interview him under caution, with a view to possible prosecution. Mr Page had no lawyer present and declined to be interviewed. Mr Page says the officer then formally arrested him and took him to the nearest police station, where he says he was locked in a squalid cell, his shoelaces, belt and tie removed. He says he was told that if he wanted to wait for his own chosen lawyer he would have to spend the night in the cell.

He says: 'I had no choice but to agree to be interviewed there and then.' He was then told that it was alleged he had begun his speech with racist comments. According to Mr Page's account, the officer then asked him what it was he had said. Mr Page says the two then had a bizarre conversation in which he alleges the police officer asked him if he were a racist. Mr Page also says the Sergeant appeared to indicate a dislike of traditional country people, called him an eccentric and remarked that people like him caused a lot of trouble because they offended moderates. In late January 2003 the Crown Prosecution Service decided that there was insufficient evidence to take the case further.

Plenty of people might dislike Mr Page and his views or see him as an eccentric. They would be entitled to their opinions, as he is to his. Our society contains many different sorts of human being and some of them are destined not to get on with each other. What is important about this astonishing account is that the power of the law and the resources of the police are being deployed to investigate speeches and personal, private opinions. If the police are allowed to form judgements on whether we are eccentric or not, how long before they are forming judgements on whether we are institutionally racist, xenophobic or homophobic? Mr Page, who is well-known and articulate, is able to resist. But how many others are not? In an era when few local newspapers report the courts as thoroughly as they once did, how many individuals have been pursued in this way without anyone ever hearing about it? How many now fear that, if they speak their minds, they risk such treatment? It is impossible to know. But it is disturbing that English police officers think that such interrogations are part of their duties.

One other incident needs to be recorded here. It involves Anne Robinson, the TV presenter, who was rude about the Welsh people on a BBC TV programme *Room 101*. There were many complaints about her rudeness and following these accusations, North Wales Police took it upon themselves to suggest to the BBC that they should not repeat the programme. This is interesting in itself. I asked the North Wales Police under what law they had the power to take such action and they have yet to reply. When the programme was repeated, they sent officers hundreds of miles to interview Greg Dyke, Director General of the BBC but eventually wrote to him to say that they would be seeking a prosecution. However, this was not because the very idea was preposterous but because there was said to be insufficient evidence.

A very short time ago, anyone in England would have thought all these cases were comical, silly bungles by heavy-handed, inexperienced and humourless juniors, without any greater significance. This kind of thing does not happen here, we would have thought; therefore we may safely laugh at it. And yet this kind of thing does happen here, not by mistake but through the conscious and deliberate actions of powerful public officials. A pattern is perceptible in these incidents which is not reassuring. It seems likely that similar prosecutions and investigations will happen with increasing frequency and seriousness. Such speech codes have been rigorously enforced on many university campuses for some years (the author, for example, has had his microphone switched off in mid-speech by student officials following baseless allegations of racism. Such officials frequently find their way into national politics, and the expansion of the universities means that many police officers, lawyers and court officials will have been exposed to – and possibly infected by – such attitudes during their education.) They are now spreading into the country as a whole as the intolerant campus consensus infects the police and the prosecuting authorities. New European Union Provisions, under the Racism and Xenophobia directive, threaten to provide a legal basis for more official widespread persecution of certain opinions. One major purpose of this book is to warn that there is now a real threat to liberty of thought and speech in this country, a threat which cannot be lightly dismissed by any observant or alert citizen. I hope the warning will, for once, be heeded.

Index

Page, Leo 132–4
Page, Robin 301–2
Parker, Philip (Assistant Recorder)
170–1
Parker, Lord 221
Parliamentary Bills (alphabetical order):
Anti-Terrorist Bill (2001) 9
Criminal Justice Bill (1948) 190–1
Criminal Justice Bill (1966) 246
Felonious Use of Firearms Bill
(1887) 158
Firearms Bills (1883) 158
Pistols Bill (1893 and 1895) 158–9
Regulation of Carrying of Arms Bill
(1881) 158
Paterson, Sir Alexander 138–9, 146,
185, 195
Payne, Sarah 201
Peel, Sir Robert: founding of
Metropolitan Police 51, 54, 64,
65–6; early opposition 101–4;
limiting of police powers 104–5,
107; as prison reformer 113, 114
Penal discipline, reformatory projects …
English Prison Commission 1895–1939
(Forsythe) 140, 141
Pentonville Prison 113–14
Persistent Offenders Committee
131–2
'Peterloo Massacre' (1819) 102, 157
Phillips, Sir David (Chief Constable of
Kent) 41, 43
Pitt, William 1
Pilkington, PC John 64
Playfair, Giles 114
Police Advisory Board: working parties
reports (1966) 64–9, 72

police: alleged institutional racism 18,
261, 263, 271–2, 300; chief officer
elite 27–9, 50, 82; as servants of the
state 38–9, 47; graduate entry 50,
269–70; revisions to constables' oath
51; force mergers (1966) 79–83, 101;
militancy 79; formation of national
force 79, 82, 107; influence of
American culture 85–7;
independence and neutrality
105–6; 'canteen culture' 271 *see also*
Bramshill Police College
Police Complaints Authority 30, 108,
271, 290, 295
Police Federation, The 28, 46, 78, 281
Police Foundation (pro-drugs charity)
224–5
police manpower 46–7, 48–50, 66, 94,
99–100; female officers 47–50;
recruitment and retention 50, 65,
70, 72, 77, 269–70; sickness 97 *see
also* Unit Beat Policing
Police Powers and Politics (Baldwin and
Kinsey) 95
Police Research and Development
Branch 89, 95
Police Superintendents Association
173
Police … Camera … Action (TV) 87
policing: crime prevention 26, 87, 288;
demise of foot patrols 29, 41–2,
53–5, 58–61, 65–9, 76, 82, 85, 99;
reactive policing 29–31, 73, 91;
high-speed chases 30; CCTV
cameras 32, 50, 71–2; restraining
equipment and weapons 33, 201–2;
relationship with public 33–4, 39,

Police Powers (1929) 51–3, 54, 104–5

Royal Parks Police (London) 42

Ruggles-Brise, Sir Evelyn 135–6, 138, 146

Ruggles-Brise, Sir John 221

Russell, Bertrand 137, 139, 147

Ryan, Michael 150

Salisbury Review 228–9

Scargill, Arthur 106

Scarman, Lord 273, 274–82

Scotland, justice system in 5–6

Scott, Alistair 300–1

Scottish Scout Movement 153

Seay, Davin 220

Second Amendment Sisters (feminists; USA) 178

Sedley, Lord Justice 172, 282, 299

Select Committee on Capital Punishment, Parliamentary (1930) 202

self-defence 168–74; right to bear arms (UK) 39, 148–9, 154–7, 158–9, 182

'Seven Bishops', acquittal of (1688) 236

sexual offences 34–7

Sharp, Martin 223

Sheehy Report 46

Shelburne, William 101–2

Shenstone, William 101

Short, Edward 160

Sidney Street incident (1910) 159

Simpson, Sir Joseph (Commissioner of Metropolitan Police) 54, 240

Skeates, Edwin 170

Snell (criminal) 264

Snell, Superintendent John 24–5

Softly Softly (TV) 57, 83

Soskice, Frank (*later* Lord Stow Hill) 62, 78, 163, 246

Spectator 227

Sportsman's Association 153–4

St Johnston, Eric (Chief Constable of Lancashire; *later* Sir Eric and first Chief Inspector of Constabulary) 85, 88, 101; reform of Lancashire force 55–6, 58; as BBC TV advisor 57–8; belief in foot patrols 58–60; introduction of Panda cars 59–61 *see also* Unit Beat Policing

Stanley, Lord, of Alderley 175

Statute of Northampton (1328) 155

Statute of Winchester (1285) 155

Staunton, George 273

Stephen Lawrence Inquiry: … by Sir William Macpherson of Cluny, The (1999) 18, 260–8, 271–2, 283, 284

Stevens, Sir John 257

Stonham, Lord 83

Strachan, Crispian (Chief Constable of Northumbria) 29

Strangeways Prison riot (1990) 10, 144

street crime 10, 47, 22–3, 118, 214, 231

'Streetwise-Effective police patrol' (Audit Commission; 1996) 96

Stroud News and Journal 301

Stroup, Keith 227

Sun 257

Sunday Telegraph 144

suspended sentences 77, 101, 143

Task Force (TV) 57